Creative
Communities

Creative Communities

ART WORKS IN ECONOMIC DEVELOPMENT

MICHAEL RUSHTON
EDITOR

Sponsored by the
National Endowment for the Arts,
Office of Research & Analysis

BROOKINGS INSTITUTION PRESS
Washington, D.C.

Copyright © 2013
THE BROOKINGS INSTITUTION
1775 Massachusetts Avenue, N.W., Washington, D.C. 20036
www.brookings.edu

Library of Congress Cataloging-in-Publication data
Creative communities : art works in economic development / Michael Rushton, editor.
    pages   cm
  "Sponsored by the National Endowment for the Arts, Office of Research and Analysis."
  Includes bibliographical references and index.
  Summary: "Examines the impacts of arts and cultural consumption and production on local economies. Topics include location choices of arts entrepreneurs; links between the arts and non-arts sectors; public policies to foster local arts; and the arts' effects on incomes in cities across the United States and the United Kingdom"—Provided by publisher.
  ISBN 978-0-8157-2473-5 (pbk. : alk. paper)
  1. Artists and community—Economic aspects. 2. Arts—Economic aspects. 3. Art and state—Economic aspects. 4. Regional economics. 5. Economic development.
I. Rushton, Michael, 1959-
  NX180.A77C73 2013
  338.4'77—dc23   2013005090

9 8 7 6 5 4 3 2 1

Printed on acid-free paper

Typeset in Minion

Composition by Oakland Street Publishing
Arlington, Virginia

Printed by R. R. Donnelley
Harrisonburg, Virginia

Contents

Foreword

Since I took over as chairman of the National Endowment for the Arts in 2009, I have spent a lot of my time in pursuit of creative placemaking, which seeks to integrate art and design in community planning and development, build shared spaces for arts engagement and creative expression, and increase local economic activity through arts and cultural activities. This goal has borne fruit in national programs such as Our Town, Art Place, and other NEA-supported initiatives under my tenure.

Another focus of mine for the last four years has been to bolster research and evidence sharing about the value and impact of the arts in American life. Without good data and analysis—much of it grounded in economic theory—we cannot hope to strengthen communities through the arts or to achieve any of the other goals that we have set for the National Endowment for the Arts, the largest nationwide funder of the arts. Consequently, I have amped up resources and expectations for research at the NEA. For example, in October 2012, the NEA's Office of Research and Analysis published a five-year research agenda that includes a system map and measurement model for understanding "how art works." (See www.nea.gov/research/How-Art-Works/index.html.) This volume thus marks the convergence of two of my major themes as NEA chairman: the arts as an engine in transforming communities for the better, and the arts as an integral, measurable component of the U.S. economy.

In 2011, the NEA's Office of Research and Analysis issued a public call for research papers attempting to measure economic activity resulting from "the creation of arts districts, the construction of performing arts centers and museums, and arts-favorable tax policies and other incentives for productivity

and innovation in fields such as architecture and design, visual and performing arts, and literary and media arts." In its call for papers, the NEA placed special emphasis on New Growth Theory, popularized by Paul Romer and others.

Why the emphasis on New Growth Theory? Admittedly, there have been
numerous well-intentioned and often compelling studies of the arts' local
economic impact, yet a common weakness has been that it is nearly impossible to tell whether the arts' effects on, say, local tourism spending could have
been replicated by the introduction of non–arts-related activities—for example, the construction of a sports facility. The argument is not so much that
such studies are overestimating the effects of the arts; rather, a case can be
made that those effects are *under*valued, simply because the tools used are not
precise enough to account for the effects independently of other economic
variables.

New Growth, with its assumption that new ideas lead to new economies of
scale without a diminution of resources, seemed a natural fit when discussing
why the arts matter in stark economic terms. In any case, we were prepared to
explore the theory's potential. And indeed, some of the papers that we received
chose to address the theory in relation to the arts and economic development. Some, but not all: other papers examined links between arts participation and scientific innovation; the effects of cultural tax districts on giving to
the arts; and the impact of per capita cultural spending on local economic
growth, among other topics.

On the strength of those draft papers, the Brookings Institution hosted a
one-day symposium entitled "The Arts, New Growth Theory, and Economic
Development." Sponsored by the Brookings Metropolitan Policy Program,
the event featured not only the authors of the chapters that appear in this volume but also the urban economist Edward Glaeser, happiness researcher Carol
Graham, and top officials and analysts from the U.S. Patent and Trademark
Office, the Bureau of Economic Analysis, and the Department of Housing
and Urban Development. The agenda and video from that day are available
at www.arts.gov/research/Brookings/index.html.

Where do we go from here? One of the big lessons learned at the Brookings event was that we need long-term, reliable data to more effectively track
the arts' unique effects on economic development, whether related to New
Growth Theory or not. I am pleased to note that through a historic partnership with the U.S. Department of Commerce's Bureau of Economic Analysis,
we will have that resource ready for the use of all economists and policymakers
who care about cultural value. Specifically, the NEA and BEA are creating an

Arts and Cultural Production Satellite Account, which, beginning with preliminary estimates later in 2013, will provide annual figures on arts and cultural industry revenues, expenditures, workers, compensation, and value added to the GDP. This is a landmark opportunity for both the arts and cultural sector and the nation as a whole.

In closing, I wish to thank Michael Rushton of Indiana University for his editorship of this volume and for his spirited collaboration with us in 2012 when we commissioned the original symposium papers.

Rocco Landesman
Chairman (2009–12)
National Endowment for the Arts

Acknowledgments

This volume would not have been published and the symposium where these papers were first presented would not have taken place without the initiative and support of the National Endowment for the Arts. For their support of the project from its conception to publication, thanks are due to Rocco Landesman, Joan Shigekawa, Sunil Iyengar, Ellen Grantham, Bonnie Nichols, and Joanna Woronkowicz. Many thanks also to the Brookings Institution for hosting the symposium and especially to Bruce Katz of the Brookings Metropolitan Policy Program.

Creative
Communities

MICHAEL RUSHTON

1

Introduction

This volume presents original research findings on the impacts of cultural consumption and production on local economies. The chapters are based on papers presented at "The Arts, New Growth Theory, and Economic Development," a May 2012 Brookings Institution symposium sponsored by the National Endowment for the Arts. The central theme of the symposium was that the arts are not an amenity or a sector that exists in isolation but that they are wholly integrated into local economies. Indeed, the complex role of art in local growth is what has made empirical research in the field so challenging and the new research in this volume so welcome to scholars and policymakers who seek to advance public knowledge about the dynamic relationship between art and economic growth.

The following chapters investigate the arts in local economies from a range of viewpoints, presenting original data derived from quantitative and qualitative methods. Topics investigated include location choices by arts entrepreneurs; links between the arts and non-arts sectors; public policies to foster local arts organizations; and the arts' effects on incomes in cities across the United States and the United Kingdom. There is no single method of parsing the complex factors at work, and these chapters should inspire further research along various lines to advance knowledge about the place of the arts in economic development. A brief review of the evolution of arts policy and of thinking about economic growth is presented below, followed by a survey of the contributions of these chapters and suggestions for future research.

Public Policy and the Arts

Until around the turn of the twenty-first century, public arts policy in the United States received relatively little attention. There was enough of a committed interest group to keep public funding of the arts alive at the federal, state, and local levels, although budgets were generally small; however, the greatest public support of the arts came from income tax–deductible charitable donations to nonprofit arts organizations, not from public funding.[1] Typically, the only time that arts policy was newsworthy was when public controversy arose over specific works of art that had received, usually indirectly, some form of government support.

In the 1960s, the rationales for direct public funding of the arts tended to center on the benefits to the public of being able to enjoy fine arts: classical music, opera, ballet and modern dance, some theater, and the visual arts.[2] First, there was the case for equity: the fine arts are part of a fulfilling life that ought to be made available to all, including those who have low incomes or who live far from major art centers. Public funding of nonprofit arts organizations could enable those organizations to undertake outreach activities to underserved populations and to keep ticket prices in check. Second, there was a rationale based on the potential for market failures in the arts: public subsidies are a means of encouraging the production and consumption of forms of art that provide public benefits, especially art forms that would be unlikely to flourish in a purely market-oriented environment. Because the fine arts provide public as well as private benefits, they do not represent purely private consumption. For example, people may benefit from my attending the opera even if they themselves never attend. They might be pleased that the traditions of operatic performance are being preserved so that they have the option of attending one day in the future (or that their children and grandchildren have that option), they might take special pride in knowing that their community is considered a center of culture, or they may simply feel good because others in the community are enjoying art of high quality.

However, even those who enjoy the arts a great deal might find those rationales for public funding somewhat weak. If the real concern is about inequality in the United States, are health, education, and housing not more pressing concerns than art museums and classical music performances? Are the claimed external benefits of private arts consumption of any significant magnitude, or do they simply represent wishful thinking by those who themselves happen to value the arts and their associated public subsidies?

More recently, however, two new kinds of economics-based cases have been made for active public support of the arts. One is the so-called "economic impact" of the arts. In many studies commissioned by arts advocates, impact is calculated by measuring direct consumer spending on the arts (usually restricted to the nonprofit sector), then inflated by a Keynesian-style "multiplier" that generates an estimate of the complete impact on aggregate income resulting from arts expenditures. Although some arts advocates, impact studies in hand, proclaim that the arts warrant public subsidy because of the great amount of total income generated by arts expenditures, the problems with the analysis are clear: the estimated benefits from increased expenditures on the arts do not account for the concomitant *reduction* in non-arts expenditures in the public sector (if the increase in arts spending was the result of a shift in budgetary allocations) or in the private sector (if the increase in arts spending was financed through a tax increase). The analysis works on the naïve assumption that an increase in aggregate demand (if indeed there is one) generates an equal increase in aggregate income, and it fails to acknowledge that *all* sectors of the economy, from plumbing and auto repair businesses to coffee shops, also have an economic impact, yet they do not obviously warrant public funding as a result.[3]

But a second class of economic argument deserves to be taken more seriously. Suppose that increased levels of arts activity serve to increase productivity and wages. If such effects could be demonstrated, then indeed public investments in the arts would have, at least in theory, a solid economic rationale besides any aesthetic case for public support. But by what mechanisms might the arts in fact increase wages? What evidence is there of such an effect? The new research studies presented in the chapters in this volume provide some valuable insights into these questions.

That is not to say that this volume covers the whole of arts policy. Questions surrounding the role of the arts in local economic development are important, but they must be considered alongside the "old school" arts policy issues that have always been present: what is the appropriate response to the widely differential access to the arts that arises from individuals' geographic location or socioeconomic circumstances? What is an appropriate balance between investing resources in arts education for the young and supporting current artists and organizations? What is the importance of preserving genres of art that could not survive unaided in the marketplace? These are important questions that go beyond considerations of the arts and productivity or of attracting the creative class. While the importance of the individual issues covered in this volume must be recognized, it is important not to lose sight of the fact that they are parts of a larger whole.

The Arts and New Growth Theory

"New growth theory" (NGT) arises from theoretical and empirical findings that first gained traction in the 1980s.[4] The key aspects could be listed as follows. First, NGT treats advances in growth-enhancing technology as a result of the conscious, strategic decisions of individuals, firms, and governments to invest in the acquisition of skills and knowledge and in potential innovation. It has long been known that in advanced economies, technological change—not the accumulation of current-technology physical capital—is responsible for most of the long-run growth in income per person.[5] NGT *models* technological change (a reason why NGT is often also referred to as "endogenous growth theory") rather than treating it as something that simply "happens" to firms and workers.[6]

Second, NGT recognizes that new technologies are not perfectly guarded by the firms that develop them. There are "knowledge spillovers": firms and individuals in close proximity to others that are developing new ideas get the chance to benefit from those ideas. That is one reason why firms and individuals in the knowledge-based sector gain such benefits from locating near other firms in the sector, thereby forming "clusters." Visual artists value being in New York City and songwriters value being in Nashville not only because there is a thick market of buyers for their products but also because they benefit from being around other painters and songwriters, among whom they find inspiration and develop their ideas. Furthermore, there can be important knowledge spillovers between sectors. An implication is that "technology" is not something that a firm anywhere in the world can simply buy and apply locally. What workers and machines are capable of producing (and it is productivity that determines income) depends on location, which is one reason why producers in knowledge-based industries are willing to pay such a high premium to be able to locate in densely packed cities and why skilled knowledge workers find their productivity and pay highest not where their sort of talent is scarce, but where it is plentiful.[7]

Third, unlike the inputs of physical capital and labor, knowledge and innovation are not subject to decreasing returns. New ideas are non-rival public goods, and once generated they can be used in a countless number of firms and applications. That fact helps explain the observation that over the long term, industrialized countries have seen (the recent recession notwithstanding) growth *rates* in per capita income rise rather than fall since the Industrial Revolution.[8]

What then is the place of the arts in contemporary thinking about economic growth? When economists talk about "the arts" in a local economy, they are talking about a tradable good, one with local production and consumption, imports and exports. Some works of art might be produced locally—a painting, a music recording—and sold elsewhere. Live performances might attract visitors. There also is local consumption of locally produced art—a painting purchased in a local gallery—as well as imports of recordings, books, and films. The effects of the arts on productivity in the local economy could come through consumption or production of the arts or both.

On the arts-consumption side, a vibrant cultural scene, whether based on local or touring artists, may attract to the city mobile, highly skilled individuals who serve to raise average productivity levels in the immediate term because of the knowledge and talents that they bring to the local economy and who in the long run serve to increase the productivity of the broader workforce through interaction and knowledge transfer. That is the essence of so many cities' efforts to brand themselves as "cool" and thereby attract those workers known (not without some controversy over definition and measurement) as the "creative class."[9] The positive effects may accumulate: skilled workers who could benefit from being around other skilled workers might migrate to a city that has built up a strong presence of such workers, even if the new migrants themselves have no interest in the "coolness" of the city—they simply find benefits in being in proximity to other workers, some of whom may have been attracted by the city's cultural life. All of this is not to suggest that a lively arts scene is the only way for a community to gain appeal as a residential choice for skilled professionals; good public schools, safe streets, and outdoor recreation also are important, and for some professionals they will be the primary amenities. But culture certainly matters to a segment of the "creative class," and therefore it becomes an important consideration in local economic development policy. Furthermore, the scale of the cultural sector matters in that a larger cultural scene and potential audience results in increased possibilities for cultural diversity and specialization. As the cultural sector and its audiences grow, the potential for sustaining more esoteric arts appealing to a smaller part of the local population is enhanced.

On the arts-production side, consider the effects of local arts production (even if not for local consumption) on the productivity of the workforce. First, the arts themselves are an income-generating sector of the economy. As a creative industry, the arts benefit from the knowledge spillovers that can occur when increased numbers of creators work in close proximity. Clusters in visual art, music recording, publishing, theater, and film production generate jobs and incomes themselves, apart from any effects that they may have on other sectors of the economy, and the scale and importance of the arts-production sector in this respect is unfortunately often overlooked.[10] Second, there are cross-sectoral effects, which may occur through direct links—for example, media and advertising firms draw benefits from locating in cities with a vibrant artistic production scene. But there also are intangible effects arising from a more broadly defined "culture of innovation," whereby a city, through its working artists, develops an ambience that serves to foster creative thinking among the greater variety of knowledge workers who reside there.

The possibilities above represent a selection of those regarding the arts and economic development, but much research remains to be done. The evidence on correlations between clusters of "Bohemian" artists and high-tech entrepreneurship is just that: evidence on correlations, without much indication of whether new investments in artistic clusters help create new growth in other knowledge industries.[11] The rationale for the symposium that resulted in the chapters in this book, then, was to get beneath the surface to investigate relationships between the arts and economic growth, generate new results, and inspire further research.

New Findings

In chapter 2, Jenny Schuetz brings her analysis down to the level of the city block, examining new art galleries and their locational choices and effects on neighborhoods. She looks at galleries in Manhattan, finding that new galleries have a strong preference for locating in what are known to be "gallery districts" and especially for being close to "star" galleries. She also notes that they prefer using old building stock or being close to historical districts (lending support to Jane Jacobs's famous dictum that "old ideas can sometimes use new buildings . . . new ideas must use old buildings")[12] and that they prefer locations where there is high population density and high household income. She finds that "far from seeking out blighted neighborhoods in need of gentrification, galleries prefer to locate in high-amenity neighborhoods that are likely to attract residential and commercial investment." She finds the evidence that galleries spur renewal of neighborhoods rather weak; instead, galleries seem to anticipate neighborhood renewal rather than create it.

In chapter 3, Ann Markusen, Anne Gadwa Nicodemus, and Elisa Bradbury, analyzing evidence from California, find that the strength of local arts communities is difficult to predict from socioeconomic data. Instead, individuals seem to respond to the availability of the arts, lending credibility to the claim that arts entrepreneurs and local policymakers willing to invest in capacity building are capable of influencing the spending patterns of locals. This finding underscores that the economic value of arts production does not lie solely in its ability to generate a product for export (the so-called "export base theory"); it can also generate local economic growth and net new jobs within the region. A local market for the arts can, of course, lead to an export market, but it need not start that way. Investments in the arts generate increased local incomes by further increasing demand for local goods and services and by attracting human capital and entrepreneurship to the region.

What might states do to enhance capacity building in the arts at the local level? In chapter 4, Richard Maloney and Gregory Wassall consider in depth three Massachusetts communities that have benefited from the state's John and Abigail Adams Arts Program for the Creative Economy (Adams Arts). While it is too soon to be able to say much about the long-term outcomes of the program, the authors were able to go into those communities and, in interviews with a variety of local stakeholders, learn about the program's implementation. They find that a culture-based local economic development strategy is not something that can be successfully implemented simply by having a funded program on offer by the state. To develop a coherent plan that results in an actual economic strategy requires skilled practitioners who have the time and energy to devote to the project, in partnership with local organizations and local government.

In chapter 5, Lauren Schmitz turns to another type of local arts funding program, namely the earmarked tax revenue of Colorado's Scientific and Cultural Facilities District (SCFD). Earmarked taxes for the arts have become widespread across the United States as a means of providing somewhat stable sources of public funding for the arts.[13] The tax revenues, which can be based on sales taxes (as is the SCFD), property taxes, tobacco taxes, hotel/motel taxes, and others, generally require voter approval by referendum. There is some research on whether publicly funded grants to arts organizations affect their ability to raise funds privately; this study asks whether earmarked funding also affects fundraising. Comparing the trends in fundraising for organizations not eligible for SCFD funding with trends for those that are, she finds no evidence that the earmarked funding "crowds out" earned revenues from fundraising—a positive argument for using public policy to increase the total revenues flowing to the nonprofit arts sector.

The next two chapters deal with links between the arts and related, innovation-based sectors of the economy. In chapter 6, Robert Root-Bernstein and his colleagues from Michigan State University survey professionals in science, technology, engineering, and mathematics (STEM), examining their artistic experiences when they were children and their current activities for evidence on whether arts participation influenced their success and level of innovation in their professional work. In particular, they find that rates of patenting by STEM professionals and rates of entrepreneurship in founding new companies were higher when a professional had more of a background in the arts and participated more in the arts. That is an especially striking result: despite the popular advocacy for the impact of arts education on other aspects of students' academic performance, there is little evidence that goes beyond the simple correlation that students in schools with high levels of arts activity score better on tests than students in schools with lower levels of arts activity. Such studies fail to indicate whether it is the arts that make the difference or whether other factors play a role in the school or the student cohort. Root-Bernstein and colleagues take individuals who have succeeded academically (well enough to be professionals in a technically demanding field) and ask about the links between their cultural lives and their subsequent activity in innovation and patenting. This is clearly a promising avenue for future studies with new, larger sets of data.

In chapter 7, Douglas Noonan and Shiri Breznitz focus on new media arts—digital art, computerized animation, and Internet and interactive art— and on whether cultural districts and research universities lead to increased activity in that field. Using data from U.S. metropolitan areas, they find that cultural districts and the presence of major research universities had little impact on the trend in the share of total employment devoted to arts-related industries, defined broadly. That said, *innovation* in media arts was associated with cities containing cultural districts. There is some evidence that the presence of art schools made a difference in these trends; there also is some evidence that arts-related employment, defined more narrowly, may have been affected by the presence of research universities, although the results for cultural districts remained unchanged. This finding points to a need for deeper understanding of cultural districts and for considering exactly what they are expected to provide for local economies.

In chapter 8, Roland Kushner discusses the local environments most conducive to arts entrepreneurship. Using data since the year 2000 on a sample of U.S. counties, he examines factors associated with the formation of new nonprofit arts enterprises. He finds that faster-growing, more densely populated counties whose residents were more highly educated had a higher ratio of new to old arts organizations. Further, higher cultural spending in the county—but not necessarily higher levels of arts philanthropy—tended to favor new firm growth.

The last two chapters in the volume present analyses that employed econometric techniques, specifically within the context of new growth theory models, to consider the influence of arts activities on local economic growth in the United States and the United Kingdom. In chapter 9, Peter Pedroni and Stephen Sheppard embark on an analysis of U.S. cities to examine how investments in nonprofit cultural spending affect per capita income in the long run, beyond any immediate stimulus effects. The authors model economic growth for an urban area while explicitly recognizing that investment in the arts necessarily comes with an opportunity cost. In theory, it is quite possible for a city to overinvest in the arts, as such investment might come at the expense of more valuable investments in other infrastructure. That said, the authors do find a long-term relationship between arts spending and per capita income: in the median case, a rise in arts spending did in fact lead to a permanent increase in per capita income. (They also find that a rise in per capita income from some other source tended to lead to permanent increases in nonprofit arts spending). However, when they look at individual cities, they find counterexamples, suggesting that overinvestment in the arts might be more than a theoretical possibility.

In chapter 10, Hasan Bakhshi, Neil Lee, and Juan Mateos-Garcia used data from cities in the United Kingdom to investigate the impact of the arts on income. Given that, as noted above, the arts affect the local economy on two dimensions—by providing opportunities for both arts consumption and arts production (and influencing other productive sectors through knowledge spillovers)—the impact of the arts on incomes in the local economy might be positive or negative: positive when the arts increase the productivity of employees but negative when the arts make a city such a desirable place to live that employees are willing to accept lower wages in return for living in an area that provides such amenities. They used a standard model in which the wage of an individual is a function of his or her education and experience, variables capturing the nature of the local economy, and—of particular interest here—the level of local arts activity. They find that although they observed a simple positive correlation between wages and arts employment in cities, when they corrected for individual and local economy characteristics the positive correlation disappeared; indeed, with some measures of cultural employment, the relationship was negative. In other words, the consumption-side effect of workers being willing to accept lower wages in exchange for living in an area with an active cultural scene seems to dominate the production-side effect.

While that was found to be the case for wages in general, when they looked only at wages of those working in creative industries, the positive effect appeared to dominate, lending support to the theory that clustering leads to knowledge spillovers and productivity gains.

Looking Ahead

Future directions in economic research, like future directions in artistic creation, are to a degree inherently unpredictable: researchers do not know what new ideas will take hold and spur further works and innovation. They can, however, at least speculate on which avenues of research hold promise.

First, there is much to be learned about how artists and arts organizations in a city affect the productivity and growth of other sectors. What art forms or types of employment matter the most, in what neighboring sectors? Must the working artists be gathered into a "district," or can they simply be present in the same city or metropolitan area, even if dispersed? Are there certain policies or types of infrastructure that enhance the transmission of productive externalities between the arts and other sectors? What is inside the "black box" of positive spillovers between the arts and innovation in STEM industries? How does art education make a more innovative engineer? How does a theater district influence patenting rates? In this volume, Root-Bernstein and colleagues, Noonan and Breznitz, Pedroni and Sheppard, and Bahkshi and colleagues all present new findings on such spillovers, and hopefully there will be more to come.

Second, what policies foster the growth of the arts in local economies? How does a city ensure that "the arts" is not defined only by a core of long-established major arts institutions but also includes entrepreneurship, innovation, and competition? Is the opportunity to use the arts as a key component in economic development strategy restricted only to high-income, highly educated communities that can rely on existing demand for the arts and capacity for leadership in the arts, or are possibilities open to other communities, even to those starting with little? What state and local policies best foster the development of a strong local arts scene? Here the chapters by Markusen and by Kushner consider the development of local nonprofit capacity in the arts; the chapter by Schuetz looks at entrepreneurial choices by new galleries; and the chapters by Schmitz and by Maloney and Wassall examine regional and state policy implementation and effects.

This is an exciting time to be studying the role of the arts in local economic growth. The original research presented in this volume serves as an invitation to explore a field ripe for future case studies and new approaches to modeling the complex relationships that exist between artists, arts organizations, and their cities.

Notes

1. Tyler Cowen called the tax deductibility of charitable contributions "the genius of the American system": *Good and Plenty: The Creative Successes of American Arts Funding* (Princeton University Press, 2006).

2. See, for example, William J. Baumol and William G. Bowen, *Performing Arts: The Economic Dilemma* (New York: Twentieth Century Fund, 1966), especially pp. 370–86.

3. Bruce A. Seaman, "Arts Impact Studies: A Fashionable Excess," in *Economic Impact of the Arts: A Sourcebook,* edited by Anthony Radich and Sharon Schwoch (Washington: National Conference of State Legislatures, 1987).

4. Paul M. Romer, "The Origins of Endogenous Growth," *Journal of Economic Perspectives,* vol. 8, no. 2 (Winter 1994), pp. 3–22; David Warsh, *Knowledge and the Wealth of Nations: A Story of Economic Discovery* (New York: Norton, 2006).

5. The seminal empirical study is Robert M. Solow, "Technical Change and the Aggregate Production Function," *Review of Economics and Statistics,* vol. 39 (August 1957), pp. 312–20.

6. Paul M. Romer, "Endogenous Technological Change," *Journal of Political Economy,* vol. 98, no. 5, part 2 (1990), pp. S71–S102.

7. Edward Glaeser, *Triumph of the City* (New York: Penguin, 2011).

8. Paul M. Romer, "Crazy Explanations for the Productivity Slowdown," *NBER Macroeconomics Annual,* vol. 2 (1987), pp. 163–210.

9. Richard Florida, *The Rise of the Creative Class* (New York: Basic Books, 2002).

10. Elizabeth Currid, *The Warhol Economy: How Fashion, Art, and Music Drive New York City* (Princeton University Press, 2007).

11. Richard Florida, "Bohemia and Economic Geography," *Journal of Economic Geography,* vol. 2, no. 1 (2002), pp. 55–71.

12. Jane Jacobs, *The Death and Life of Great American Cities* (New York: Random House, 1961), p. 188.

13. Michael Rushton, "Earmarked Taxes for the Arts: U.S. Experience and Policy Implications," *International Journal of Arts Management,* vol. 6, no. 3 (2004), pp. 38–48; Michael Rushton, "Support for Earmarked Public Spending on Culture: Evidence from a Referendum in Metropolitan Detroit," *Public Budgeting and Finance,* vol. 25, no. 4 (December 2005), pp. 72–85.

JENNY SCHUETZ

2

Causal Agents or Canaries in the Coal Mine?
Art Galleries and Neighborhood Change

Art galleries serve several important functions within the arts industry. Economically, galleries are places of arts consumption, generally focusing on visual arts such as painting and sculpture. If artists visit galleries to learn about their peers' work, galleries may also contribute to enhanced arts production. Galleries are almost always for-profit entities; the main distinction between galleries and museums is that museums typically display original art but do not offer it for sale, while galleries display art in order to sell it. Like many forms of arts production discussed elsewhere in this volume (see chapters 3 and 8), the retail art market is diffuse and highly entrepreneurial: it is made up mostly of small, independently owned firms—single dealers or small partnerships. Although art galleries are an essential component of the overall arts industry, as economic entities they are quite different from a symphony orchestra, a publicly funded museum, or an independent novelist or painter. In many respects, the upper echelon of art galleries is similar to the high-end retail market: the best-known galleries are businesses whose primary function is to sell expensive luxury goods. Outside the top tier, galleries resemble small businesses in other retail segments: they operate in a highly competitive industry with low barriers to entry and experience relatively high turnover.

Art galleries also have the potential to enhance the cultural and economic life of surrounding neighborhoods. In cities across the United States—from

The University of Southern California's Lusk Center for Real Estate generously funded the creation of the Manhattan Gallery Database. New York University's Furman Center provided several administrative datasets and technical assistance in the use of the data. Thanks to Ann Markusen, Doug Noonan, and Michael Rushton for helpful comments. Marie Sullivan provided outstanding research assistance.

Los Angeles to Santa Fe to Provincetown, Massachusetts, and Naples, Florida—clusters of galleries attract visitors who "gallery hop" through the neighborhood. Some visitors may be serious art collectors intending to purchase new works; others may attend exhibit openings as social events or may simply enjoy viewing art in a more informal setting than a traditional museum. Local governments, chambers of commerce, and business improvement districts in many cities have established monthly "art walks" through designated areas, encouraging locals and tourists to mingle, browse, and buy—if not a $10,000 original painting, then at least drinks and dinner from nearby restaurants. Through such mechanisms, art galleries may draw in additional commercial activity and create social cachet for the neighborhood, benefiting both businesses and residents.

In this chapter, I present evidence from Manhattan that I used to test the hypothesis underlying local efforts to develop gallery districts: that art galleries can spur neighborhood economic and physical development. First, I investigated whether art galleries locate in blighted neighborhoods in need of revitalization; second, I compared signs of physical redevelopment across otherwise similar neighborhoods with and without art galleries. Keeping in mind the economic purpose of art galleries—to sell art—is essential to understanding the location choices that gallery owners make. I begin by discussing the best-known case study of the establishment of art galleries as a stage in the process of economic development: New York's Soho neighborhood. The emphasis is to place Soho within the context of other Manhattan neighborhoods and conduct a counterfactual thought experiment: what would Soho's fate have been if galleries had not chosen to locate there? I then lay out hypotheses for gallery location choices more generally, drawn from theoretical models. The empirical analysis uses New York City as its context, describing the characteristics of Manhattan's four dominant art gallery centers—Chelsea, Midtown, Soho, and the Upper East Side—to demonstrate that gallery location choices are a reflection of a gallery's access to long-standing physical amenities. I present evidence that neighborhoods with art galleries experience no more physical redevelopment than otherwise similar neighborhoods without galleries once the underlying amenities are taken into consideration. I conclude with some policy implications and directions for future research.

Why Soho?

Much of the attention given to galleries as potential agents of gentrification can be traced back to case studies on a single neighborhood in New York

City, the downtown area known as Soho (South of Houston).[1] Several detailed historical studies have described Soho's trajectory: what was a blighted postindustrial area in the mid-twentieth century was infiltrated in the 1960s by artists looking for cheap apartments and studios; the artists were followed by galleries in the 1970s and 1980s; and the galleries were followed by mainstream retail and high-end residential tenants in the 1990s and afterward.[2] Artists were drawn to the space by both relatively cheap rents and the availability of buildings with high ceilings, open floor plans, and large windows, suitable for working studios. Galleries likewise were attracted by those physical attributes as well as by the social ties between artists and gallery owners. Researchers have argued that the presence of artists and galleries reduced visual blight and increased the social cachet of the neighborhood, drawing in more affluent households and eventually mainstream retailers, restaurants, and cafes.[3]

These historical analyses provide richly detailed accounts of events that occurred in Soho, establishing the chronological relationship between the in-migration of artists and galleries and subsequent neighborhood change. How-ever, the studies do not constitute evidence that the relationship was causal. A major limitation of the case study method is that lacking an appropriate comparison group, it does not illuminate the counterfactual scenario: what would have happened to Soho had artists and galleries not moved in? An advantage of larger-scale statistical analysis is that comparison neighborhoods can be identified—areas that initially were similar to Soho but that did not attract galleries—to serve as the counterfactual case. An obvious concern with arguing that artists and galleries caused Soho to gentrify is the potential for selection bias: if artists and galleries were drawn to Soho because of place-specific amenities and those amenities had an independent impact on the economic trajectory of the neighborhood, then Soho's gentrification may have been due to its initial amenities rather than the presence of artists.

A simple comparison of Soho to the rest of Manhattan illustrates the poten-tial selection bias involved. In 1970, only five art galleries were located in Soho, a fact that provides an insight into the neighborhood's condition and ameni-ties before its rapid growth in galleries.[4] Confirming the findings of the case studies, at that time Soho was ranked as economically disadvantaged relative to other Manhattan census tracts on several standard indicators: average house-hold income, share of the population in poverty, share of the population with college or graduate degrees, and average monthly residential rent (table 2-1). But was Soho typical of other low-income Manhattan neighborhoods, or did it have traits that made it especially attractive to galleries? The third column in

Table 2-1. *Comparison of Soho with Other Manhattan Tracts, 1970*[a]

Measure	Soho	Other Manhattan tracts	Other low-income Manhattan tracts
Income (dollars)	35,345	52,712	31,981
	(5,841)	(32,416)	(5,538)
Percent in poverty	21.53	16.95	24.58
	(5.66)	(10.12)	(8.60)
Percent college educated	9.06	19.04	5.34
	(9.55)	(16.02)	(4.54)
Monthly rent (dollars)	296	572	348
	(130)	(314)	(62)
Distance to CBD (miles)	1.83	3.48	4.27
	(0.14)	(2.22)	(2.14)
Percent pre-1940 housing	91.29	65.67	70.65
	(10.40)	(26.31)	(26.18)
Distance to museums	0.94	1.14	1.30
	(0.06)	(0.65)	(0.63)
Tracts (number)	7	277	139

Sources: Author's calculations using Geolytics' Neighborhood Change Database (www.geolytics.com/USCensus,Neighborhood-Change-Database-1970-2000,Products.asp).

a. Tract averages, weighted by population. Standard deviations shown in parentheses. Distance to central business district (CBD) calculated using latitude-longitude coordinates of census tract center and the Empire State Building. Distance to museums is a nearest-neighbor index measuring average distance from census tract center to five nearest museums. Location of museums assembled from *The Rough Guide to New York City 2006* (New York: Penguin Group) and museum websites.

table 2-1 compares Soho to all other Manhattan census tracts with below-median household income (approximately $42,000 in 2000 inflation-adjusted dollars). Soho was slightly better off than other low-income areas on three measures (higher household income, lower share in poverty, and a higher share of the population that was college educated) and had lower monthly rents, which might have been viewed as advantageous by gallery owners.

The bottom panel of the table offers further evidence that Soho enjoyed some location-specific advantages over other low-income areas and indeed over some more affluent areas. In particular, Soho is closer to Manhattan's central business district (CBD), it had a larger share of pre–World War II housing stock, and it is closer to museums. Soho's building stock was not just old; it was architecturally and historically significant, as recognized in 1973 by the designation of most of the central neighborhood as the Cast Iron Historic District.[5] In addition, Soho benefited from the presence of New York University, which functions as an anchor institution for the neighborhood, and of Washington Square Park, a notable open space; it also abutted the already gentrifying neighborhood of Greenwich Village. As discussed in more detail below, those physical attributes—which predate both artists and galleries—could have been instrumental in attracting galleries to the neighborhood and in drawing higher-income households and commercial uses. Therefore, to isolate the impact of galleries on Soho's subsequent change, its trajectory must be compared to that of other Manhattan neighborhoods that had similar physical amenities and population characteristics but that did not become home to art galleries.

What Influences Gallery Location Decisions?

To develop a conceptual framework for gallery location decisions, I drew on both qualitative neighborhood case studies and economic theories about retail location choices. In explaining gallery movements into both Soho and Chelsea, historical researchers have highlighted the importance of the physical building stock.[6] Galleries that display very large artworks may require high-ceilinged open spaces such as those found in older manufacturing and warehouse buildings. It also seems plausible that gallery owners are sensitive to building aesthetics and prefer distinctive or attractive buildings in which to display their art. Standard retail location models suggest that galleries should choose locations that are attractive and convenient to potential consumers.[7] Because art collectors are likely to be highly affluent individuals, galleries should locate in high-end residential or commercial areas. In general, high population density and proximity to amenities such as employment centers and transportation infrastructure increase the volume of potential consumers. However, for luxury retailers such as galleries, access to the CBD or public transportation may be considered less important or even a drawback: high-end galleries may prefer to have a small and exclusive clientele rather than a large volume of casual visitors. Proximity to museums and other cultural institutions may be beneficial in drawing art-loving visitors to a neighborhood.[8] Retail location theory suggests that galleries benefit from agglomeration economies: locating near other galleries should increase the volume of potential consumers without the drawback of price competition, because consumers choose artworks based on aesthetic characteristics rather than price.[9] A recent empirical study has documented high spatial concentration among galleries and the preference of newly opening galleries to locate near existing gallery clusters.[10] Some important distinctions between gallery clusters and the arts districts discussed in other chapters in this volume (see, in particular, chapters 7 and 5) are that gallery clusters occur naturally, do not have specific zoning or tax status, and have no formal boundary designations.

As suggested by the Soho example, most of the factors that are likely to attract galleries to a neighborhood arguably exert independent impacts on the probability that the neighborhood will undergo economic or physical change. Distinctive and attractive architecture appeals not only to gallery owners but also to real estate developers who wish to sell or lease the space for housing or for retail or entertainment venues.[11] For example, many of the cast iron buildings in Soho are now occupied by high-end furniture stores, restaurants, and lofts, with an Apple store occupying a prominent storefront. Proximity to employment centers, museums and cultural institutions, and affluent residential populations increases the value of buildings for various real estate types, including housing and retail, entertainment, and office space.[12] Therefore it seems likely that neighborhoods with high levels of physical and economic amenities will attract investment, even in the absence of galleries.

Empirical Analysis

I explored two research questions in the context of New York's art market: In what types of neighborhoods do galleries choose to locate? Do neighborhoods with galleries experience more redevelopment? New York City offers a rich setting in which to conduct statistical analysis of art gallery location patterns. New York, specifically Manhattan, is the largest art market in the United States, with roughly twice as many art galleries as Chicago or Los Angeles.[13] During the 1990–2003 period, more than 4,500 galleries (total for the period) operated in Manhattan; two-thirds of them were contained in just four neighborhoods: Chelsea, Midtown, Soho, and the Upper East Side (figure 2-1). Comparing the economic and physical characteristics of those neighborhoods with one another and the rest of Manhattan allowed me to test which of the hypotheses discussed above explains galleries' location choices. The first stage of the analysis focuses particularly on location-specific neighborhood amenities that predate the emergence of gallery clusters; the second stage examines whether and how galleries influence patterns of redevelopment in the surrounding neighborhood. I tested whether city blocks that housed art galleries experienced more redevelopment—including adaptive reuse, new construction, and changes in land use patterns—than initially similar blocks without galleries.[14]

Figure 2-1. *Manhattan Gallery Locations, 2000*

Source: Manhattan Gallery Database. See Jenny Schuetz and Richard K. Green, "Is the Art Market More Bourgeois than Bohemian?" working paper (University of Southern California, Lusk Center for Real Estate, July 2011), pp. 7–11 (forthcoming, *Journal of Regional Science*, 2013).

Galleries' Choice of Neighborhood

As is true for other types of arts and cultural venues described in this volume, art galleries are not uniformly distributed within cities. In 2000, nearly 70 percent of Manhattan's 955 galleries were located in just four neighborhoods: Chelsea, Midtown, Soho, and the Upper East Side (figure 2-1). Even within those neighborhoods, galleries tended to cluster along certain streets or blocks (Madison Avenue on the Upper East Side, 57th Street in Midtown, and between 24th and 26th Streets along Tenth Avenue in Chelsea). Each of the four dominant gallery neighborhoods in Manhattan has certain amenities that may be attractive to gallery owners, although the amenities vary somewhat across the four neighborhoods (table 2-2).

The Upper East Side is Manhattan's oldest gallery cluster, dating back to the 1950s, and some individual galleries have existed for at least forty years. For decades it has been a prestigious residential neighborhood, attracting high-income residents and accordingly high real estate prices. Seventy percent of the land is used for residential purposes, double the figure for Manhattan's overall residential land share. Even by Manhattan standards, the building stock is quite old, and it is considered both historically and architecturally noteworthy; between 1967 and 1998, six separate historic districts were created in the Upper East Side, covering nearly 80 percent of the land area.[15] Adding to the prestige of the neighborhood, since the nineteenth century the Upper East Side has been home to many of New York's oldest and best-known museums and cultural institutions, including the Metropolitan Museum of Art (1870), the Guggenheim Museum (1959), and the Frick Collection (1935). The stretch of Madison Avenue from 59th Street to 86th Street, along which most galleries are located, also contains numerous luxury retailers. Zoning may constrain the location of galleries within the Upper East Side: galleries (and other retail uses) are allowed along most north-south avenues but not in the central residential areas of east-west cross streets.

Midtown also has been well known as an established gallery neighborhood since the 1950s. It is a predominantly commercial area, with 40 percent of the land used for office space, including space for financial services firms, law firms, and other highly paid professional services businesses. A luxury shopping district has developed around the intersection of Fifth Avenue and 57th Street, at least since 1940, when Tiffany's opened its flagship store at that corner.[16] Most of Midtown's galleries cluster around 57th Street, on or near that intersection. Galleries do not occupy only ground-floor showrooms in Midtown; often they are stacked in multilevel buildings. Midtown also houses

Table 2-2. *Comparison of Manhattan's Big Four Gallery Neighborhoods, 2000*

Measure	Manhattan	Chelsea	Midtown	Soho	Upper East Side	Other neighborhoods[a]
Galleries						
Galleries	955	140	125	194	207	14.19
Galleries/acre	8.94	34.42	25.66	115.19	74.30	4.08
Lagged galleries/acre	8.09	7.38	21.96	141.31	72.51	2.83
Land use and building characteristics						
Residential (percent)	34.26	30.95	8.78	34.00	70.70	33.83
Retail (percent)	2.55	3.41	6.96	8.85	3.36	2.10
Office (percent)	6.01	8.55	42.02	13.36	4.72	4.12
Loft + industrial (percent)	3.30	19.33	9.40	24.06	0.15	2.50
Pre-1940 structures (percent)	75.61	86.27	79.29	90.77	90.48	74.16
Other amenities						
Historic district (percent)	20.97	35.88	1.51	64.11	87.96	16.92
Commercially zoned (percent)	35.09	79.63	99.18	90.60	34.15	30.02
Cultural institutions/acre	1.91	1.48	2.67	0.59	7.18	1.39
Subway lines/acre	1.37	1.97	4.31	5.34	2.51	0.53
Tax lots (number)	43,648	2,367	2,207	1,603	2,657	1,221
Population characteristics						
Population/acre	141.85	116.49	56.54	144.89	228.97	97.33
Median household income	51,037	56,271	68,222	47,339	122,365	47,266
Bachelor's, professional, or graduate degree (percent)	46.10	61.66	64.23	46.22	79.54	43.64
Median rent	960	907	1,340	846	1,377	931
Census tracts (number)	290	11	18	7	14	9.23

Sources: Author's calculations using data from New York City Department of Finance, Real Property Assessment Database (RPAD), Neighborhood Change Database (www.geolytics.com/USCensus, Neighborhood-Change-Database-1970-2000,Products.asp), Manhattan Gallery Database, and New York City Department of City Planning, Landmarks Preservation Commission. All New York City administrative datasets provided to author courtesy of New York University's Furman Center.

a. Average across twenty-six other neighborhoods.

several major cultural institutions, including the Museum of Modern Art (1937) and the venerable main branch of the New York Public Library at Fifth Avenue and 42nd Street (1911). Although Midtown has a large number of subway stations connecting to nearly all subway lines, galleries are not clustered immediately around the stations. Virtually all the land in Midtown is zoned to allow commercial uses, including galleries. The residential population is relatively small, but it is more affluent and highly educated than Manhattan's overall population. Reflecting the high underlying land values, the price of Midtown real estate—commercial and residential uses—is among the highest in any part of Manhattan. Relatively little land had been designated part of a historic district as of 2000, the end of the study period.[17]

As discussed, Soho first attracted art galleries during the mid-1970s. The number of galleries continued to grow rapidly through the mid-1990s before declining somewhat through the early 2000s. Soho has a diverse mix of residential and commercial land uses, with an unusually large share of loft and industrial buildings (24 percent); the share in Manhattan overall is only about 3 percent. The central part of Soho, in which the vast majority of galleries are located, is composed of architecturally notable cast iron buildings, originally constructed as factories in the 19th century.[18] In 1973, the area of Soho containing those buildings (West Broadway on the western edge, Crosby Street on the east, Houston to the north, and Canal Street in the south) was designated the Cast Iron Historic District. Historic district status protects building exteriors from demolition or changes that would damage their architectural integrity, but it allows fairly flexible renovation and reuse of interior space. Many of Soho's cast iron buildings were vacant at the time of the historic designation and have undergone adaptive reuse since then, with extensive reconfiguration to fit the interiors for residential, retail, restaurant, office, and other tenants. Most of the buildings have also undergone exterior restoration and maintenance since the 1973 designation. Like Midtown, virtually all of Soho has commercial zoning that accommodates galleries. The population is the least affluent of the populations of the four main gallery neighborhoods, with incomes and residential rents slightly below Manhattan's average as of 2000, when the study ends.

Chelsea, which is the newest of Manhattan's gallery districts, rose to prominence in the late 1990s, while Soho was in decline. The neighborhood is quite mixed in terms of both land use and population. The western edge of Chelsea, which borders the Hudson River and former railroad yards, was originally developed for manufacturing and warehouses, and like Soho, it retains a fair number of industrial structures (19 percent of land was occupied by loft or industrial space as of 2000). The southern edge of Chelsea, abutting Greenwich Village, and the eastern part, along Fifth Avenue, have long been occupied by residential and mainstream commercial enterprises, including the historic "Ladies' Mile" shopping area along Fifth Avenue. Some of the residential areas, which historically served affluent residents (including the author

Clement Clarke Moore), have been designated historic districts since the early 1970s.[19] Other parts of the neighborhood contain superblocks of high-rise public housing. A smattering of galleries is located along Fifth Avenue, but most are clustered along Chelsea's western edge near Tenth Avenue in converted lofts and industrial spaces. As in Midtown, some buildings house multiple galleries stacked vertically on several floors. Chelsea has received considerable large-scale investment during the past ten to fifteen years, including the Chelsea Piers entertainment complex, the northern extension of Hudson River Park along the western edge, and most recently the highly renowned redevelopment of unused rail yards into High Line Park.[20]

The descriptive analysis of Manhattan's four gallery neighborhoods suggests not only that place-based amenities may be relevant in galleries' location decisions but also that galleries may value different types of amenities. The large display spaces available in formerly industrial buildings could explain galleries' presence in Soho and Chelsea but not in Midtown or the Upper East Side. Older, architecturally notable buildings may draw galleries to Soho and the Upper East Side, but they are less relevant for Chelsea and Midtown. One possible interpretation is that different types of galleries—perhaps varying by the genre or period of the art displayed or by the aesthetics of the gallery owner—prefer different types of neighborhood amenities. Another striking fact that emerges from considering the trajectory of gallery neighborhoods is the degree of persistence in gallery clusters. Two of the four neighborhoods have been home to a large number of art galleries for half a century, and even after Soho's much documented "decline," it retains nearly 20 percent of Manhattan's galleries.[21] The persistence of galleries in certain neighborhoods is consistent with strong agglomeration economies: for newly opening galleries in particular, one of the best ways to attract visitors is to locate among other, more established galleries in a neighborhood with a reputation as a gallery district.

To provide a more systematic test of the factors that affect gallery location decisions, I estimated a series of regressions modeling the number of galleries in a census tract or city block as a function of the lagged presence of galleries and various characteristics, such as building vintage, land use shares, presence of historic districts, and property values.[22] In general, the regressions provide support for some of the hypotheses suggested by the neighborhood descriptive analysis. The presence of notable or "star" galleries in the neighborhood five years earlier was the most robust predictor of current gallery locations: galleries seek to locate where other well-known galleries have established a foothold. The number of galleries in the census tract or block is positively associated with the share of pre-1940 building stock as well as the share of land in historic districts, suggesting some preferences for architectural styles or characteristics. The presence of museums or other cultural institutions is also positively predictive of the number of galleries in a tract or block; such institutions may also attract culturally minded visitors to the neighborhood. The regressions provide somewhat weaker evidence that the lack of commercial zoning may constrain galleries' location choices. Almost all blocks in Manhattan have some commercially zoned land, so zoning likely affects location choice at a very fine level of geography (that is, galleries can operate on blocks that face north-south avenues but not in the middle of east-west residential streets). The assessed value of buildings (per square foot) is positively correlated with the number of galleries in the neighborhood in all estimations, although the correlation is not always statistically significant. Building values should reflect the quality or desirability of the building itself and the value of amenities in the neighborhood. When population characteristics are added to the regression, it appears that galleries are more prevalent in neighborhoods with high population density and high household income, as are luxury retailers.

Taken together, the regression results suggest that far from seeking out blighted neighborhoods in need of gentrification, galleries prefer to locate in high-amenity neighborhoods that are likely to attract residential and commercial investment. Certainly two of the main gallery neighborhoods—Midtown and the Upper East Side—have been wealthy and high-value neighborhoods for many decades, while even Soho and Chelsea have distinctive place-based amenities that the rest of Manhattan does not enjoy. As a first estimation, then, it appears somewhat unlikely that art galleries will be effective mechanisms of neighborhood economic development because they tend not to move into initially blighted areas in need of regeneration.

Galleries and Neighborhood Transformation

As other chapters in this volume suggest, the impact of arts-related activities may be tested using a variety of economic indicators, including productivity and innovation (see chapters 7 and 10), income (chapter 9), and expenditures or employment in the arts themselves (chapters 3, 5, and 8). Impacts can also be measured at different levels, from metropolitan area to neighborhood to individual organization. Here I focus on identifying the impact of art galleries on the surrounding physical environment at two highly local levels: census tract and city block. Does the presence of art galleries cause changes in land use patterns and building stock in the immediate vicinity of the galleries? The form of this question arises directly from the qualitative neighborhood histories, which argue that the arrival of artists and galleries in neighborhoods such as Soho led to adaptive reuse of formerly industrial structures to create residential and retail buildings and to the reduction of visual blight in those neighborhoods.

Manhattan is a challenging setting in which to examine physical neighborhood changes. Because it is an island, land availability is strictly limited by immovable boundaries. The existing building stock is old and quite dense compared with that in many U.S. cities, while the regulatory environment—both formal zoning and public pressure—make the development process long, costly, and uncertain.[23] The demand for additional built space puts enormous upward pressure on land values, which should encourage greater development, yet natural and artificial supply constraints limit the rate and quantity of development. That raises questions about the best way to measure neighborhood change. The most straightforward metrics capture the quantity of new development, such as the number of new buildings or new residential units. But in Manhattan, development of new buildings may take from three to five years (or longer), so there may be a long lag between the initial stimulus—such as the arrival of a gallery—and the completion of new construction or an increase in the total number of residential units.[24] Alternatively, qualitative studies suggest that the arrival of galleries often prompts change in use of existing buildings, either to house a gallery itself or to convert neighboring buildings from lower-value uses (warehouses, garages, and industrial space) to higher-value uses (residential, retail, and office space). Depending on the initial condition of the building and the degree of remodeling needed, adaptive reuse of an existing property could be apparent in as little as one year. Existing properties also can be reconfigured or expanded to offer more leasable space, such as by converting a basement or laundry room into a residential or commercial unit or by adding floors on top of the existing structure. Such changes also allow property owners to capture more rents in response to rising property values, with less time and money expended than with demolition and redevelopment. In summary, to track the nuances of physical change in Manhattan requires the use of a variety of metrics on the quantity, type, and size of the built environment.

To illustrate the types of change that have occurred in Manhattan, table 2-3 shows the transition of two blocks with many galleries. These blocks were selected because each had the largest number of galleries per block in its neighborhood for the beginning year. Block 697 in Chelsea (located on 25th and 26th Streets between Tenth and Eleventh Avenues) had six lots that changed uses between 2000 and 2003, in each case moving from a lower-value use (warehouse, garage, factory) to a higher-value use (office, store, loft, museum). In five of these cases, one or more galleries were located in a building that changed use type. Lots 23 and 42 also acquired galleries during 2000–03, but they did not change building uses. Note that galleries were located in several different classes of building: warehouse, office, store, loft, factory, and museum. None of the lots on block 697 experienced changes in the size of the building (lot size or number of stories and units), and no demolition or redevelopment occurred on the block. In some cases, physical changes made during adaptive reuse were relatively minor or observable only in the interior; in others, they were comprehensive restorations of interior and exterior spaces that were widely visible to the neighborhood.

Block 1293 in Midtown (57th and 58th Streets between Madison and Fifth Avenues) illustrates not only changes in building use but also two examples of demolition and redevelopment between 1995 and 2000. On lot 12, a six-story loft building dating from 1930 was demolished and replaced by a sixteen-story retail building in 1996. Three adjacent lots (13, 14, and 15) that housed five- or six-story lofts and one walk-up apartment building were combined, and the existing buildings were demolished and replaced by a single twenty-four-story office building occupying the larger lot. Note that on this block, four of the five changes in building class occurred in buildings without galleries, while the building with the largest number of galleries (lot 26) did not change use or size. That illustrates the challenge of making a causal link between galleries and redevelopment: did the presence of galleries cause neighboring property owners to change uses or redevelop larger buildings, or did galleries choose to locate on a block experiencing development pressures for other reasons, such as increased demand for retail and office space in Midtown?

In a more systematic analysis of the relationship between galleries and physical change, I next compared various metrics of change across city blocks with and without galleries (table 2-4). The indicators of change were the percent of lots on a block that changed use type or size; the change in the total number of buildings, stories, and residential units on the block; and the change in the block's share of land that was residential or vacant. Each of the change metrics was calculated over a four- or five-year period (1990–95, 1995–2000, 2000–04), while the presence of galleries was measured in the first year of each period. The first two columns in table 2-4 show the average of each metric, comparing blocks that had at least one gallery at the beginning of the period with blocks that initially had no galleries. In comparing all city blocks in Manhattan, it appears that blocks with galleries underwent more change on almost all measures. For blocks with at least one gallery, approximately 7 percent of lots underwent a change in building class; on non-gallery

Table 2-3. *Chelsea and Midtown Land Uses, Selected Blocks*

Panel A. Chelsea, Block 697, 2000–03[a]

Lot	Building class 2000		Building class 2003		Square feet	Stories	Units	Year built	Galleries 2000	Galleries 2003
1	V1	Vacant	G6	Parking lot	19,750	0	0	0	0	0
5	E9	Warehouse	O9	Office	7,406	6	1	1926	2	3
8	G2	Garage	K9	Store building	5,896	1	1	1926	0	1
10	G6	Garage			6,448	1	1	1910	0	0
13	E1	Warehouse	L2	Loft	24,687	4	1	1910	0	1
23	L1	Loft			9,890	9	1	1917	0	12
27	E9	Warehouse			9,875	1	1	1942	0	0
31	E1	Warehouse			19,760	10	1	1928	1	0
42	F2	Factory			12,343	12	6	1927	0	3
47	F2	Factory	P7	Museum	22,219	10	4	1910	12	13
56	G1	Garage	L3	Loft	9,875	2	3	1929	0	1
60	G1	Garage			9,875	1	1	1929	0	0

a. "Square feet," "Stories," "Units," and "Year built" did not change between 2000 and 2003 for any of the lots on block 697. Blank space indicates that the variable did not change between 2000 and 2003.

Table 2-3. *Chelsea and Midtown Land Uses, Selected Blocks*
Panel B. Midtown, Block 1293, 1995–2000[a]

Lot	Building class 1995	Building class 2000	Square feet 1995	Square feet 2000	Stories 1995	Stories 2000	Year built 1995	Year built 2000	Galleries 1995	Galleries 2000
1	O3 Office	K9 Store	6,225		15		1931			
7	O3 Office		3,012		21–22		1926		1	4
9	L8 Loft	K9 Store	2,800		6		1916			
10	L8 Loft	K9 Store	3,815		6		1930			
12	L8 Loft	K9 Store	4,317		6	16	1930	1996	2	
13	L8 Loft		1,600		5		1953			
14	L8 Loft	O3 Office	2,312	6,221	6	24	1939	1998	1	
15	C7 Walk-up apartment		2,309		6		1930			
26	O4 Office		12,900		40–42		1929		14	25
47	J1 Theater	K1 Store	5,020		1		1930			
51	K3 Store		2,500		5		1930			
52	O9 Office	K9 Store	4,650		7		1930		2	2
59	O3 Office		18,000		25		1965			1
69	O4 Office		21,975		34–35		1930		1	3
7501	R5 Commercial condominium		26,592		51		1990			

Sources: Manhattan Gallery Database and New York City Department of Finance, Real Property Assessment Database (RPAD).

a. Blank space indicates that the variable did not change between 1995 and 2000. Lots 13, 14 and 15 were combined and redeveloped between 1995 and 2000. Building class, size, year built, and galleries for all three lots in 2000 are indicated in the row for Lot 14.

Table 2-4. *Change across City Blocks with and without Galleries*[a]

Change metric	All Manhattan blocks			Chelsea blocks		
	Gallery	No gallery	Difference	Gallery	No gallery	Difference
Any change (percent)	10.98	9.84	1.142**	14.12	13.29	0.826
	(12.56)	(14.99)		(15.14)	(20.87)	
Use change (percent)	7.30	5.76	1.547***	12.04	8.54	3.496*
	(10.61)	(11.99)		(14.96)	(17.08)	
Size change (percent)	4.84	5.02	-0.186	3.52	5.43	-1.909
	(6.71)	(9.74)		(4.26)	(12.67)	
Buildings	0.58	0.34	0.244***	0.40	0.36	0.046
	(2.50)	(2.88)		(1.96)	(2.18)	
Stories	2.24	0.86	1.384***	3.43	1.22	2.204
	(14.59)	(11.61)		(22.31)	(5.34)	
Residential units	24.36	15.13	9.235*	39.89	26.72	13.171
	(137.20)	(165.38)		(101.28)	(81.87)	
Residential land share (percent)	2.65	1.47	1.184***	2.75	1.21	1.544**
	(7.53)	(7.63)		(6.48)	(5.38)	
Vacant land share (percent)	-0.42	-0.75	0.334	-0.61	-0.17	-0.439
	(3.90)	(7.61)		(5.58)	(13.07)	
Number	1,167	4,665		89	229	

Sources: Author's calculations using New York City Department of Finance, Real Property Assessment Database (RPAD) (1991, 1996, 2000, and 2004) and Manhattan Gallery Database (2012).

a. The first three metrics report percent of lots in census tract undergoing change over five years. "Buildings," "Stories," and "Residential units" report changes in the number of each metric for the tract. Changes in building stock were calculated for 1990–95, 1995–2000, 2000–04. Gallery presence is given for the initial year of each period. Standard deviations are in parentheses.

*Significant at the 10 percent level; **significant at the 5 percent level; ***significant at the 1 percent level.

blocks, the figure was 5.76 percent. Blocks with galleries also saw larger increases in the total number of buildings, total number of stories, and total residential units than did blocks without galleries. The size of additional construction measures was quite small—gallery blocks gained 0.58 buildings, 2.24 stories, and 24.36 residential units over the five-year period—reflecting the lengthy and costly redevelopment process in Manhattan. Gallery blocks saw a greater increase in residential land share but not a significantly larger decrease in vacant land share.

However, comparing outcomes across all city blocks in Manhattan does not address the underlying differences in the location of galleries explored previously. That is, blocks on which galleries were located tended to be in higher-amenity, higher-income neighborhoods like Midtown and the Upper East

Side, while many of the non-gallery blocks were located in low-amenity, low-income neighborhoods, which are less likely to experience development for a variety of other reasons. A cleaner analysis would limit the comparison to blocks within the same larger neighborhood to control for the differences across neighborhoods that may affect gallery location choices and physical changes. For example, the last three columns in table 2-4 compare each of the change metrics across blocks with and without galleries, but the sample is limited to Chelsea. The results indicate fewer statistically significant differences between gallery and non-gallery blocks within the neighborhood than the all-Manhattan comparison revealed. Gallery blocks did have a larger share of lots that changed building class (12.04 percent versus 8.54 percent) and a greater increase in residential land share (2.75 percentage points versus 1.21 percentage points). But most of the metrics do not show statistically significant differences between gallery and non-gallery blocks. The difference between the all-Manhattan and Chelsea comparisons suggests that galleries locate in larger neighborhoods that are more likely to undergo future change but that within smaller areas, the presence of galleries has less of an impact on development patterns.

Manhattan's relatively restrictive zoning raises some concerns about whether the building stock can be redeveloped effectively in response to gentrifying influences. Perhaps galleries do increase underlying property values, but the surrounding buildings cannot be altered because of constraints. Comparing changes across blocks within the same neighborhood helps control for differences in zoning across Manhattan that might conflate the effect of galleries with the effects of tighter zoning. One possible explanation for the larger changes in blocks with galleries than in blocks without galleries across all neighborhoods is that galleries tend to locate in less restrictively zoned areas. But the lack of difference in block-level changes within neighborhoods could be explained only by the opposite relationship: galleries would have to be systematically located on more restrictively zoned blocks within the same neighborhood for zoning to cause downward bias in the estimated effects of galleries. To control for that possibility, a measure of initial zoning is included in the regression analysis.

Regression analysis conducted at both the census tract and city block level largely confirms the results of the difference in means shown in table 2-4.[25] The number of baseline galleries in the census tract is positively correlated with tract-level changes across a variety of metrics, including share of lots that change building class, increase in total number of buildings, and increase in residential land share. However, almost none of the results remain statistically significant after controls are added for initial neighborhood characteristics, such as building vintage, historic district status, amount of commercial zoning, and building dimensions. Analysis at the city block level provides slightly more robust evidence that presence of galleries correlates with neighborhood change. The number of galleries per block is positively associated with the percent of lots changing building class and the increase in residential land share, after baseline neighborhood amenities are controlled for. However, there is some evidence that galleries, rather than cause change themselves, choose to locate on blocks that are more likely to change. One possible interpretation is that gallery owners are adept at identifying blocks in early stages of transition that are not observable in the building metrics—for instance, blocks where a property owner has filed for a building permit but construction has not yet started or where an existing building has had an upgrade in tenants (for instance, from a lower-end to a higher-end retail store). The presence of a gallery on the block may be an indicator that (re)development is already under way.

Policy Implications and Future Research

Examining the relationship between the arts and economic development is a broad undertaking with many possible approaches. Various chapters in this volume illustrate the challenges of conducting empirical analysis on this topic. Researchers must determine what types of arts-related activity should be studied, what kinds of organizations conduct the activity, what the right measures of economic impact are, and what level of geography should be included. These seemingly technical questions are relevant for policymakers as well as academic researchers: if policymakers seek to enhance the economic well-being of neighborhoods, cities, or regions through expansion of creative industries, it is critical that they understand what types of activities and organizations provide the most bang for the taxpayer's buck. Moreover, understanding what makes an area attractive to artists and creative workers will help policymakers devise more effective targeted tax incentives or other economic subsidies. In this chapter, I explore one type of creative business—art galleries—that has been frequently cited by qualitative research as a possible mechanism for arts-led neighborhood regeneration. Unlike some of the arts venues discussed elsewhere in the volume, art galleries are generally for-profit businesses engaged in the sale (but not the production) of art. In economic terms, galleries have more in common with luxury retail stores than with graphic design studios or artists' workshops.

Contrasting somewhat with the conclusions of neighborhood case studies, the results of statistical analysis suggest that art galleries tend to locate in relatively high-amenity, affluent neighborhoods, not blighted marginal areas in need of regeneration. Types of amenities that attract galleries include older building stock, historic districts, and museums and other cultural institutions, although specific amenities vary across neighborhoods; galleries also are attracted by commercial zoning. Galleries have a strong propensity to locate near existing gallery clusters, suggesting some level of path dependence and possibly the need for a critical mass to sustain a gallery cluster. Galleries appear to be more sensitive to physical and economic amenities than to real estate values. On the occasions when galleries locate in relatively lower-income, lower-rent neighborhoods, the neighborhoods tend to have high levels of place-specific amenities, which may portend gentrification for the neighborhood even in the absence of galleries. Results also provide at best weak evidence that galleries spur physical development. Although simple correlations suggest that tracts and blocks with galleries undergo more change in land use patterns and building stock than blocks without galleries, the differences largely disappear once initial neighborhood amenities are accounted for. Galleries are like the canary in the coal mine: once galleries appear on a block, change is already under way.

These results have somewhat mixed implications for policymakers interested in encouraging arts-related economic development. If physical amenities are important to galleries' location choice, policymakers should consider the availability of such amenities across neighborhoods in deciding whether and where to establish gallery-oriented arts districts or art walks. Offering financial subsidies such as reduced property taxes may not be effective in attracting galleries to neighborhoods that lack the desired type of building stock or that are too remote from established cultural institutions. In addition, because galleries benefit strongly from proximity to other galleries, attracting a critical mass—and potentially some better known, well-established galleries—may be necessary to create an enduring gallery cluster in a neighborhood without a prior reputation as an arts center. One of the key questions in the field of arts and economic development is what types of arts venue are likely to generate the greatest increase in economic activity. These results suggest that galleries may not be the most effective or efficient target for economic development. Because galleries' economic success depends on access to affluent collectors, they are less likely than arts-production facilities to venture into marginal neighborhoods to begin with. Moreover, galleries are typically much smaller and attract a lower volume of visitors than museums or performing arts venues, which could explain the observed lack of spillover effects in surrounding neighborhoods. Subsequent chapters in this volume suggest that other types of arts activity may give policymakers more bang for their buck in terms of increased economic output. This is, however, an important area for future research. Analysis that directly compares the spillover impacts of different types of artistic venues within the same geographic context would be helpful in determining the most effective policies.

The analysis in this chapter focuses on the art market in Manhattan, so some caveats apply in attempting to extrapolate the results to other cities. Manhattan offers a useful setting for conducting large-scale quantitative research because of its unusually large inventory of galleries, the presence of four well-established gallery clusters, and not least, the availability of rich datasets that contain geographically and chronologically granular data on art galleries and neighborhoods' physical condition. Beyond that, it is difficult to know whether the setting is likely to overstate or understate the effect of galleries on surrounding neighborhoods. On the one hand, the unusual density of galleries and presence of notable or "star" galleries in Manhattan would seem propitious for attracting the volume and type of visitors that might revitalize a marginal neighborhood. As shown in table 2-3, Chelsea and Midtown have some blocks that have more than twenty-five galleries each—a density that is unlikely to occur in many other U.S. cities. On the other hand, the cost and difficulty of negotiating the development process in Manhattan may make it difficult for the physical environment to adapt to rising property values; cities with a more flexible development process or more available land might respond more visibly to gentrifying influences. The stringency of zoning in Manhattan may constrain the overall level of changes observed in the building stock, but it is unlikely to explain the lack of difference in redevelopment across blocks with and without galleries in the same neighborhood.

Although no equivalent datasets for either galleries or physical indicators exist for other U.S. cities, some comparative work could be undertaken using publicly available data, such as ZIP Business Patterns (ZBP) or U.S. economic census data, or proprietary datasets such as the National Establishment Time Series (NETS). At a minimum, the ZBP could be used to examine the degree and persistence of galleries' spatial concentration within other U.S. cities or metropolitan areas, down to the ZIP code level. Combining the ZBP with demographic and economic characteristics from the decennial U.S. census or the American Community Survey (ACS) would allow examination of whether art galleries in other cities also locate in high-income neighborhoods with older housing stock. The role of art galleries in neighborhood revitalization has so far been studied mostly by qualitative researchers; complementing their studies with larger-scale statistical analysis would help place gallery neighborhoods within the larger urban context.

Notes

1. Neighborhood boundaries in New York, as in other cities, may be defined in a variety of ways, and colloquial neighborhood names do not always reference the same spatial boundaries. For the purposes of the empirical analysis in this chapter, neighborhood boundaries are defined by the New York City Department of City Planning projection areas, which overlay colloquial names on geographically contiguous clusters of census tracts.

2. Sharon Zukin, *Loft Living: Culture and Capital in Urban Change* (Rutgers University Press, 1989), p. 2–6. Harvey Molotch and Mark Treskon, "Changing Art: SoHo, Chelsea, and the Dynamic Geography of Galleries in New York City," *International Journal of Urban and Regional Research,* vol. 33 (Spring 2009), pp. 517–41; Aaron Shkuda, "From Urban Renewal to Gentrification: Artists, Cultural Capital, and the Remaking of the Central City," Ph.D. dissertation, University of Chicago, 2010, chapter 1.

3. Molotch and Treskon, "Changing Art," p. 519; Zukin, *Loft Living,* pp. 111–25.

4. All data on art galleries were drawn from the Manhattan Gallery Database, described in more detail in Jenny Schuetz and Richard K. Green, "Is the Art Market More Bourgeois than Bohemian?" working paper (University of Southern California, Lusk Center for Real Estate, July 2011), pp. 7–11 (forthcoming, *Journal of Regional Science,* 2013).

5. Landmarks Preservation Commission, *Soho Cast-Iron Historic District Designation Report* (New York: 1973) (www.nyc.gov/html/lpc/downloads/pdf/reports/SoHo_HD.pdf).

6. Molotch and Treskon, "Changing Art," p. 524; Shkuda, "From Urban Renewal to Gentrification," p. 14.

7. Brian Berry, *Geography of Market Centers and Retail Distribution* (Englewood Cliffs, N.J.: Prentice Hall, 1967); David L. Huff, "Defining and Estimating a Trading Area," *Journal of Marketing,* vol. 24 (Fall 1964), pp. 34–38; Gabriel Picone, David Ridley, and Paul Zandbergen, "Distance Decreases with Differentiation: Strategic Agglomeration by Retailers," *International Journal of Industrial Organization,* vol. 27 (Fall 2009), pp. 463–73.

8. David Halle and Elisabeth Tiso, *Far West in New York: Contemporary Art, Mega Projects, Preservation, and Urban Change,* unpublished manuscript (2012), chapter 4; Chin-tao Wu, *Privatising Culture: Corporate Art Intervention since the 1980s* (London: Verso Books, 2003).

9. Picone, Ridley, and Zandbergen, "Distance Decreases with Differentiation," p. 465.

10. Schuetz and Green, "Is the Art Market More Bourgeois than Bohemian?" pp. 25–26.

11. Hans Koster, Jos van Ommeren, and Piet Rietveld, "Upscale Neighborhoods: Historic Amenities, Income, and Spatial Sorting of Households," working paper presented at the Urban Economics Association meeting, Miami, November 2011.

12. Jan Brueckner, Jacques-Francois Thisse, and Yves Zenou, "Why Is Central Paris Rich and Downtown Detroit Poor? An Amenity-Based Theory," *European Economic Review,* vol. 43, no. 1 (1999), pp. 91–107.

13. Data on art galleries across metropolitan areas are available from the U.S. Census Bureau's County Business Patterns dataset (www.census.gov/econ/cbp/).

14. Primary data on art gallery locations come from the Manhattan Gallery Database (see Schuetz and Green, "Is the Art Market More Bourgeois than Bohemian?" pp. 7–11, for a full description of the database). Detailed information on land use patterns and building characteristics for every tax parcel in Manhattan is taken from New York City administrative records kept by the Department of Finance, the Department of City Planning, and the Landmarks Preservation Commission. Those datasets were combined with economic and demographic characteristics at the census tract level taken from Geolytics' Neighborhood Change Database. Analytical techniques used include mapping and spatial analysis, descriptive statistics, and multivariate regression analysis. Full details on data and statistical methods are available in Jenny Schuetz, "Do Art Galleries Transform Neighborhoods?" working paper, University of Southern California, Lusk Center for Real Estate (2012), pp. 10–20.

15. Treadwell Farm (1967) was one of Manhattan's earliest historic districts, but it is quite small. Carnegie Hill (1974, expanded 1993), Metropolitan Museum (1977), and Upper East Side (1981) cover the largest areas. Maps of all historic district boundaries are available on the Landmarks Preservation Commission website (www.nyc.gov/html/lpc/html/maps/historic_district.shtml).

16. Corporate history for Tiffany's and Co. is available at www.tiffany.com/About/TheTiffanyStory/default.aspx#p+1-n+6-cg+-c+-s+-r+-t+-ri+-ni+1-x+-pu+-f+/5/0/6.

17. Two historic districts were added to Midtown after 2000, both relatively small: one around Madison Square Garden, the other to the east near Murray Hill.

18. Photographs of some of the cast iron buildings that still house galleries can be found in Schuetz, "Do Art Galleries Transform Neighborhoods?" p. 38.

19. See Landmarks Preservation Commission, *Chelsea Historic District Designation Report* (1970) and *Ladies' Mile Historic District Designation Report,* vol. 1 (1989) for details on district designations. Historic districts in Chelsea include Greenwich Village (1969), Chelsea (1970, extended 1981), and Ladies Mile (1989). Galleries mostly fall into the area belonging to the West Chelsea Historic District, but it was not designated until 2008, after the study period.

20. Halle and Tiso, *Far West in New York,* chapter 4.

21. For discussion of Soho's decline, see Molotch and Treskon, "Changing Art," pp. 524–25; Halle and Tiso, *Far West in New York*, chapter 1.

22. Full details on the data and estimation techniques can be found in Schuetz, "Do Art Galleries Transform Neighborhoods?" pp. 10–20.

23. Edward L. Glaeser, Joseph Gyourko, and Raven Saks, "Why Is Manhattan So Expensive? Regulation and the Rise in Housing Prices," *Journal of Law and Economics,* vol. 48 (Fall 2005), pp. 331–70.

24. For analysis of the time required to complete a development project in New York City, see Furman Center for Real Estate and Urban Policy, *State of New York City's Housing and Neighborhoods 2006* (New York University, 2006).

25. Full regressions results can be found in Schuetz, "Do Art Galleries Transform Neighborhoods?" p. 44–52.

ANN MARKUSEN, ANNE GADWA NICODEMUS,
and ELISA BARBOUR

3

The Arts, Consumption, and Innovation in Regional Development

Economic development strategy at the state, regional, and local levels has been dominated by economic (or export) base theory, which posits that exports drive overall growth, whether measured by employment, output, or value added. The dominance of export base theory directs policy attention and incentives chiefly to businesses whose output is exported from the city or region. In the United States, where economic development is practiced principally at the state and local level, public sector development agencies are preoccupied with outside export-type enterprises, which they try to attract to the local area, rather than with local startups, especially those aimed at area consumers.[1]

Although arts advocates often stress the local multiplier effects of additions to arts capacity and programming enabled by public funding, they largely fail to demonstrate that such additions can produce net increases in growth and jobs unless the additions draw tourists or produce commodified goods for export. This chapter revisits export base theory, probing its origins and showing its limitations, and reviews cross-sectional and longitudinal evidence from national studies questioning the causal relationship between exports and growth. Despite caveats since its inception, economic base theory—which distinguishes between locally consumed and externally consumed goods and services and assumes that the former evolve in lockstep with the latter (despite evidence to the contrary)—is a guiding principle of economic developers at state and local levels. We argue that export base practices are based on a trun-

Our thanks to Todd Gabe and Greg Schrock for feedback on earlier versions of the arguments; to Bill Beyers for his partnership on the empirical findings; and to Michael Rushton, Kevin Rafter, Doug Noonan, and Jenny Schuetz for feedback on the content.

cated view of regional growth potential, one that is especially antagonistic to arts and culture.

We offer an alternative, consumption base theory, which posits that investments in certain types of consumption base activity can create net new jobs and income by

—offering residents opportunities to spend more of their discretionary income on new locally produced goods and services

—seeding innovations that later expand into export markets

—nurturing organizations and occupations that re-spend more of their earnings locally than others do

—attracting and retaining entrepreneurs, firms, and workers.

We explore this theory in the context of arts and culture. First, an increase in local arts activity can capture a larger share of residents' discretionary income, creating sustainable jobs. This is a phenomenon broader than import substitution, in which people simply buy locally the same items and services that they previously imported. The argument here is that given local access to new types of arts and cultural programming, people will change the composition of their spending toward the arts and away from other consumer goods and services. Or, put another way, proximity to arts and cultural offerings will alter people's tastes and preferences (or tap into latent preferences) in ways that change the basket of goods and services that they spend their money on.

Second, new arts and cultural offerings first serve a local market (as do offerings in other fields), which functions as a testing ground. Musicians (other than the classically trained, orchestra-bound types) may begin in a garage, move out into pubs and cafes, and build a local group of fans before exporting their work. New plays, choreography, and visual art are created and honed in local venues. Most successful arts and cultural innovations are first rooted and nurtured in local consumption markets and marketed farther afield only when they are proven and mature.[2]

Third, because most arts activities are highly labor intensive, higher shares of income generated locally may be re-spent locally. A visiting orchestra or Broadway troupe, whose performers drive in for a night and take their incomes with them, would not have much local effect, nor would a museum exhibit in which the artwork is shipped in from elsewhere. But if residents patronize local artists who live and work in the community, their expenditures are apt to recycle locally at higher rates, supporting other workers, businesses, and landlords. Furthermore, it is widely believed that artists spend higher shares of their income on fellow artists' work—unlike workers in most other occupations—and often do so locally, so that the multiplier effect is again larger.

Fourth, arts offerings may attract and retain residents, entrepreneurs, firms, and workers in non-arts sectors. Their productions contribute to the quality of life in a town or region. Retirees, in particular, appear to be drawn to arts-rich communities, as are self-employed people who are able to live and work wherever they wish. Employers often credit the arts with increasing their appeal to both managers and skilled workers, and some find that arts-rich locations help them attract customers, too.

Finding empirical evidence for consumption base growth is challenging. If arts and culture are treated as non-basic, as in the export base model, economists would expect the size of arts and cultural capacity and participation to expand and contract with overall area employment—that is, to be explained by export base dynamism. However, longitudinal analysis is difficult to conduct because good time series data on the supply of and demand for arts and culture do not exist.[3]

As a second best, researchers can do a cross-sectional analysis to explore whether cities and regions, taking population size and other factors into account, exhibit the comparable arts and cultural capacities and participation rates that would be expected under export base assumptions. They can also explore whether larger, denser cities have relatively larger arts and cultural complexes, an outcome observed in historical research and attributed to greater economies of scale in cultural production.[4] Where regions' and cities' arts capacities and participation rates diverge from these expectations, a plausible case can be made for the ability of arts and cultural activity to independently generate jobs and output.

We used cross-sectional data on California regions and cities (at times compared with other U.S. cities, metros, and regions) to explore whether nonprofit arts and cultural activity appears to be a non-basic sector, as economic base theory assumes, or whether there are large variations in its distribution, a finding that would support a consumption base argument. The probe also examines whether the marked differentials discovered can be explained by differences in resident populations' demographics (proxies for tastes and preferences) and economic functional roles.

We show that nonprofit arts capacity (supply) and participation (demand) by region and city in California do not correlate closely with overall size of population, which export base theory would predict. Nor do they correlate closely with demographic features of urban and regional populations, proxies for differences in tastes and preferences. The empirical analysis finds highly differentiated rates of arts organizations per capita and arts revenues per capita at both the regional and city level, as well as disparate arts-participation rates among regions. Regression of presence of arts organizations and arts participation on a set of local resident socioeconomic and local economy characteristics found that those differentials could not be fully explained. Furthermore, when comparing the Los Angeles and San Francisco Bay regions, there was no evidence that nonprofit arts activity, either arts offerings or participation rates, was driven by the concentration of for-profit cultural industries.

The chapter concludes by hypothesizing that over the longer run, evolutionary capacity building by individuals and organizations can create a nonprofits arts and cultural sector that helps to create and sustain jobs and boost incomes as well as provide products with intrinsic artistic value. This process may succeed in large part because area residents are envisioned as active participants, not passive consumers, in the process. Among the California regions, the San Francisco Bay Area is a particular standout: its arts-participation rate, presence of nonprofit arts organizations (number of organizations and aggregate budget), and share of employed (including self-employed) artists are far above what can be explained by demographic factors, economic roles, or the presence of cultural industries. In addition, the sparsely populated and heavily forested Northern and Sierra regions also host very high numbers of arts organizations per capita as well as participation rates that are above the state average. We illustrate the plausibility of the growth potential of arts capacity building with a short explication of one small rural town's successful effort to reverse long-term decline by investing in an arts center that serves the local area. In closing, We suggest implications for arts advocates, public sector economic development agencies, and arts agencies and recommend routes for further research.

The Heavy Hand of Export Base Theory

Nonprofit arts and cultural activities are broadly thought of, by economists and others, as serving a local area. Live theaters, art fairs, dance studios, and music venues rely heavily on local or regional patronage. Because of export base theory, a fashion in the field of regional science for more than half a century, economic developers, politicians, and even arts advocates believe that the only growth-generating jobs and sales are those associated with sales outside of the city or region. Indeed, the best economic impact analyses of the nonprofit arts sector consider only those expenditures and associated jobs that are created and supported by tourists traveling to a locality or by the sales or travels of art performers to venues elsewhere.[5] Even self-employed artists have been championed as partial exporters of their visual work, music, performances, and publications.[6] If artists are overrepresented in a city or metro area, their excess numbers are assumed to reflect successful sales outside the region, not higher local patronage. In contrast, the cultural industries—motion pictures and television, recorded music, advertising, publishing, broadcasting, design—are mainly the province of the for-profit sector and are assumed to be principally export oriented.[7] Although arts impact assessments based on these types of assumptions have been skillfully questioned by economist Bruce Seaman,[8] most arts advocates think that demonstrating how the arts create jobs is the only way to garner public and legislative support.

What is the causal theory behind such export base practices? The seminal debate on export base theory was conducted by Douglass North and Charles Tiebout in the 1950s. Economic historian North, then teaching at the University of Washington and likely influenced by Canadian Harold Innis's staples theory, argued that a region's growth is constrained by its ability to export. Income from exports is circulated to local workers and suppliers (indirect effects) who then re-spend it, at least in part, in the regional economy. Also at the University of Washington, Tiebout, in a brilliant critique, pointed out the logical flaw in this argument: the world economy as a whole does not export, yet it continues to grow. Tiebout posited, among other critiques, that an internal division of labor could produce growth, echoing Adam Smith's famous characterization of capitalist production and trade.[9] Put another way, export growth may follow rather than lead output growth.

As evidence for his hypothesis, North wrote an account of nineteenth-century (1790–1860) American economic growth in which he argued that most of it was attributable to exports of slave-grown cotton. Tiebout's position received empirical support in economic historian Diane Lindstrom's book on nineteenth-century Philadelphia, in which she showed that there were no appreciable exports from the Philadelphia region, a prominent center of population and output growth, during the same period. What drove Philadelphia's expansion was an elaborating internal division of labor within industry and agriculture.[10]

Export base theory was quickly distilled into economic base multipliers that became a well-used economic development tool in analyses that often completely ignored the seminal theoretical debate. Furthermore, few longitudinal comparative studies have ever been conducted. A number of economists have run cross-sectional and longitudinal tests of the export base hypothesis using nations as units. For thirty-seven developing countries over the period 1950–81, Jung and Marshall found evidence that supported the export promotion thesis in only four cases.[11] Five countries increased output but reduced exports, while four countries experienced export growth but output reduction. Ghartey concluded that export-driven development appeared to explain growth in Taiwan but not Japan or the United States.[12] In a five-country study, Sharma and his colleagues found that Japan and Germany experienced export-led growth from 1960 to 1987, but in the United States and the United Kingdom, output growth induced export growth.[13] Through the mid-1990s, then, there was no compelling empirical evidence for the claim that exports drive overall growth.

In addition, the evidence is incontrovertible that output for local consumption grows faster than exports as a town grows into a city and a city into a metropolis.[14] In other words, the multiplier is not stable—local activity tends to increase faster than export activity as a region expands. Furthermore, the local consumption base expands faster in some regions than in others of the same size. Yet economic development policy remains stubbornly myopic about the value of investments in local-serving capacity and insists, as if it were a creed, that exporting enterprises and industries be privileged. The low status of arts and culture in economic development and with government agencies generally is a by-product of such thinking.

A Consumption Base Alternative

Expansion in local consumption can also be a source of sustainable city and regional growth. The theoretical case for its potential encompasses several phenomena. First, changes in regional tastes and preferences and thus in consumer spending in favor of goods and services that are locally produced can produce job growth without any expansion in the export base. This phenomenon is much broader than economists' notion of import substitution. The latter generally refers to the efforts of a region to produce for itself the same goods and services that it previously imported. However, the demand for output from local consumption–oriented sectors may also rise when residents shift their purchases to new types of goods and services that have become available locally, such as live theater and music and opportunities to study art and participate in the making of art. For instance, if area residents can now hear live music at a local club, they may be more apt to spend their discretionary income there than at the local mall. Such shifts can be facilitated with strategic and sustained investments in the local consumption base.

In a second and related phenomenon, new local capacity may generate added jobs and incomes because it generates higher indirect and induced multiplier effects. An ethnic folk arts organization may buy more of its materials, instruments, and business services (the indirect impact) locally than does a small retail import shop at the mall. Workers in some occupational groups may be more likely than others to spend their incomes locally. Professional athletes and performing artists make an interesting comparison. The mounting of professional sports events, a mix of locally oriented (ticket sales) and export-oriented (advertising revenue) activity, involves fewer direct employees and more indirect and often external-to-the-region expenditures—for trainers and training camps, transportation services, personnel and hotel services at out-of-town games, and players who live elsewhere. In contrast, with the exception of those involved in touring plays, exhibitions, and music acts, most artists who perform in a metropolitan region also live there. Artists likely spend high shares of their incomes locally, including on ongoing music, dance, and visual art lessons and space. Furthermore, performing artists are widely believed to be significant patrons of other arts activities, so larger shares of their incomes may be cycled through the local economy. Accurate multipliers for forecasting total employment effects of new economic development projects, whether the projects serve the export or the local market, must account for activity-specific induced effects and occupation-specific consumption patterns.

A third and potentially expansive way that increments to the local consumption base may produce sustained growth is through their innovative potential. New export sectors often begin as local-serving experiments. A product or service that is pioneered locally, with local support and feedback, may blossom into something attractive to consumers or producers elsewhere, enabling job growth and diversifying the community's economic base. Cortright offers the example of microbrewing in Portland.[15] Microbrewing was first developed by small breweries serving local customers, but the breweries' returns from local demand for their products enabled them to move through the experimentation and development stages and eventually into marketing and capacity investments to reach consumers farther afield. Similarly, a locally oriented dance troupe may mature into one that tours and brings additional income back home. Entire towns have changed their fortunes by fostering arts and cultural distinctiveness—country music in Branson (Missouri), Shakespeare in Ashland (Oregon), New Orleans's unique jazz scene. Many such specializations never materialize when economic development resources are denied to local-serving startups.

Fourth, superior local consumption offerings help to attract skilled workers, managers, entrepreneurs, and retirees to a region to live and work, as argued by quality-of-life and creative city researchers.[16] Such recruits bring their human capital, companies, and retirement incomes into the regional economy, increasing its size and diversity.

Economists and policymakers have no easy longitudinal data with which to explore the relative contributions of these forces to overall urban growth and development. While all are important, the potential for arts and cultural capacity and activities to expand the economy by capturing larger shares of residents' discretionary income and the relatively high propensity for arts and cultural purchases and payroll to be spent locally are the least well explored. As economy-wide evidence for the power of the local-serving sector, however, Markusen and Schrock found that over the period from 1980 to 2000, local-serving occupations in the thirty largest U.S. metros outpaced job growth in export base occupations by four to one.[17]

If arts and cultural activity belongs purely to the non-basic sector, so that the extent of arts and cultural activity is dictated by the success of the area's economic base, then differences should not appear in per capita number of arts and cultural organizations, arts employment as a share of the entire workforce, and patronage rates from place to place—allowing, of course, for some modest differences in tastes and preferences. Furthermore, it may be possible to explain city and regional differences in nonprofit arts and cultural capacity, arts-participation rates, and artists' employment on the basis of population size, socioeconomic characteristics of the population, and the presence of commercial cultural industries.

Evidence on Spatial Differentials in Arts Capacity and Participation

Have people and organizations made differential investments in local-serving arts capacity at the city and regional levels that cannot be explained by population size or socioeconomic features of the population? A study of California's arts and cultural ecology recently completed for the James Irvine Foundation found marked differentials in the number of arts organizations per capita and in arts-participation rates across the state's cities and regions.[18] The study speculates that those differences have resulted from decades-long cultivation in some areas of local-serving arts capacity that sustains jobs and income. The findings also show that the concentration of world-class cultural industries in Los Angeles has not been accompanied by a parallel expansion in arts nonprofits and that arts-participation rates there are slightly below the state average. These results question the contention that only export-serving arts and cultural activities produce growth.

The methodology employed in the study involved use of several datasets.[19] Estimates of the number of and average budget totals of regional arts and cultural organizations were based on National Center for Charitable Statistics (NCCS) data for 2008–10, drawn from Internal Revenue Service reports, and Cultural Data Project (CDP) data for 2007–09. Because the CDP data are not a random sample and under-represent smaller and especially ethnic, folk, and traditional arts organizations, all CDP data points are benchmarked against the NCCS. For data on socioeconomic characteristics of residents and economic features of California cities, the researchers relied on the American Community Survey (2006–08), the 2000 U.S. census (housing unit density), the California Department of Finance (current city population estimates, 2009), the California consumer price index, and Foundation Center data for 2008 on annual giving. Arts-participation data were drawn from the Survey of Public Participation in the Arts for 2002 and 2008, but because of small sample sizes, analysis of effective demand could be pursued only at the regional scale. The study relied on local knowledge, both from the Irvine Foundation's arts program and the Public Policy Institute of California, to define meaningful regions (respecting contiguity, metropolitan polarity, and relative ecological and socioeconomic homogeneity in low population areas) that were large enough to ensure statistical significance with the datasets used (figure 3-1).

The regional-level analysis finds that California's largest metros—Los Angeles and the San Francisco Bay Area—host the lion's share of arts organizations and, on average, larger organizations (table 3-1). The Bay Area hosts a high number of arts organizations per capita and has the highest per capita nonprofit arts budget while the relatively populous, but less metro-centric, Inland Empire and San Joaquin Valley regions host relatively few arts organizations per capita and rank low in per capita nonprofit arts budgets.

But exceptions preclude an inference that differences among regions in per capita numbers and budgets simply reflect population size or economies of scale in the arts. Some of California's least populous regions show a strong commitment to arts capacity. The thinly populated and non-cosmopolitan Sierra (5.6 organizations per 10,000 people) and North Coast and North State (5.2 per 10,000) regions host more arts organizations per capita than the state average, though their nonprofits' budgets are on average smaller (table 3-1). The multiplicity of smaller organizations in these rural areas suggests that residents want and have invested in a full range of artistic disciplines and offerings, even if they are modest in scale. In contrast, the Los Angeles (LA) region hosts fewer arts organizations per capita than the state average, though average annual budget size is quite high: $913,000, almost 50 percent higher than

Figure 3-1. *Author-Defined Regions Based on County Groups Used by the James Irvine Foundation and the Public Policy Institute of California.*

Source: Based on Ann Markusen and others, *California's Arts and Cultural Ecology* (San Francisco: James Irvine Foundation, September 2011), figure 2 (http://irvine.org/news-insights/publications/arts/arts-ecology-reports). See Technical Appendix, A2, for counties included in each region.

the state average. Yet LA's per capita nonprofit arts budget is 10 percent lower than that in the Bay Area, a region with only half the population that LA has.

To probe explanatory factors for differences in both per capita numbers of arts organizations and per capita nonprofit arts budgets, the model includes characteristics of residents and economic features of place. The former include income, wealth, educational attainment, race/ethnicity, immigrant status, and age variables. Economic features of place include population size and density, primary city status, jobs per capita, and city government and private philanthropic funding for arts activity. If residents' characteristics explained all of the variation, one might conclude that demand alone explains arts presence, even though past investments in capacity could have attracted more art lovers to the area and produced more art lovers among the existing population. But we hypothesize that place matters: that individual, philanthropic, and public sector efforts to build arts capacity could account for marked differentials.

Table 3-1. *Characteristics of California Arts and Cultural Organizations by Region, 2009*

Region	Population	Number of organizations	Percent California nonprofits	Average number of organizations per 10,000 people	Total arts nonprofit budgets per capita[a]	Average annual budget[a]
Los Angeles metro	14,325,209	3,749	35	2.6	238.84	912,607
Bay Area	7,378,178	3,190	30	4.3	266.08	615,422
Inland Empire	4,167,153	538	5	1.3	34.70	268,808
San Joaquin Valley	3,984,340	672	6	1.7	25.94	153,828
South Coast and Border	3,364,890	848	8	2.5	102.98	408,638
Sacramento metro	2,155,116	583	5	2.7	145.75	538,775
Central Coast	1,458,990	605	6	4.1	124.81	300,982
Northern Valley	686,772	168	2	2.4	26.68	109,061
North Coast and North State	421,202	218	2	5.2	115.92	223,965
Sierra	313,658	175	2	5.6	56.93	102,039
Total	38,255,508	10,746	100	2.8	171.49	610,485

Sources: Ann Markusen and others, *California's Arts and Cultural Ecology* (San Francisco: James Irvine Foundation, September 2011), table 9 (http://irvine.org/news-insights/publications/arts/arts-ecology-reports). Data obtained from National Center for Charitable Statistics (NCCS) (nccs.urban.org) and Cultural Data Project (CDP) (www.culturaldata.org).

a. In 2010 U.S. dollars.

The regression analysis was done at the city level, including all California cities with a population in excess of 20,000 (N = 237). The move from region to city did not alter arts organizational differentials by size. On average, smaller cities had higher numbers of arts organizations per capita than larger cities, mirroring the regional pattern. The smallest cities—the bottom one-fifth, ranked by population size—hosted 14 arts organizations per 10,000 residents, on average, while the top one-fifth, the largest cities, hosted 3 per 10,000 residents.

Which of the factors that distinguish cities are most important, after controlling for the others? Ordinary least squares (OLS) regressions were used to evaluate the relative importance of the city features noted above in predicting number of organizations per capita, after controlling for regional location of cities in addition to the city features listed.

The city features most closely and positively associated with a higher number of arts and cultural organizations per capita were job density, level of private philanthropic funding for the arts, level of residents' educational attainment, and personal wealth of city residents (table 3-2). *Regional* location did not prove to be a statistically significant predictor of the prevalence of per capita organizations after controlling for the other factors, which is strong evidence that *community-level* characteristics of places play the more important role in explaining arts and cultural activity.

The job density finding is of particular interest. Job density, the number of people working in a community divided by the number of people living there, distinguishes job centers (places with a high number of jobs relative to the residential population) from bedroom suburbs, retiree enclaves, and other communities with fewer jobs relative to population. Job center cities are more likely to host businesses whose owners, managers, and employees contribute to local arts and culture through patronage or contributions. Businesses may feel that strong arts and cultural offerings enhance employee motivation, help them attract and keep employees, and encourage retail customers. Workers commuting from nearby communities may attend venues or participate in arts and cultural events at lunchtime or after work, and because they are familiar with the area, they may bring their families and friends there on the weekends. Job centers are apt to generate more in property taxes, which may be available to fund arts and culture, among other priorities, since business property tax rates are higher than residential rates.

The jobs-per-capita measure is not strongly correlated with either city size or central city status; therefore historic city-centeredness is not at work here. Those findings may reflect the fact that the larger California metro areas,

Table 3-2. *Determinants of Per Capita Nonprofit Arts and Cultural Organizations, California, 2008–09*[a]

Determinant	Organizations per capita (logged)
Population (logged)[b]	− ***
Housing unit density (logged)[c]	
Principal city[d]	
Jobs per capita (logged)[d]	+ ***
Median household income (logged)[d]	− ***
Gini index of income inequality[d]	
Income, dividend, and net rental income per household (wealth proxy)[d]	+ ***
Percent of the population over age 25 with a bachelor's degree or higher[d]	+ ***
Percent of the population that is non-white or Hispanic[d]	
Percent of population that is foreign born[d]	
Percent of the population under age 18[d]	
Private philanthropic arts funding (logged)[e]	+ ***
City arts-related public expenditure (logged)[f]	
Regional dummies	
Sacramento metro	
Bay Area	
Central Coast	
San Joaquin Valley	
Los Angeles metro	
Inland Empire	
South Coast and Border	
Adjusted R^2	0.66

Sources: Ann Markusen and others, *California's Arts and Cultural Ecology: Technical Appendix* (San Francisco: James Irvine Foundation, September 2011), table A7 (http://irvine.org/news-insights/publications/arts/arts-ecology-reports). Data from National Center for Charitable Statistics (NCCS) (nccs.urban.org) and Cultural Data Project (CDP) (www.culturaldata.org).

a. N = 237 (for cities with populations of 20,000 or more and with further exclusions as specified). Results that did not meet a significance level of $*p < .10$ are not shown.$*p < .10$; $**p < .05$; $***p < .01$.

b. California Department of Finance (www.dof.ca.gov).

c. U.S. Census, 2000 (www.census.gov/prod/www/abs/decennial).

d. American Community Survey, 2006–08 (www.census.gov/acs).

e. Foundation Center (foundationcenter.org).

f. California State Controller's Office (www.sco.ca.gov).

especially Los Angeles and the Bay Area, are quite polycentric, especially compared with East Coast and Midwestern cities. Communities like Long Beach, Culver City, Santa Monica, Pasadena, San Jose, Oakland, and Berkeley are both job centers and arts and cultural hubs. Analytical work at the community level suggests a mosaic of diversified hubs within the state's arts and cultural ecology, a complement to the finding that arts organizations are dispersed across the entire state, with a higher-than-average number of arts organizations per capita in smaller, mainly northern, regions.

This analysis, based on the James Irvine Foundation California study, is exploratory. It offers plausible evidence for arts and culture as a source of endogenous job creation, but it is not definitive. Several caveats should be noted. First, as noted above, longitudinal analysis would provide a more satisfactory test of the impact of nonprofit arts on longer-term growth. Second, some portion of the nonprofit arts sector's output of goods and services is sold to consumers outside of the region, and the analysis (like most economic base analysis) does not take that possibility into account—that is, it does not break down the sector indicators (employment, output, revenues) into export and local base components. San Francisco and Sierra arts nonprofits could be earning portions of their revenues from visitors. Third, the longer-term formation of a local population is not independent of past arts capacity additions—one of the consumption base tenets. Over time, if the consumption base theory is correct, art lovers might be found disproportionately among in-migrants (and arts-indifferent people among the out-migrants).

Fourth, with few exceptions (see below with respect to artists), the study does not explore the relationship between the arts and cultural nonprofit sector and the overall size of regional economies, again a phenomenon more appropriate for analysis over time. It focused on nonprofit arts enterprises, which are rarely studied, because new data were available and because the capacity-building theory gives central place to decisions by groups of local people to construct an organization, fund it, design and offer programming, and attract participants.[20]

Artist Density and Commercial Arts Employment

Evidence on the density of artists in the Bay Area workforce compared with that in other metro areas supports a capacity-evolving interpretation (table 3-3). The Bay Area was third among the nation's top twenty-nine metros in artist density (including self-employed artists), lower than the Los Angeles and New York metro areas but much higher than many others with larger populations. Subsequent research found that by 2006, the Bay Area location quotient had risen to 249, or second place, displacing Los Angeles to third, and that the Bay Area held that position through 2009.[21]

Could the Bay Area's outsized nonprofit arts and cultural sector and artist pool result from the presence of complementary for-profit cultural industries?

Table 3-3. *Artistic Concentrations, Top 29 U.S. Metro Areas by Employment, 2000*

Metropolitan area	Total	Performing artists	Visual artists	Authors	Musicians
Los Angeles	2.99	5.44	2.34	2.71	1.95
New York, NY–NJ	2.52	3.71	2.01	2.99	1.85
San Francisco–Oakland, CA	1.82	1.85	1.83	2.51	1.12
Washington, DC–MD–VA–WV	1.36	1.51	1.01	2.27	1.08
All 29 metro areas	1.34	1.60	1.26	1.45	1.12
Seattle	1.33	1.15	1.48	1.48	1.06
Boston, MA–NH	1.27	1.24	1.02	2.00	1.15
Orange County, CA	1.18	1.21	1.36	0.92	0.98
Minneapolis–St. Paul, MN–WI	1.16	1.12	1.10	1.33	1.16
San Diego, CA	1.15	0.90	1.27	1.10	1.25
Miami	1.15	1.48	1.05	0.82	1.28
Portland, OR–WA	1.09	1.12	0.99	1.50	0.87
Atlanta	1.08	1.05	1.11	0.97	1.15
Baltimore	1.08	0.96	1.10	0.92	1.30
Chicago	1.04	0.83	1.14	1.27	0.84
Newark, NJ	1.02	1.07	0.97	1.24	0.83
U.S. average	1.00	1.00	1.00	1.00	1.00
Dallas	0.99	1.08	1.11	0.73	0.87
Philadelphia, PA–NJ	0.96	0.90	1.04	0.94	0.88
Phoenix	0.96	0.70	1.13	0.88	0.94
Nassau–Suffolk, NY	0.93	0.83	1.10	0.84	0.76
Kansas City, MO–KS	0.90	0.59	1.16	0.82	0.76
Denver	0.90	1.08	0.82	0.98	0.79
Tampa–St. Petersburg, FL	0.89	0.83	0.89	0.76	1.08
San Jose, CA	0.84	0.75	0.95	0.95	0.61
Cleveland	0.79	0.61	0.79	0.74	1.05
Riverside–San Bernardino, CA	0.77	0.79	0.84	0.61	0.76
Pittsburgh	0.76	0.63	0.74	0.79	0.91
Houston	0.74	0.65	0.75	0.66	0.91
Detroit	0.74	0.61	0.82	0.73	0.74
St. Louis, MO–IL	0.71	0.52	0.79	0.67	0.80

Source: Ann Markusen and Greg Schrock, "The Artistic Dividend: Urban Artistic Specialization and Economic Development Implications," *Urban Studies*, vol. 43, no. 10 (2006), pp. 1661–86, table 1, p. 1667. Data include employed and self-employed people whose major occupation is in the arts (musicians, writers, visual artists, performing artists) from 2000 Census Public Use Microdata Sample (PUMS) data, from Steven Ruggles and others, "Integrated Public Use Microdata Series: Version 3.0" (Minnesota Population Center, University of Minnesota, 2004).

Table 3-4. *Metro Employment by Sector, Los Angeles and Bay Area Artists, 2000*

Employment	Los Angeles	Bay Area[a]	San Francisco–Oakland	San Jose	Santa Rosa–Vallejo
Total employed	76,090	32,921	24,688	4,677	3,556
Self-employed (%)	40	45	44	36	64
Private employer (%)	54	42	43	52	25
Nonprofit/public employer (%)	6	13	13	12	11

Sources: Ann Markusen and others, *Crossover: How Artists Build Careers across Commercial, Nonprofit and Community Work* (Project on Regional and Industrial Economics, University of Minnesota, for the James Irvine Foundation, 2006), table A1 (http://irvine.org/news-insights/publications/arts). Census 2000 data are from Steven Ruggles and others, "Integrated Public Use Microdata Series: Version 3.0" (Minnesota Population Center, University of Minnesota, 2003).

a. The Bay Area encompasses the three metro areas of San Francisco–Oakland, San Jose, and Santa Rosa–Vallejo. Counties in each metro area include Los Angeles County (Los Angeles); Santa Clara County (San Jose); Marin, San Francisco, and San Mateo counties (San Francisco PMSA); Alameda and Contra Costa counties (Oakland PMSA); and Sonoma, Santa Rosa, and Solano counties (Santa Rosa–Vallejo).

If commercial arts activity fosters complementary nonprofit arts activity, the shares of artists working in the commercial and nonprofit arts sectors should be similar across Los Angeles and the Bay Area metros, and artists working in the nonprofit arena, as a share of the total regional workforce, would be if anything higher in LA, which has greater commercial arts activity. In 2000, the share of artists working for private sector employers was much larger (54 percent) in Los Angeles than in the Bay Area (42 percent), while the self-employment rate of artists in the Bay Area was higher, as was the share working for the nonprofit and public sectors (table 3-4). In addition, the share of nonprofit arts workers in the Bay Area's total workforce was almost 30 percent higher than in LA. Los Angeles's prominence as a commercial arts capital did not translate into a higher per capita number of nonprofit arts organizations or a higher per capita nonprofit arts budget (table 3-1 above). There is little evidence, therefore, for the belief that prominent commercial arts and cultural regions cultivate higher levels of nonprofits arts activity than regions with much more modest cultural industry complexes.

Evidence on Spatial Differentials in Arts Participation

If a city's supply of arts nonprofits is not fully explained by the socioeconomic characteristics of residents, the demand side must also be at work. The unexplained variation could be attributed to tastes and preferences, the inference being that the Bay Area and other northern regions are populated by people who, other things equal, love the arts more. But perhaps it is that higher shares of the population participate in the arts in places where the supply is strong—that availability encourages people to consume more arts and cultural activities and less of other goods and services.

Do participation rates vary spatially and can they be explained by socio-economic and other variables? Californians participate in the arts at a higher rate than Americans as a whole, and although the participation rate fell from 2002 to 2008, it dropped more slowly in California than in the nation as a whole. Demographic factors do influence arts participation among California adults, but even after controlling for differences in age, family income, race/ethnicity, sex, education level, and metropolitan status, the odds of a California adult attending at least one event were 25 percent higher than for other American adults.

Regionally, participation rates were markedly higher in the Bay Area than in the rest of the state, average in the Los Angeles area, and below average in the Sacramento, South Coast and Border, Inland Empire, and San Joaquin Valley regions (table 3-5). Small sample sizes in the Survey of Public Participation in the Arts prevent greater spatial disaggregation, but the residual "rest of state," which encompasses the Northern, Mountain, and Central Coast regions, also had a relatively high participation rate (60 percent).

The high San Francisco Bay Area participation rate accounts for much of the variation between Californians and the rest of the nation. After controlling for the demographic factors noted above, the odds of a Bay Area resident attending an arts event were 81 percent higher than for other Californians.[22] The analysis also finds that the per capita presence of arts and cultural organizations is correlated with attendance at the regional scale.

Inferences about the Contribution of Locally Oriented Arts to Regional Growth

The findings on differences among cities and regions with respect to the presence of arts organizations and residents' participation in arts offerings suggest that place is a powerful crucible shaping California's arts and cultural ecology. We believe that the vibrancy of the Bay Area's arts scene and that of the smaller Northern and Mountain regions are the result of an evolutionary process whereby residents build and invest in nonprofit arts and cultural organizations aimed at the local market.

Table 3-5. *Arts Participation by California Region, 2008*[a]

Region	Participation (percent)	Number of annual arts participants (thousands)	Number of attendances at selected arts events (thousands)
San Francisco Bay Area	66	3,716	22,855
Los Angeles metro	54	5,422	24,594
South Coast and Border	52	1,101	3,852
Sacramento metro	50	735	1,504
San Joaquin Valley/ Inland Empire	42	2,466	9,780
Rest of state	60	974	4,515
Total	54	14,414	67,100

Sources: Ann Markusen and others, *California's Arts and Cultural Ecology* (San Francisco: James Irvine Foundation, September 2011), table 6 (http://irvine.org/news-insights/publications/arts/arts-ecology-reports). Data from the National Endowment for the Arts, "Survey of Public Participation in the Arts Combined File, 1982–2008" (www.nea.gov/research/2008-sppa.pdf).

a. Participation defined as numbers/shares of resident adults attending at least one arts event in the preceding year. Regions aggregated to ensure statistical reliability of relatively small sample sizes.

This expansion of capacity drew both artists and arts-loving migrants from elsewhere as well as previously more arts-oblivious local residents into the creative sphere. Census net migration data show that in 2000, the Bay Area's ratio of incoming artists to all artists was higher than for any other large U.S. metro area. Its rate of net artist in-migration (total in-migrants divided by total out-migrants) for 1995–2000 (1.37), the last period for which data are available, was exceeded only by that of Los Angeles (2.16), where commercial sector opportunities are a powerful draw.[23] Indeed, the rate for Los Angeles, which attracts more than two in-migrating artists for every one that leaves, exceeds the rates for all the major U.S. metro areas.

The place-based analysis takes the story a step further. It confirms that certain communities—in particular, job centers that also attract and retain well-educated, wealthier residents—are currently more apt to provide a home to arts organizations, regardless of region. These communities are able to capture more philanthropic arts funding, which in turn reinforces a "virtuous cycle" of arts presence and attendance. Indeed, by 2008, Bay Area arts nonprofits enjoyed an extraordinarily high amount of private philanthropic funding, $23.50 per capita, while the figure was $17.30 in Los Angeles and below $2.00 in outlying regions (table 3-6). Note that funding figures include awards

Table 3-6. *Private Philanthropic Funding for Arts and Culture,*
per Capita by Region, 2008
U.S. dollars

Region	Per capita funding
Bay Area	23.5
Los Angeles metro	17.3
Central Coast	16.1
Sacramento metro	6.5
South Coast and Border	3.8
Northern Valley	3.8
North Coast and North State	1.4
Inland Empire	1.1
Sierra	1.1
San Joaquin Valley	0.6

Sources: Ann Markusen and others, *California's Arts and Cultural Ecology* (San Francisco: James Irvine Foundation, September 2011), table 11 (http://irvine.org/news-insights/publications/arts/arts-ecology-reports). Philanthropic data from Foundation Center, 2008 (foundationcenter.org); population data from California Department of Finance (www.dof.ca.gov). Data cover giving from private philanthropies (not individuals) located outside the region and state as well as within California.

from foundations based outside the region, including elsewhere in the state and the nation.

A final speculation concerns art education, which is important in encouraging local arts consumption. As cities, regions, and small towns built arts capacity over the decades and broadened participation, a strong preference for arts and culture could have placed a premium on quality arts programs in the schools and adult educational forums, further enhancing both the supply and demand for the arts. Arts learning in childhood and/or adulthood is a strong predictor of adult attendance at arts events currently included in the Survey of Public Participation in the Arts.[24]

A Case Study in Locally Oriented Arts Development

Over a couple of decades of scrutiny, researchers have generated a large number of qualitative case studies of arts capacity building and its impact on cities and towns.[25] As an example of successful local consumption base building, we offer the following case.

Live theater and music performances, local art fairs, and opportunities to take lessons in art or to rent space to do art work can increase the share of the local dollars that go into artists' and art organizations' bank accounts, substituting for DVDs, CDs, and non–arts-related purchases of commodities and services from elsewhere. In the late 1980s, a visual artist, John Davis, moved to an abandoned farmhouse outside New York Mills, Minnesota, a declining Finnish farming community three and a half hours northwest of the Twin Cities.[26] He started an artist's retreat, believing that visiting artists would bring creative ideas into the region while the idyllic rural atmosphere would enhance their work. Davis then sought out "the artist in every person in the county" in a campaign to convince community leaders, the city council, and a local landowner to renovate an 1885 brick building on Main Street as the New York Mills Regional Cultural Center. He solicited the help of farmers whose oil portraits were stashed away in their barns and people who had never considered singing in a choir as art, and many such people came to support the development of the center, which opened in 1992. Between 1992 and 1997, seventeen new businesses opened, and employment increased by 40 percent. By the year 2000, the tiny town's population had grown to 1,200, twice its pre-center size. By 2005, the center hosted six to eight gallery exhibitions a year, some showcasing emerging local artists or historic community photos, and many performances.

Today, the New York Mills Cultural Center acts as a community and tourist hub. A tractor emblazoned on the New York Mills water tower heralds the town's mission, "cultivating the arts." The downtown landscape has changed dramatically, with a new medical clinic and renovated storefronts replacing abandoned buildings. Visiting and area poets, authors, and storytellers share their work through readings and workshops. Touring theater, music, and dance groups perform in the gallery. The center helps local artists overcome the disadvantages of working far from a major city by holding a monthly forum that brings together area artists to network and critique each others' work. In addition, the center works with other organizations to educate artists about the business side of the arts. Visiting artists offer activities such as jazz improvisation workshops, build public sculptures with community members, and interact with community youth. People travel from miles around to attend events and participate in workshops. Thus a local commitment of development dollars has resulted in a facility that captures local and regional consumer expenditures as well as enables local artists to develop their careers.

Conclusion

This chapter questions the primacy of economic base theory and makes a theoretical case for a consumption base counterpart. Investments in the non-profit arts and cultural sector are especially good candidates for nurturing economic development, particularly because of special features of their organization and because their intrinsic contributions are so powerful.

The chapter shows that there are wide variations among California's cities and regions in the presence of nonprofit arts organizations, artists' employment, and arts-participation rates across cities and regions and that they cannot be fully explained by the socioeconomic characteristics of residents, economic roles within the region, or the presence of commercial cultural industries. For both a very large region, the San Francisco Bay Area, and a small town in Minnesota, New York Mills, we offer a plausible interpretation of what occurred over time in arts capacity building and its results. Longitudinal analysis of these ideas is needed, an arduous but possible research task.

These findings have implications for both economic developers and arts advocates. They suggest that judicious investment in local-serving arts and cultural capacity may be especially fruitful for economic development. Arts advocates should free themselves from a single-minded emphasis on economic impact analysis, which is not very convincing for reasons well articulated by others, and make the broader case for the preeminence of the arts in the consumption base.

For cities and regions hoping to increase their arts and cultural offerings, this chapter underscores the huge significance of nonprofit organizations as major innovators, creators, producers, and presenters of arts and cultural experiences and stresses the need for governments at all levels to understand nonprofit organizations, with respect to size, focus, missions, governance structures, and spatial differentiation. In addition, comparable research is needed on the size, character, and location of the for-profit arts and cultural sector, testing causal theories about its location, including its synergy with the nonprofit and public arts sectors.

Notes

1. See Ann Markusen, *Reining in the Competition for Capital* (Kalamazoo, Mich.: W. E. Upjohn Institute for Employment Research Press, 2007) for theoretical, empirical, and policy analysis of business incentive competition among U.S. and European regions, states, and localities.

2. See also chapter 7 in this volume for an exploration of innovation in arts and culture and its relationship to growth.

3. Pathbreaking new research using IRS 1099 data on arts nonprofits, compiled by the Urban Institute, is being done by Steven Sheppard and his colleagues at Williams College. See Peter Pedroni and Steven Sheppard's longitudinal analysis in this volume, which shows that big infusions of investment in arts nonprofits can have a lasting impact on regional growth.

4. See Judith Blau, *The Shape of Culture* (Cambridge University Press, 1989), for an excellent history of arts and cultural capacity distributions among large U.S. cities up through the 1970s. In chapter 4, Blau hypothesizes that large places may have large institutions but fewer numbers of them, a scale phenomenon, and also raises the possibility that within regions, supply may create its own demand.

5. See William Beyers and GMS Research Corporation, *An Economic Impact Study of Arts, Cultural, and Scientific Organizations in the Central Puget Sound Region* (Seattle, Wash.: ArtsFund, 2011) (www.artsfund.org).

6. Ann Markusen and Greg Schrock, "The Artistic Dividend: Urban Artistic Specialization and Economic Development Implications," *Urban Studies,* vol. 43, no. 10 (2006), pp. 1661–86.

7. See Andy Pratt, "The Cultural Industries Production System: A Case Study of Employment Change in Britain, 1984–91," *Environment and Planning A,* vol. 29 (1997), pp. 1953–74; and Ann Markusen and others, "Defining the Creative Economy: Industry and Occupational Approaches," *Economic Development Quarterly,* vol. 22, no. 1 (2008), pp. 24–45.

8. Bruce Seaman, "Arts Impact Studies: A Fashionable Excess," in *Economic Impact of the Arts: A Sourcebook,* edited by Anthony J. Radich and Sharon Schwoch (Washington: National Conference of State Legislatures, 1987), pp. 43–76.

9. Harold Innis, *The Fur Trade in Canada: An Introduction to Canadian Economic History* (Yale University Press, 1930); Douglass North, "Location Theory and Regional Economic Growth," *Journal of Political Economy,* vol. 63 (1955), pp. 243–58; Charles Tiebout, "Exports and Regional Economic Growth," *Journal of Political Economy,* vol. 64 (1956), pp. 160–69.

10. Douglass North, *The Economic Growth of the United States:1790–1860* (Saddle Hills, N.J.: Prentice Hall, 1961); Diane Lindstrom, *Economic Development in the Philadelphia Region, 1810–1850* (Columbia University Press, 1978).

11. Woo Jung and Peyton Marshall, "Exports, Growth, and Causality in Developing Countries," *Journal of Development Economics,* vol. 18 (1985), pp. 1–12.

12. Edward Ghartey, "Causal Relationship between Exports and Economic Growth: Some Empirical Evidence in Taiwan, Japan, and the U.S.," *Applied Economics*, vol. 25 (1993), pp. 1145–52.

13. Subhash Sharma, Mary Norris, and Daniel Wai-Wah-Cheung, "Exports and Economic Growth in Industrialized Countries," *Applied Economics*, vol. 23 (1991), pp. 697–708.

14. See, for instance, Richard Pratt, "An Appraisal of the Minimum-Requirements Technique," *Economic Geography*, vol. 44, no. 2 (1968), pp. 117–24.

15. Joseph Cortright, "The Economic Importance of Being Different: Regional Variations in Tastes, Increasing Returns, and the Dynamics of Development," *Economic Development Quarterly*, vol. 16, no. 1 (2002), pp. 3–16.

16. See Robert McNulty, R. Leo Penne, and Dorothy R. Jacobson, *The Economics of Amenity: Community Futures and the Quality of Life* (Washington: Partners for Livable Places, 1985); Charles Landry and others, *The Creative City in Britain and Germany* (London: Anglo-German Foundation for the Study of Industrial Society, 1996); Richard Florida, *The Rise of the Creative Class* (New York: Basic Books, 2002); Charles Landry, *The Creative City: A Toolkit for Urban Innovators* (London: Earthscan, 2003).

17. Ann Markusen and Greg Schrock, "The Distinctive City: Divergent Patterns in American Urban Growth, Hierarchy, and Specialization," *Urban Studies*, vol. 43, no. 8 (2006), pp. 1301–23. For more general treatments of the potential for local-serving economic development investments to produce growth, see Ann Markusen, "A Consumption Base Theory of Development: An Application to the Rural Cultural Economy," *Agricultural and Resource Economics Review*, vol. 36, no 1 (2007), pp. 1–13; and Ann Markusen and Greg Schrock, "Consumption-Driven Regional Development," *Urban Geography*, vol. 30, no. 4 (2009): pp. 1–24.

18. Ann Markusen and others, *California's Arts and Cultural Ecology* (San Francisco: James Irvine Foundation, September 2011 (http://irvine.org/news-insights/publications/arts/arts-ecology-reports).

19. For data limitations, methodology, and variable definitions, see the "City Characteristic Data Source" and "Analysis by City Characteristics" sections of Markusen and others, *California's Arts and Cultural Ecology: Technical Appendix*.

20. Most economic impact and growth studies done on regions use chiefly for-profit sector data and do not include the self-employed, excluding a very large number of artists and related workers. See, for instance, Los Angeles County Economic Development Corporation, *Report on the Creative Economy of the Los Angeles Region* (Los Angeles: Otis College of Art and Design, 2009). See chapter 8 in this volume on entrepreneurship and capacity building in the nonprofit arts sector.

21. Carl Grodach and Michael Seman, "The Cultural Economy in Recession: Examining the U.S. Experience," *Cities* (http://dx.doi.org/10.1016/j.cities.2012.06.001).

22. NEA participation data are generated by an add-on to the Current Population Survey data and thus include California respondents' arts participation outside of California. However, it is unlikely that Bay Area residents would travel more frequently

to participate outside of the state than would residents of other large California metro regions.

23. Markusen and Schrock, "The Artistic Dividend," table 4.

24. Nick Rabkin and E. C. Hedberg, *Arts Education in America: What the Declines Mean for Arts Participation* (Washington: National Endowment for the Arts, 2011).

25. See, for example, chapter 4, on three New England towns, in this volume.

26. Ann Markusen and Amanda Johnson, *Artists' Centers: Evolution and Impact on Careers, Neighborhoods, and Economies* (Minneapolis, Minn.: Project on Regional and Industrial Economics, University of Minnesota, 2006), pp. 91–94 (www.hhh.umn.edu/projects/prie/PRIE—publications.html); Dana Gillespie, Carlos Questa, and Padraic Lillis, *Bright Stars: Charting the Impact of the Arts in Rural Minnesota* (Minneapolis, Minn.: McKnight Foundation, 2006).

RICHARD G. MALONEY *and* GREGORY H. WASSALL

4

A Case Study in Cultural Economic Development: The Adams Arts Program in Massachusetts

Today municipalities face many pressing financial challenges, which typically include declining tax revenues, reduced federal and state aid, and increased demand for local services. As a result, local leaders are continuously searching for new economic development strategies to reinvigorate their tax base. During the past decade, the idea that the arts and culture sector can play an important, if not leading, role in local economic development has rapidly grown in popularity. However, despite widespread interest in this idea, the process through which municipalities move from initial consideration to implementation of a specific initiative remains unclear. This chapter addresses one element of this process by exploring how three Massachusetts municipalities (Hyannis, Gloucester, and Fitchburg), with financial support from the Adams Arts Program for the Creative Economy, implemented and sustained cultural economic development initiatives.[1] Through interviewing local leaders in the three communities, we identified the human and institutional resources involved and the parts that they played in turning proposals into reality. Our findings will interest local leaders and policymakers in similar municipalities who are considering investing in cultural economic development as an economic revitalization strategy.

Background

Academic thinking about the relationship between art and economic development has evolved over the past several decades. The traditional theory of regional economic development relies on the classification of industries into the export and service sectors. Export industries sell to entities outside the region and, if successful, cause economic growth inside the region. Initially, advocates of cultural economic development argued that the arts were an export industry and that they could help drive economic development.[2] Certainly there are examples of art and entertainment driving local economies— Las Vegas, Los Angeles, and Orlando, for example—but for the most part, evidence suggests that the arts industry plays a minor role in the economic base of most urban areas.[3]

Recently, the argument that creativity and creative people drive economic development has received growing support.[4] According to this argument, the nexus between the arts and economic development is different: in urban areas with concentrations of highly educated creative people, the productivity of such people drives economic growth. Because artists are often regarded as the most creative of creative people, they may play an especially important role. In Richard Florida's version of this argument, young, mobile, highly educated entrepreneurial types are attracted to a vibrant arts community; therefore, basing an economic development strategy on attracting artists and building arts and cultural organizations will create jobs and growth in the long run.

In reality, those explanations are too simple. A variety of amenities may attract young, creative professionals to an urban area, including old standbys such as cheap housing and quality schools; however, attracting such people does not automatically guarantee economic growth. The important question is whether art and culture, however defined, are truly an important force for greater economic growth or simply a by-product of it. Other chapters in this volume address that question more directly, primarily at the macro level; this chapter discusses cultural economic development initiatives at the municipal level.

The John and Abigail Adams Arts Program

Established by the Massachusetts legislature in 2004 and administered by the Massachusetts Cultural Council (MCC), the John and Abigail Adams Arts Program for the Creative Economy (Adams Arts) is the successor to a cultural economic development program that was in operation from 1997 to 2003. While the previous program served only a handful of applicants each year (no more than twelve) and awarded a small amount of funding (less than $290,000 annually), the Adams Arts program is better funded and has awarded far more grants. (See table 4-1 for the number and amount of Adams Arts grants awarded during 2005–10.) The Adams Arts grant application process is also more sophisticated, requiring applicants to provide detailed information regarding their project objectives and specific economic development goals.[5] The Adams Arts

Table 4-1. *Grants Awarded in the John and Abigail Adams Arts Program*

	Type of grant					
	Cultural economic development		Planning		Total	
Year	Number	Dollar amount	Number	Dollar amount	Number	Dollar amount
2005	22	900,000	0	0	22	900,000
2006	33	1,290,175	0	0	33	1,290,175
2007	27	1,240,000	10	52,820	37	1,292,820
2008	27	1,241,000	9	39,371	36	1,280,371
2009	29	1,208,750	9	41,750	38	1,250,500
2010	23	786,000	5	17,500	28	803,500
Total	161	6,665,925	33	151,441	194	6,817,366

program awards grants for planning (up to $5,000–$10,000, depending on the year) and implementation (up to $75,000–$100,000, depending on the year) to applicants who develop realistic local cultural economic development initiatives in collaboration with a minimum of three community organizations; usually four to seven organizations are involved. A local government department or a nonprofit organization must take the lead, but private sector companies are encouraged to participate in the partnership. Each proposal is vetted for quality by a panel of experts organized by the MCC. The grants must be matched by funding provided by the community at a ratio of 1:4 (planning grant) or 1:1 (implementation grant). The MCC employs a broad definition of the term "cultural economic development," so broad that even "stimulat[ing] increased participation and engagement in cultural and creative activities by residents and visitors" has been deemed an acceptable proposal objective.[6] The Adams Arts program is the oldest local cultural economic development grant program funded by a state arts council in the United States.

We view the Adams Arts program as a relatively pure example of a microlevel experiment in cultural economic development. Our original intent in studying it was to determine how effective this strategy would be in encouraging local economic development. Because the program is still in its relative infancy—some projects are just under way and others have only recently been completed—there are not enough mature projects to allow us to tackle the statistical question of whether the program has had an overall salutary effect on local economic development.[7] However, the program is established enough to permit us to examine the process through which the communities attempted to reach their economic development goals.

What Communities Receive Adams Arts Grants?

While selecting the communities for our sample, we examined what types of communities were successful in obtaining Adams Arts grants. To answer that question, we collected information about the Adams Arts program from 2005 to 2010; to provide context, we collected demographic information from the American Community Survey (ACS) on 243 Massachusetts communities.[8] In addition, we used an existing database on cultural nonprofits in Massachusetts.[9] Using the ACS and the nonprofit data, we drew up a socioeconomic profile of the towns that received Adams grants and compared it with that of the group of towns that did not receive Adams grants over the 2005–10 period.

Between 2005 and 2010, 168 grants were made to 35 communities; of those communities, 26 received more than one grant during this period. The "average" Adams Arts grant town received 4.8 grants during the period; the average town that received more than one grant received 6.1 grants. Clearly some communities were highly motivated to secure the grants and to do so more than once; others seemed to have had little interest in the process.

Table 4-2 profiles the communities receiving at least one Adams Arts grant (35); the communities receiving more than one Adams Arts grant (26); and the communities receiving no Adams Arts grants (208). The communities that received Adams Arts grants had more than three times as many residents than those that did not. Adams Arts grant communities had median family incomes that were $17,000 lower than median incomes of nongrant communities and a lower percentage of college and high school graduates. The communities that received grants were typical of larger, more urban communities in general. The differences between grant and nongrant communities were magnified further when only communities that received multiple grants were counted as grant communities. In addition, communities that received Adams Arts grants contained more cultural nonprofits per capita; they also had higher nonprofit spending per capita and higher cultural nonprofit net assets per capita.

Although this profile may change after more grants are made, it seems clear that small communities were not getting involved in the process, perhaps because of the complexity of putting together a coalition to apply for a grant and/or the absence of any paid official who could spearhead the effort. It also seems that among larger communities, the grant recipients tended to be older, urban blue-collar communities with a history of support from and engagement with cultural nonprofits. Comparably sized well-to-do suburban communities tended not to apply for funding. While at this time it is impossible to state definitively why that was so, we speculate that one of the reasons is that

Table 4-2. *Demographic Profile of Communities That Receive Adams Arts Program Grants*

Number of grants received	Percent high school graduates	Percent college graduates	Percent with graduate degree	Median family income (dollars)	Population
No grant	92.0	39.1	16.3	86,713	14,136
At least one	86.2	33.2	14.2	69,516	66,717
More than one	84.4	30.7	12.9	61,369	78,439

these communities were simply not interested in attracting large numbers of art patrons or artists.

Methodology

To a greater or lesser degree, every community encompasses a range of ongoing cultural activities within its borders. Because cultural activities take place in every community, outsiders (that is, researchers) may find it difficult to determine quickly which communities have made a formal sustained commitment to cultural economic development and which simply have a lot of cultural activity. To address this issue, we examined municipalities that had been awarded Adams Arts funding a minimum of three times, including in 2009 (the fieldwork was conducted in 2009 and early 2010).

We also created two other requirements for inclusion in our sample. Grant requirements stipulated that each applicant identify which collaborating local institutions were the lead organization and which were partners. To achieve a better understanding of the role of local government in the implementation process, we considered only municipalities that listed the local government as either "lead" or "partner." In addition, we decided to focus on "midsized" municipalities, those that had a population of 30,000 to 50,000. That decision was based on the assumption that communities of that size were small enough to enable us to access important local leaders yet large enough to have the resources and expertise necessary to establish and support a formal economic development strategy.

The grant protocol also required each community to state the names of the local individuals who supported the proposal, along with their organizational affiliations. Those people, through their participation in meetings and in the grant writing process, had become, in effect, local experts on cultural economic development (regardless how great or small the role that they played in the process). This list of names served as the primary source of respondents.

After we applied our criteria to the successful 2009 Adams Arts grant applicants, four communities qualified: Hyannis,[10] Fitchburg, Gloucester, and Pittsfield. We decided that it was necessary to visit each community several times to conduct interviews and gain a better understanding of its cultural economic development initiatives, but because we had a limited amount of time to conduct the fieldwork, we removed Pittsfield from the study due to its distance from Boston, leaving Hyannis, Fitchburg, and Gloucester as the final case study communities. By using specific criteria to select our sample, we hoped to observe common elements that would enable us to draw some conclusions about the examined municipalities.

The fieldwork consisted of nineteen semi-structured interviews with local elected officials, government employees, arts leaders, arts educators, public school officials, college administrators, and chamber of commerce officials in the three municipalities. The interviews were recorded, transcribed, and analyzed to reveal underlying patterns and themes. In order to ensure the quality of the data, the respondents were guaranteed anonymity so that they could speak candidly about their experiences and their communities.

The respondents were employed in the nonprofit sector or the public sector. In the nonprofit sector, individuals were employed by the local university, cultural institutions, arts service organizations, chambers of commerce, and community organizations. In the public sector, individuals were employed by the public schools and the local government.

The background of the respondents was strikingly similar across the three communities. Almost universally, the respondents

—had been born in the community or had lived there for many years, or both

—were middle aged, white, and graduate school educated

—had worked in the community for many years

—were female.

As a group, the respondents were not representative of their respective local populations, which tended to be younger, less educated, and more likely to be members of a minority group.

Findings

The elements present in each community that were primarily responsible for the development and implementation of the local cultural economic development initiatives were

—a vibrant partnership of leaders of important local institutions

—an intermediary organization

—the local government

—grant funding and technical support provided by the Massachusetts Cultural Council.

On occasion, we observed some overlapping of elements. For example, the local government could also serve as the intermediary organization. In addition, there were strong indications that the local government consistently played an important part regardless of its level of engagement with the initiative. With the current dataset it is impossible to determine definitively which factor was the most important (if any) or to ascertain the level at which each factor needs to be present in each community, but it is clear that all four are necessary.

Two additional factors were present in two of the three communities:

—a college: Fitchburg State University in Fitchburg and Cape Cod Community College in Hyannis

—local print media, in Hyannis and Fitchburg.

It is difficult to state definitively the impact of these two elements because they were not present in all three communities. Overall, the findings, while requiring additional refinement, indicate the emergence of a model of local cultural economic development initiative implementation.

Vibrant Community Partnerships

One of the distinctive factors in the three communities was the presence of a vibrant, sustained partnership between leaders of cultural and community organizations and the local government. Naturally, some cultural leaders, local government administrators, and elected officials were aware of each other prior to the awarding of the first Adams Arts grants in 2005; however, the data indicate that they did not engage with each other on a regular basis. The grant requirements strongly encouraged applicants to collaborate with organizations from different sectors to develop their cultural economic development initiatives, and that stipulation was the catalyst that brought these individuals and institutions together in a sustained and purposeful manner. The respondents indicated that the process of developing and implementing the initiative increased the connections among the partners.

The members of the partnership varied depending on the available cultural and community assets, but in all cases included leaders from local cultural organizations and government and community leaders. In Hyannis, where the town was the lead applicant, the partnership was driven and sustained by town administrators who provided the expertise and sustained engagement necessary to move the project forward. In Fitchburg, where the lead applicant was the city economic development office, the partnership was originally driven by that office with the support of the mayor and a small group of community and cultural leaders. Due to financial constraints, the economic development office was eventually restructured, leaving it incapable of effectively leading the initiative, and at that point a group of local cultural leaders volunteered to take the lead. At the time of the fieldwork, the group appeared to be becoming overwhelmed by the amount of work and lack of resources. In Gloucester, the local arts service organization, Society for the Encouragement of the Arts (seARTS), was the lead applicant; however, the partnership was actually driven by a few energetic cultural leaders with minor support from the city. SeARTS was very involved in the partnership, although administrative, fiscal, and strategic challenges limited its ability to lead the initiative; eventually local cultural leaders took the lead on a volunteer basis.

While all the partnerships consisted of individuals working in the public and nonprofit sectors—with the occasional participation of leaders of chambers of commerce and business improvement districts—members of the local business community generally were not well represented in the grant partnerships. Respondents from the nonprofit and government sectors indicated that it had been difficult to develop a sustained relationship with local business leaders. However, most respondents agreed that business leaders could (and should) play a larger role in developing future cultural economic development initiatives.

Partnerships in the Three Municipalities

FITCHBURG. In Fitchburg, the most important actors in the cultural economic development process were leaders who worked in the nonprofit and public sectors at Fitchburg State University, the local arts service organization (Fitchburg Cultural Alliance), the Massachusetts Cultural Council, local cultural organizations, and the public schools. Some of the leaders had participated in a tourism/place-marketing initiative that received funding from the original MCC cultural economic development program, which ended in 2003. As a result, they were familiar with the grant process, and when the Adams Arts program was announced, they were able to connect with people at the university, city government, and public schools to organize a partnership and develop a new initiative.

According to the respondents, Fitchburg State University played an important and unique role in supporting the cultural economic development effort. Possessing a strong cultural events office, experienced staff, an undergraduate program in theater, and a graduate program in arts education, the university is increasingly committed to engaging with the city on cultural matters and supporting initiatives that have a positive impact on local residents' quality of life. University leaders believe that in order to attract high-quality students and faculty members, Fitchburg needs to offer a variety of cultural offerings, and the university is working with city officials to achieve that goal. However, due to the poor economy and flagging state support, the university faces multiple financial challenges. As local cultural economic development is not its primary purpose, the university currently plays an important but supporting role in the cultural economic development process.

Respondents in Fitchburg indicated that positive coverage in some local newspapers of the Adams Arts program–supported initiative had increased attendance at cultural events and the sense among residents that theirs is a vibrant, successful community. However, the major newspaper in Fitchburg, the *Sentinel and Enterprise*, was not considered by respondents to be a supporter of local cultural economic development efforts. Respondents speculated that editors at the *Sentinel* still regarded Fitchburg as a depressed mill town and did not recognize recent changes in the community. However, they also acknowledged that they had not been in regular contact with the paper and that the lack of contact had limited their ability to have an impact on its editorial focus.

The research revealed that Fitchburg cultural institutions also were engaged in the partnership but that it was the individual leaders of the institutions and their willingness to volunteer their time and energy that made the difference. Even so, respondents consistently stated that lack of financial and administrative resources limited their ability to adequately support significant cultural economic development efforts. While many committed and talented people were involved, they struggled to coordinate and sustain their efforts.

HYANNIS. The partnership in Hyannis displayed notable sophistication, with different organizations contributing their particular strengths to the project (for example, access to funding, knowledge of local artists, connections within the business community, and expertise in gallery management). Respondents indicated that individual leaders were "very receptive to partnering," and early participants made sure to get the right partners involved from the start. County-level assistance was also extremely valuable in Hyannis because full-time public sector professionals provided expert funding and marketing support. Local chambers of commerce were also part of the partnership, and their participation was considered vital. The ensuing partnership was called "very collaborative," and it had continued to meet regularly despite changes in personnel because people took new jobs or moved out of the community. That continuity suggests that the partnership was not exclusively dependent on the efforts of individuals with a vested interest in a particular project.

Respondents reported that while it was skeptical of the initiative at first, the *Cape Cod Times* (the largest paper on the Cape) published articles supporting the effort. It is difficult to be certain why the role of local print media in Hyannis differed from that in Fitchburg, but one reason might be that full-time town administrators in Hyannis who supported the initiative were in more frequent contact with the press and had developed better public relations skills than the local cultural leaders in Fitchburg. As newspaper coverage in Hyannis increased, a respondent noted that "excitement grew" in the community; however, the data cannot confirm exactly how and why excitement grew or whether the respondent's perception was accurate.

Unlike the college in Fitchburg, the local college in Hyannis—Cape Cod Community College, which has a smaller enrollment than Fitchburg State University and does not offer bachelor's or master's degrees—was not a member of the partnership. However, town officials were considering contacting specific faculty members who taught in the arts to discuss participating in some way.

Respondents frequently mentioned that Cape Cod has a certain community cohesiveness. The sense that "we are all in this together" was given as one reason why partnerships with leaders of local organizations have been relatively easy to develop and maintain. This attitude may stem from the fact that Cape Cod, being connected to the rest of Massachusetts by only two bridges, is physically somewhat separate from the rest of the state. In addition, the Cape is well known as a popular summer vacation region, where many local businesses are either expressly seasonal in nature or benefit from the presence of thousands of tourists. While determining the exact nature of this sense of cohesiveness and interdependence requires further study, Hyannis respondents are well aware of the challenges presented by the cyclical local economy, and to some extent they appear to coordinate their efforts in order to thrive during the slower winter months.

GLOUCESTER. In Gloucester, there was a general consensus about the importance of a few actors: leaders of cultural institutions and other community leaders, the tourism agency (although the agency was staffed by volunteers in 2009 because the only employee had been laid off), the MCC, and (mentioned less frequently) the local chamber of commerce and local artists. However, there was substantial disagreement about the effectiveness of the city, the local arts service organization (seARTS), and the Mayor's Committee for the Arts. Most respondents stated that the participation of these three institutions was vital; however, they noted that the organizations were not always able to contribute effectively because of lack of resources, that they were distracted by other pressing local concerns, and that they struggled to achieve consensus regarding strategic objectives. These challenges, resulting in a weakened partnership, had a negative impact on the cultural economic development policy process in Gloucester.

Unique to Gloucester is its history of support for the cultural as well as the fishing industries, both of which are considered an important part of the community's identity. Its dual identity has frequently resulted in competition for resources and attention, and because the resulting tension is deeply rooted in the history of the community, it is not likely to be resolved in the near future. Several respondents stated that the city was determined to maintain its dual identity; however, city leaders struggled to cope with reduced revenues and to address existing urban problems, which limit its ability to support cultural initiatives.

Intermediary Organizations

Intermediary organizations played an important part in each community by helping to establish the initiative partnership, facilitating communication among the partners, and generally advocating for the arts. The intermediary organizations in each community functioned somewhat differently.

GLOUCESTER. In 2000, local cultural leaders came together to found seARTS, in part to obtain a cultural economic development grant offered by the MCC. By 2010, seARTS articulated a focused vision of arts support, research, advocacy, and communication—traditional activities for an arts service organization. However, its early years were marked by conflict and indecision among its opinionated leaders as they struggled to define the role that the organization should play in the community. That internal conflict, which alienated several early board members and supporters, and the inability to secure enough funding to hire a full-time professional staff member for a sustained period of time limited the organization's ability to support the cultural economic development initiative.

FITCHBURG. Founded in 1978, the Fitchburg Cultural Alliance initially served as a forum for artists and interested members of the community to gather and discuss arts issues. Today, the alliance operates a gallery space on Main Street, where eight artists have studio space, and it works to engage the community by offering many local cultural activities. In recent years, the alliance has benefited from the stewardship of a small group of committed volunteers who are leaders in the Fitchburg cultural community. While the organization has supported the local cultural economic development initiative to a fair degree, the lack of paid administrative staff has limited its ability to maintain and increase its influence and effectiveness.

HYANNIS. Located in Barnstable, the Arts Foundation of Cape Cod serves as the primary arts advocacy organization for the entire Cape. However, the local government—the primary supporter of the initiative in this community—assumed the role of intermediary organization while the foundation advised the town on artistic matters and provided marketing support. Because the local government had previously worked with cultural organizations, artists, and local businesses to support tourism initiatives, effective lines of communication between many of the partners already were established; it was therefore unnecessary to employ the local arts service organization to establish or manage those relationships. The town also used its financial and administrative resources (in paying for and building artists' spaces), planning expertise (in creating the Walkway to the Sea), and marketing resources (in installing signage on local roads indicating the location of the artists' spaces and the walkway) to support the various elements of the cultural economic development initiative. Representatives of town government participated in local meetings about the project and took the lead in planning new initiatives, such as the recently established arts district. While the Arts Foundation contributed in a more limited fashion than arts advocacy organizations in Gloucester and Fitchburg, its advisory role on artistic matters was critical to town administrators, who recognized that their own abilities did not lie in that area. Arts advocacy organizations in Hyannis, with their deep understanding of the local art scene, helped establish trust between artists and local government by providing a professional point of contact through which the government and the arts community could engage. According to one respondent, artists tend to be suspicious when approached by local government, so it is important not to minimize this unique contribution.

Role of Local Government

The data indicate that local government made three contributions to the initiative partnership:

—direct services, by providing direct funding, signage, and infrastructure improvements

—indirect services, by providing meeting space and marketing, communications, and social media assistance; encouraging government employees and officials to attend meetings; speaking publicly about the importance of the arts; and giving the community opportunities to be heard

—the local "seal of approval," by announcing local government support of the project.

Hard services, which are necessary to support major cultural activities and building projects, will always be important tools in supporting local economic development projects. However, the respondents indicated that soft services also were important and became even more so during difficult financial times, when city leaders focused on more long-standing concerns facing their communities. Because soft services typically do not require much funding to implement, they are easier to maintain when the attention of city leadership is drawn elsewhere. The importance of the third service, the "seal of approval," is often overlooked. By simply acknowledging that meaningful cultural activity is available and ongoing, local governments lend credibility to the effort. In other words, the government can signal the community that using culture to promote local economic development is an idea that should be taken seriously. Likewise, winning an Adams Arts grant sends a signal to local governments, other community leaders, and potential partners that the proposed policies have proven acceptable to a state-level body of experts. This indicator of credibility can attract additional support from other local organizations and funders and convince skeptical bystanders to engage.

Although some Adams Arts program grants do not involve local governments as either lead applicant or partner, the data collected in these three communities indicate that the active participation of the local government made their efforts more successful. The most effective example, Hyannis, was the one municipality in which the city was the lead applicant. While the data cannot support the conclusion that a community needs the full participation of the local government to establish a successful local cultural economic development initiative, they do indicate the challenges facing communities that proceed without its participation.

FITCHBURG. Fitchburg's economic development office served as the lead applicant for the city's Adams Arts application, and the city leadership appeared committed to the idea of cultural economic development. However, due to political and economic concerns, city support of the resulting initiatives has been uneven. Several respondents indicated that a unified economic development vision was lacking due to differences of opinion between long-time Fitchburg residents and newer arrivals. Specifically, city employees and cultural leaders tended to advocate increasing cultural and outdoor amenities while the city council (dominated by older long-time residents) favored approaches that are rooted in Fitchburg's industrial past. Moreover, the city has found it difficult to sustain its commitment to cultural economic development because of staff reductions necessitated by financial shortfalls; at least two eliminated positions were responsible for local economic development. The young mayor's overall vision for the future of the city was considered bold and well informed, but respondents stated that local community and cultural leaders could not continue their efforts to implement their initiatives without additional support from the city.

HYANNIS. In Hyannis, the most important factor in the success of a cultural economic development initiative was the town government, specifically its leaders, resources, and ability to bring all participating members together. The actual partnership—which included the town government, the business improvement district, nonprofit cultural institutions, artists, an arts advocacy organization, and a chamber of commerce—was considered the next important factor.

GLOUCESTER. Gloucester's government did not take an active role in supporting cultural economic development initiatives at the time of the interviews. In the past, the city sponsored public art events, established the Mayor's Committee for the Arts, and publicly indicated its support; however, recent financial troubles have forced it to curtail even those limited efforts. A cultural leader was bemused that the city seemed to encourage "generic" commercial economic activity in the harbor but did not recognize arts organizations that showcased the unique qualities of Gloucester. The respondent concluded, "As a matter of fact, with all the harbor planning that goes on, there's very little attention paid to the arts and culture by city government."

Grant Funding and Support Provided by the Massachusetts Cultural Council

The funding provided by MCC has been an enormous catalyst for action in the three communities—in the words of one respondent, "We wouldn't be doing this without them, it's as simple as that." While that finding is not surprising, funding is not the entire story. Many respondents mentioned the additional services that MCC provided as being crucial to the success of their efforts, including

—assisting during the application process

—making multiple site visits

—facilitating meetings and planning efforts

—sponsoring management, finance, and planning workshops attended by cultural leaders, city employees, and elected officials.

Supporting a local cultural economic development initiative is a relatively new endeavor that brings together town officials (who often do not know much about the arts) and cultural leaders and artists (who often do not know much about politics and public administration). MCC was able to facilitate communication between the two groups and give them the tools to move forward. In addition, its "outsider" perspective enabled it to rise above local concerns and approach issues from a new perspective. In particular, respondents in Gloucester and Fitchburg indicated that they received significant guidance from MCC, which enabled them to prepare stronger applications, develop more robust projects, and establish more effective partnerships.

While respondents in Gloucester and Fitchburg often indicated their need for assistance in organizing and in facilitating meetings, those concerns did not seem to be present in Hyannis. That may indicate that local leaders there did not need that type of assistance on a regular basis because they had previous experience in developing effective partnerships.

Several respondents remarked that it was not easy for the partners to work together, and they credited MCC staffers for helping them work through their differences. A cultural leader and former government employee described this situation: "[The MCC staff member] stayed with it. . . . I know it was rough going at the beginning. So yes, I do think that [the staff member] has been effective in Gloucester, to the extent that Gloucester will allow [him/her] to be."

Additional Findings

In these three communities, pursuing an economic development strategy focused on the arts was not a foreign idea. Local leaders were well aware of their community's cultural assets. During the past ten to fifteen years, the three communities have explored small programs that link the arts to community development and quality of life objectives (through public art installations in Gloucester and Fitchburg) and to efforts to increase tourism (all three communities). The data offer strong indications that those assets are a primary reason why local leaders initially decided to apply for Adams Arts funding. The fact that local leaders were already aware of and somewhat experienced with this approach to economic development almost certainly contributed to their taking advantage of the opportunity to apply for an Adams Arts grant.

In these three municipalities, we observed that developing a cultural economic development initiative is a skill that takes time to master and remains, for at least two of the three, a fairly challenging endeavor in which observable results (positive or negative) take some time to emerge. In addition, as the initiatives received only a modest amount of funding (in relation to other traditional economic development initiatives), the data suggest that lack of both skill and funding has hampered efforts to sustain newly created cultural infrastructures. However, it is impossible to state at this time the exact nature and amount of resources required to guarantee a positive outcome.

The commitment of the people who work for and lead cultural economic development initiatives and organizations cannot be overstated. These people are local leaders who are passionate about their communities and who volunteer their limited time to support the initiatives. Over time, they can become overwhelmed, which jeopardizes the effectiveness of the partnerships, and many leaders stated that they were working too hard. Several respondents mentioned that they had recently curtailed their efforts because they were exhausted and frustrated with the pace of progress. Others wondered when the next generation of leaders would emerge to help take some of the burden off their shoulders. A cultural leader in Gloucester summed up the seriousness of the situation: "It's been hard to have a structure without staffing . . . people get burned out. I mean, how often can you volunteer?" Our findings demonstrate that without vibrant community leadership, these initiatives cannot be sustained. Therefore, we believe that it is important for communities to find ways to identify potential leaders, mentor them so that they can assume positions of authority, and provide better training and support for both emerging and established leaders.

Some of the challenges facing the three case study communities appear to be generated by the structure of the policies themselves. Initially, we considered comparing the cultural economic development goals of each project (as stated in its Adams Arts program application) with our field observations as a way to begin our conversations with the respondents; however, we abandoned this approach almost immediately for several reasons. In our initial interviews, it became clear that most of the respondents were not fully aware of their community's stated economic development goals. In fact, several respondents had no idea what they were. It also became clear that the stated goals evolved and changed over time as obstacles arose. Goals typically mentioned by respondents included increasing attendance at cultural events, encouraging people to visit downtown areas, increasing sales of cultural goods, encouraging knowledge workers to relocate to the community, encouraging artists to move to the community, and increasing cultural tourism. The variety and inconsistency of the goals made it difficult to determine which objectives were being pursued, at what time, by whom. For example, Fitchburg indicated in its 2009 Adams Arts grant application that it planned to raise artists' incomes by encouraging sales of their work (an economic development goal) while also creating a sense of place by commissioning a piece of public art (community development goal).[11] It is almost impossible to establish that the latter objective generated any measurable economic growth. This finding is not that surprising considering that the people who created these initiatives had different backgrounds and worked in a variety of occupations. As a group, they could be best described as community development experts, not economic development experts. They were interested in and involved with a wide range of issues that affected their respective communities, and, not surprisingly, their actions reflected their basic concern: improving the quality of life where they lived. Generating additional economic activity was not their exclusive concern. These factors, combined with the MCC's broad definition of economic development, made it difficult to use short-term observation to determine definitively the specific economic outcomes of each community's cultural economic development initiatives.

Finally, while respondents in all three communities agreed that their respective initiatives had been successful to some degree (with Hyannis being the most confident), we have some concerns about the efficacy of the grant program itself. Currently, it is difficult to determine, using available data, whether actual economic growth is occurring or whether resources are being shifted from one community to another. One result of broad-based initiatives to increase attendance at cultural events, encourage people to visit downtown areas, or increase sales of cultural goods is that communities could end up essentially competing against one another to attract cultural producers and consumers. Several respondents indicated that they would be pleased if, because of state-sponsored cultural economic development efforts, artists chose to relocate from adjacent communities to theirs. While further study is necessary to explore this issue, using public money to encourage economic resources to move from one community to another is inefficient and, in the long run, ineffective.

Appendix 4A

Barnstable (Hyannis)

Year awarded: 2006–10 (five grants)
Grant request: $30,000 (2006); $50,000 (2007); $40,000 (2008); $40,000 (2009);
    $36,000 (2010)
Total funding: $196,000
Project name: Harbor Your Arts (HyA)
Lead partner: Town of Barnstable
Partners: Arts Foundation of Cape Cod, Hyannis Main Street Business Improvement
    District (BID), Cape Cod Art Association, Coastal Community Capital, Hyannis
    Area Chamber of Commerce
Population (2010): 45,193

Project description (2009)

The Town of Barnstable and its Partners work cooperatively to provide resources to our arts community to foster the local economy. The Harbor Your Arts initiative began with seven artist shanties and expanded to an arts-focused revitalization of downtown Hyannis. Next steps include defining a downtown Hyannis arts district with a way finding plan and additional public art to provide connectivity between the Harbor, Pearl Street arts galleries, and Main Street.

Project goals (2009)

A defined downtown arts district will provide economic opportunities for artists and businesses, attract visitors and establish Hyannis as an arts destination. Harbor Your Arts (HyA) supports the local creative economy and business activity on Main Street and harbor area. Performing arts event attendance and revenues for shanty and Pearl Street artists underscores the success of these initiatives. Private investment in the area has begun to increase further enhancing the downtown area.

Gloucester

Year awarded: 2005–09 (five grants); no award in 2010
Grant request: $30,000 (2005); $40,000 (2006); $40,000 (2007); $35,000 (2008);
    $26,000 (2009)
Total funding: $171,000
Project name: Arts and Economic Development in Gloucester
Lead partner: Society for the Encouragement of the Arts (seARTS)

All information in this appendix was taken directly from each municipality's 2009 Adams Arts program grant application. Population data were acquired from the U.S. Census Bureau (www.sec.state.ma.us/census).

Partners: ArtsGloucester, Cape Ann Chamber of Commerce, City of Gloucester, Gloucester New Arts Festival, North of Boston Convention and Visitors Bureau, Rocky Neck Art Colony, Cape Ann Artisans Tour, Gloucester Committee for the Arts
Population (2010): 28,789

Proposed Project Summary (2008 and 2009)

This project provides innovative and effective economic opportunities for artists, businesses and the City by developing, sustaining, and promoting arts activities that are integrated into the business and cultural life of the City, creating and sustaining strategic partnerships, and developing a viable Cape Ann arts market.

Project's Economic Development Goals (2008 and 2009)

To create sustainable arts/business collaborations, develop new audiences, showcase high-quality art, increase consumer activity in under-visited locations and businesses, boost existing cultural events, extend programming into the shoulder-months and increase connectivity between downtown and the harbor.

Fitchburg

Year awarded: 1998, 1999, 2005, 2008, 2009 (five grants); no award in 2010
Grant request: $5,000 (1998); $7,000 (1999); $35,000 (2005); $6,000 (2008);
  $18,000 (09)
Total funding: $71,000
Project name: REACH Fitchburg
Lead partner: Economic Development Office, Fitchburg
Partners: Fitchburg State University: Teaching American History Grant Program, Central Mass Women's Caucus for Arts, Office of the Mayor, Fitchburg Art Museum, Fitchburg Public Schools: Department of Visual and Performing Arts, Fitchburg Historical Society, Fitchburg Cultural Alliance, Fitchburg Access Television, Fitchburg State University: Office of Cultural Affairs and CenterStage
Population (2010): 40,318

Proposed Project Summary (2008 and 2009)

The City of Fitchburg has a collective history of more than 300 years as a cultural center in North Central Massachusetts. The intent of the REACH Fitchburg project is to build on those assets to attract sustainable residential and commercial businesses by highlighting downtown Fitchburg as a "Cultural Historic District" with an installation of permanent and dynamic public art projects.

Project's Economic Development Goals (2008 and 2009)

(1) Water Street Bridge Gateway: To create a "sense of place" at the entrance to downtown through a public sculpture project; (2) To generate tourism and community interest in one of Fitchburg's most unique architects, H. M. Francis; (3) To generate revenue

through the sales of artists' work at Fitchburg Cultural Alliance at 633 Main Street (the "Storefront Artists" project).

Notes

1. In this chapter, "implementation" refers to the actions undertaken by local leaders who are self-employed or working for the local government, arts organizations, or cultural service organizations to execute a specific local cultural economic development initiative. In policy circles, implementation typically refers to efforts of government employees (bureaucrats) to execute a specific government-supported policy. In this study, most of the respondents did not work for the local government and had no training in public policy implementation. In addition, the initiatives in two of the three municipalities originated in the arts community, not the local government. As a result, the context of this study is local economic development, not policy implementation.

2. For a contrary argument, see chapter 3 in this volume.

3. See Tyler Cowen, "When Should Regions Bid for Artistic Resources?" presented at the "Lasting Effects Economic Impact Analysis Conference," Pocantico Conference Center, Tarrytown, New York, May 2004, and Bruce Seaman, "Arts Impact Studies: A Fashionable Excess," in *Economic Impact of the Arts: A Sourcebook*, edited by Anthony Radich and Sharon Schwoch (Washington: National Conference of State Legislatures, 1990).

4. For example, see Charles Landry, *The Creative City: A Toolkit for Urban Innovators* (London: Earthscan, 2003); John Howkins, *The Creative Economy* (New York: Penguin Press, 2001); Richard Florida, *The Rise of the Creative Class* (New York: Basic Books, 2002); and Edward Glaeser, *Triumph of the City* (New York: Penguin Press, 2011).

5. See appendix 4A for a description of each community's proposed project and its respective economic development goals.

6. Adams Arts Program, "Frequently Asked Questions" (www.massculturalcouncil.org/applications/adamsarts_faqs.asp).

7. According to research conducted by Hutchins and Smith, building a local creative economy takes "in the neighborhood of twenty to thirty years." See Jennifer Hutchins and Deborah Smith, "The Creative Economy in Small Places: Eight Case Studies and a Development Model," *Southern Maine Review* (February 2005), p. 41.

8. The ACS data were aggregated from a file combining annual surveys between 2005 and 2010.

9. Gregory Wassall and others, *Passion and Purpose: Raising the Fiscal Fitness Bar for Massachusetts Nonprofits* (Boston Foundation, 2008). For this study, we used 2005 nonprofit data to represent the status of these organizations in communities at the beginning of the program.

10. While commonly referred to as Hyannis, as here, the community is actually the largest village in the town of Barnstable. All activity supported by the cultural economic development initiative occurred within the village of Hyannis.

11. See appendix 4A.

LAUREN SCHMITZ

5

Do Cultural Tax Districts Buttress Revenue Growth for Arts Organizations?

W hat role should public funding play in financing the arts in the United States? A wealth of research has assessed whether lump-sum government transfers to nonprofit organizations "crowd out" private giving. However, less attention has been paid to the incidence of local voter-approved cultural tax districts in the country and the effect that they have had on the success and sustainability of participating organizations. The study presented in this chapter used a quasi–natural experiment approach to evaluate the effect of the Scientific and Cultural Facilities District (SCFD) of metropolitan Denver—the largest cultural sales tax district in the United States—on private and program-related revenues. Results indicate that there was no significant difference in the average amount of total revenue collected by the majority of organizations inside the SCFD and the average amount collected by organizations outside the district, indicating that SCFD grants to these organizations can be taken purely at face value: that is, that SCFD grants neither crowd in or crowd out other funds. These results suggest that because cultural tax districts provide organizations with an additional source of revenue, they may be an effective policy tool for strengthening and expanding local arts communities.

Local Option Taxes and the Arts

In 1988, voters in the Denver metropolitan area overwhelmingly decided to increase sales taxes in the area to support arts and cultural organizations through the creation of one of the first regional tax districts in the United States. Today, the Scientific and Cultural Facilities District distributes approximately $40 million in annual support to more than 300 organizations. Its creation has inspired other cities—Pittsburgh, Kansas City, and Salt Lake City, among others—to create similar cultural districts, tailored to the unique resources and needs of their respective regions.[1]

The United States does not have a centralized government agency to coordinate the policies of individual cultural institutions and provide funding. Instead, arts funding is a mix of public, private, and earned revenues, with roughly 43 percent coming from private donations, 13 percent from the government, and 44 percent from earned revenues.[2] This "dynamic and decentralized" mixed-market system has engendered a diverse arts landscape in which new arts organizations are fostered alongside established institutions in a fresh and innovative atmosphere.[3] Nevertheless, the turbulence of the system can be destabilizing, and many organizations struggle to gain the secure financial footing that is necessary to grow and prosper.

The system's challenges are all the more apparent during rough economic times, when both private and public funding for the arts is often scaled back dramatically. To help mitigate funding volatility and preserve long-standing cultural institutions, voters in a number of localities have created cultural tax districts. The taxes from these districts are often earmarked for a specific institution, as in the case of the Minneapolis Institute of Arts and the St. Louis Art Museum. More recently, Detroit voters in three Michigan counties saved the Detroit Institute of Arts from devastating budget cuts through a property tax increase.[4]

In the wake of the 1982 economic downturn, hefty cuts to Colorado's arts budget prompted the region's four largest cultural institutions to band together and push through legislation that established a Denver metro area local option sales tax to fund the arts. The SCFD—modeled after the St. Louis Metropolitan Zoological Park and Museum District founded in 1971—was unique in that it sought to provide a broader regional base of support that would fund large and small organizations in Denver and the surrounding suburban counties. In 1988, citizens of urban and rural counties voted 3-1 to increase sales taxes and create the SCFD. The SCFD claims that as a result, the arts landscape has been dramatically altered and that Colorado residents enjoy a much richer and more diverse selection of cultural alternatives.[5]

The tax is a sales and use tax of one-tenth of 1 percent (or one penny for every $10 purchase) within the seven-county Denver metropolitan area, which currently includes Adams, Arapahoe, Boulder, Broomfield, Denver, Douglas, and Jefferson counties; it could extend to other counties if voters approve.[6] The annual per capita tax contribution was $15.17 in 2007.[7] SCFD funds are allocated among three funding tiers, detailed in table 5-1. Each tier receives a different proportion of the tax revenue, and each is subject to separate policies concerning how funds are awarded.

Table 5-1. *Summary of SCFD Funding Tiers, 2010*

Funding tier	Number of organizations	Range of total annual operating income	Percent of SCFD funding received	Distribution process and governance
Tier 1	5[a]	$13.8 to $44.9 million	65.5 percent for tax revenues up to and including $38 million and 64 percent for revenues over $38 million, or $25,962,117 in 2010.	A set percentage of funds ranging from $3.2 to $6.8 million is earmarked for each organization. SCFD staff and the board of directors (BOD) administer funding.[b]
Tier 2	24[c]	$1.3 to $11.7 million	21 percent for tax revenues up to and including $38 million and 22 percent for revenues over $38 million, or $8,357,406 in 2010.	Funds are distributed based on a weighted average of the organization's qualifying annual income and audited paid attendance. SCFD staff and the BOD administer funding.
Tier 3	268[d]	Approximately $1,000 to $2.7 million	13.5 percent for tax revenues up to and including $38 million and 14 percent for taxes over $38 million, or $5,025,476 in 2010.	County cultural councils, appointed by county commissioners or the local city council in each of the seven SCFD counties, annually read grants, conduct interviews, and make funding decisions.[e] Staff oversees the process, and the BOD approves the annual allocations.

Source: Author's summary of information from the SCFD website (www.scfd.org) and from public information requested from the SCFD on August 13, 2012. All data are from fiscal year 2010 or 2011.

a. Between 1996 and 2006 there were four Tier 1 organizations. As part of the tax renewal in 2006, a fifth organization was moved to Tier 1 from Tier 2 because of its longevity and size.

b. The eleven-member board of directors is representative of all seven counties; members are appointed by local city councils, county commissioners, or the governor. The SCFD also employs four staff members: the executive director, two program managers and an office administrator.

c. This number varies from year to year. To qualify for Tier 2, an organization must have been in existence for at least five years and must meet the annual qualifying income threshold, which is adjusted each year based on the previous year's consumer price index. In 2012, the qualifying income threshold was set at $1,442,930.42.

d. In order to qualify for funding, Tier 3 organizations must have IRS 501(c)(3) in-state status, have local incorporation, be governed by a local board, show proof of individual Form 990 tax filings, and have been actively in existence for at least three years. They must also have an overall purpose that is in alignment with the SCFD statute's commitment to the advancement of Colorado culture. Organizations must reapply to receive funding every year through a rigorous process that includes a lengthy grant application and an interview. A total of 277 Tier 3 organizations applied for funding in 2010, but only 268 were funded.

e. The portion of Tier 3 funds received by each county is proportional to the amount of sales tax collected in each county.

SCFD distributed $40.2 million to 297 cultural organizations in 2010[8] and has distributed more than $660 million since its enactment in 1989.[9] Voters reaffirmed their support of the SCFD statute in 1994 and most recently in November 2004, with 65 percent approval.[10] The statute will now expire on June 30, 2018, unless it is reapproved again.[11]

The continued relevance of the SCFD in Colorado gives it a stamp of legitimacy that other centralized funding mechanisms may lack and makes it an interesting case for observing the effects of local option sales taxes on the arts. Since the tax was enacted, participation in the arts has increased significantly and the number of organizations that receive funding has more than doubled. The cultural community, boosted by SCFD funds, has worked to supplement arts and science education in schools with more school performances, after-school programs, and "free days"—select days when Colorado residents enjoy free admission.[12] In 2010 alone, students in the Denver metro area participated in an average of nine arts and cultural events—a 20 percent increase since 2007.[13] These results have led proponents of the tax to believe that the SCFD plays an important role in both stimulating and maintaining local economic growth: investments in local culture have not only increased direct local spending on the arts but also helped develop an educated workforce.[14]

If economic growth is a function of investments in human capital and innovation—as "new growth theory" contends—then policies that encourage the development and sustainability of the cultural sector are vital in stimulating local economic activity and broader revitalization efforts. This chapter explores the direct impact of the SCFD on the success and sustainability of the arts community itself. Arts organizations that receive SCFD funding have been coexisting alongside other arts and non-arts organizations outside the boundaries of the SCFD for more than twenty years. Our analysis attempts to isolate the impact of SCFD grants on the other funding that an organization receives by comparing the revenues of organizations inside the SCFD with the revenues of those outside the district, while controlling for any other confounding factors that may influence levels of funding.

Initial results indicate that organizations within the boundaries of the SCFD had less average total revenue and private giving than organizations outside the district. However, further analysis reveals that the results varied depending on the size of the organization. Large organizations inside the SCFD had less total and earned revenue than comparable organizations outside the district, a result that may be due in large part to the substantial number of free days that these SCFD organizations provided to the general public.

On the other hand, there does not seem to be any significant difference in the average total revenue of small organizations inside the district and the average total of those outside, indicating that SCFD grants to small organizations did not reduce overall revenues. Smaller organizations inside the district did have less average revenue from private giving, but that seems to have been offset by higher average earned revenue (for example, revenues from ticket sales and membership dues); thus, the grants' overall impact on total revenue was insignificant. These results, though not definitive, suggest that cultural tax districts may be an effective policy tool for strengthening and expanding local arts communities.

The "Crowding Out" Problem

The original crowding out hypothesis held that donors treat their contributions to public goods—for example, goods provided by charitable organizations—as perfect substitutes for government contributions to those charities.[15] That finding raised considerable doubt about the role of government spending on social services. Subsequent studies have shown that crowding out is incomplete if individual preferences are different from those assumed in traditional pure public goods models.[16] If one assumes some private satisfaction, such as receiving a "warm glow" from the act of giving,[17] neutrality between publicly or privately provided goods breaks down and government contributions to charity will incompletely crowd out private contributions.

Several studies have examined the relationship between private and public donations to various types of arts and cultural organizations. Kingma's 1989 study of public radio stations found that for every $10,000 increase in government funding, private support for public radio decreased by $0.15 per contributing member.[18] Okten and Weisbrod looked at a range of nonprofit organizations, including art galleries, and found no significant relationship between public and private donations.[19] Both Brooks[20] and Borgonovi[21] found that the relationship between public support and private transfers to arts organizations followed an "inverted U shape", meaning that low levels of public support crowd *in* private donations while higher levels may displace them.

Looking specifically at large symphony orchestras, Brooks argued that measuring crowd out for the nonprofit industry as a whole was not possible due to the unique constituencies and funding characteristics of each subsector.[22] His results show that there was no definitive link between public and private transfers; public transfers did not decrease or increase private funding. Smith, examining the impact of National Endowment for the Arts (NEA) funding on dance companies, found crowd in of about $3.00 for every $1.00 of National Endowment for the Arts funding.[23] In another study, Smith found crowd in of between $0.14 and $1.15, depending on the estimation techniques used to uncover the relationship between government grants and private donations in the data. Moreover, the type of art organization also mattered: symphony and music companies experienced crowd in while dance and ballet companies experienced crowd out.[24]

To incorporate the behavioral response of arts organizations, Andreoni and Payne investigated the demand side of the funding market, revealing a second possible reason for crowding out: the strategic response of an arts organization was to reduce fundraising efforts after receiving a grant.[25] Their empirical results confirm that government grants caused significant reductions in fundraising. Dokko, who also looked at the relationship between government giving, fundraising, and private giving, estimated that private charitable contributions to arts organizations increased by $0.60 to $1.00 per donor, on average, for every $1.00 decrease in NEA funding during the mid-1990s.[26] Moreover, those increases coincided with an average $0.25 increase in fundraising expenditures by arts organizations for every $1.00 decrease in government grants.

In sum, the majority of the empirical studies of crowd out in the arts have found partial to no crowd out as a result of government transfers. The difficulty in estimating the extent of crowd out and the diversity of results leaves a good deal of ambiguity and points to the need for more specific regional and institutional assessments. To date, no study has examined the effect of grants from a cultural tax district on private and program-related revenues. The existence of the SCFD in Colorado for more than twenty years made it possible for us to collect data on the organizations that participated in the tax district and compare that data with data on control groups that were not eligible for funding or were outside the tax district, limiting the effect of unobserved real-world factors that may have offset the degree of crowd in or out in other studies.

Estimating the SCFD's Impact

We evaluated how organizations inside the district were faring compared with those outside the district by comparing arts and non-arts organizations within the geographical boundaries of the tax district[27] to arts and non-arts (that is, social service) organizations outside the district.[28] Arts organizations in the SCFD were the treatment group, while the other three groups (in-district non-arts, out-district arts, and out-district non-arts organizations) served as control groups. In theory, that removed any other trends that may have been present in the data due to differences in geography, mission, or other social or culture-specific tendencies while ensuring a degree of comparability.

The quality of the control groups used was crucial to the quality of the estimates obtained from the analysis; good control groups and the group experiencing the policy change must evolve similarly and react similarly to other changes in the environment that drive policies to change.[29] For this study, the control groups used varied from the treatment group on several dimensions but were influenced by the same elements that affected arts organizations in the district. Mission aside, nonprofit organizations inside and outside the district were subject to similar institutional rules governing their financing, management, and operations and thus responded similarly to observable changes in economic and political forces.

At the same time, the difference in the types of goods and services that arts and social service organizations provided to different sectors of the population controlled for the problems of unobserved variation in the sample, which bias results. Those problems could include, for example, differences in the type of private donor that is attracted to give to the organizations, mission-related differences that affect reliance on government funding and/or private donations, and differences in the scale of day-to-day operations, which can influence the level of general operating support or discretionary funding.

This approach, though more accurate than a standard ordinary least squares regression, still had some drawbacks. Mainly, systematic changes in the arts financing environment and other broader historical changes cannot be accurately controlled for without data from the period before the policy was enacted. For example, estimates will be biased upward if organizations from the control group—those outside the district—gradually moved inside the district over time to take advantage of SCFD funds, though the SCFD has no direct evidence of that having occurred.[30] This analysis therefore does not definitively prove causality. Rather, the results provide a snapshot of how arts organizations inside the district were faring compared with those outside the district in 2005.

The Colorado Nonprofit Dataset

Data on nonprofit revenues and expenses were collected from individual federal tax returns filed by IRS Section 501(c)(3) organizations in the year 2005. Form 990 tax returns identify the amount of private giving (PG), government grants (GG), earned revenue (ER), and total revenue (TR) filed by an organization. PG may come from individuals, estates, corporations, and/or other nonprofit organizations. GG includes grants received from all levels of government, excluding reimbursements for services provided by the non-profit under government contract. If an organization received SCFD funding, it was subtracted from GG and reported separately in the data. ER refers to all revenue generated by an organization through program services, membership dues and assessments, interests, or other rents.

Individual tax returns were obtained from GuideStar, a nonprofit organization that has IRS 990 forms for nonprofit organizations on its website (www.guidestar.org). Data on arts organizations were collected by entering "dance," "theater," "music," "museum," or "art" for both in-district cities (Aurora, Boulder, Brighton, Denver, Broomfield, Littleton, Lakewood, Parker, Northglenn, and Evergreen) and out-district cities (Aspen, Colorado Springs, Pueblo, Ft. Collins, Greely, Vail, and Telluride) into the website's advanced search option. Similarly, data for non-arts organizations were collected by typing in "poverty," "youth services," "natural resource conservation and protection," "advocacy," or "animal protection." Each keyword could have been located in either the organization's name, the type of organization, or the organization's mission statement as posted on GuideStar.[31] The total amount of SCFD funding for each in-district arts organization in 2005 was also recorded.

A cross-section of firm-level data from 2005 was used for two reasons: data on organizations in the treatment and control groups before and after the tax was enacted were difficult to obtain because many organizations did not exist prior to 1989 or did not consistently file a Form 990 tax return, and household-level data on individual contributions to specific organizations were unavailable. Ideally, one would want to match household donations to specific arts organizations over time to measure how the SCFD sales tax affected private giving.[32] Data from 2005 were used because they captured a relatively neutral period in the macroeconomic business cycle: nonprofit revenues and donor behavior were not subject to the sharp fluctuations in national income that characterized the beginning and end of the decade. The final cross-sectional dataset contains 526 nonprofit organizations in Colorado, broken down into four subsamples:

—*In-district arts organizations*, which includes a sample of arts organizations that resided within one of the seven counties (Adams, Arapahoe, Broomfield, Boulder, Denver, Douglas, or Jefferson) that had the SCFD tax. This subsample also contains arts organizations that did not receive SCFD funding but were located within the district.[33]

—*In-district non-arts organizations*, which includes a sample of non-arts organizations that resided within one of the seven in-district counties. These organizations were not eligible for SCFD funding.

–*Out-district arts organizations*, which includes a sample of arts organizations that resided within one of the seven counties (Eagle, El Paso, Larimer, Pitkin, Pueblo, San Miguel, and Weld) that did not have the SCFD tax.

—*Out-district non-arts organizations*, which includes a sample of non-arts organizations that resided within one of the seven out-district counties.

The in-district and out-district arts datasets are representative of the following arts organizations: art museums, other types of museums (for example, cultural history), performing arts groups (theater and dance), and music groups. The in-district and out-district non-arts datasets cover social services organizations that are concerned with families and children; poor, homeless, elderly, or disabled individuals; crime and delinquency; employment issues; other types of basic human and housing-related services; and the environment.

Table 5-2 reports summary statistics for the amount of total revenue (TR), private giving (PG), government grants (GG), earned revenue (ER), and SCFD funding received by each subsample. There were more arts organizations inside the district (151) than outside the district (52). As a result, arts organizations outside the district received more funding on average than arts organizations inside the district, where funding appeared to be more spread out. That may be partially attributable to SCFD funding, which has been instrumental in expanding the arts community in the Denver metro area. Since 1989, the number of organizations that receive funding has nearly doubled, to more than 300.[34]

Arts organizations inside the district received an average of 34 percent of their TR from PG; average TR and average PG were $1,051,850 and $357,440, respectively. ER made up another 42 percent of TR, averaging $446,530. GG accounted for 7 percent of total revenue—$74,110 on average—and SCFD funding made up the remaining 17 percent of funds, averaging $180,710 per organization. Arts organizations outside the district received the same percentage (34 percent) of TR from PG; however, they averaged $369,300 and $1,099,320 in PG and TR, respectively. GG represented only 3 percent of TR ($28,510), and ER made up the remaining 64 percent ($701,520).[35]

For non-arts organizations within the district, PG accounted for 52 percent ($927,840) of TR ($1,800,530). GG made up only 15 percent ($262,860) of TR, and ER accounted for the remaining 34 percent ($616,200). Finally, the ninety-six non-arts organizations outside the district brought in an average of 37 percent of their revenues from PG ($552,560), 21 percent from GG ($324,120), and 42 percent from ER ($641,010).

Table 5-3 illustrates the differences in variable means among in-district, out-district, arts, and non-arts organizations. With the exception of popula-

Table 5-2. *Summary Statistics by Organization Type and Location, 2005*[a]

Group	Variable	Number	Mean[b]	Standard deviation[b]	Median[b]	Min.[b]	Max.[b]
In District Arts	TR	151	1,051.85	4,007.20	131.80	0.76	28,678.43
	PG	151	357.44	1,198.82	35.01	0.00	9,829.42
	GG	151	74.11	387.99	0.00	0.00	2,943.59
	ER	151	446.53	1,754.19	58.57	0.00	14,480.04
	SCFD	151	180.71	940.41	5.24	0.00	7,466.92
In District Non-Arts	TR	228	1,800.53	5,571.41	348.48	0.40	64,625.84
	PG	228	927.84	4,732.65	84.93	0.00	64,420.75
	GG	228	262.86	1,204.98	0.00	0.00	15,016.14
	ER	228	616.20	2,151.91	67.34	0.00	15,492.75
	SCFD	228	0.00	0.00	0.00	0.00	0.00
Out District Arts	TR	52	1,099.32	3,099.81	105.12	6.10	18,035.63
	PG	52	369.30	1,292.48	37.08	0.00	7,934.20
	GG	52	28.51	73.00	0.00	0.00	318.65
	ER	52	701.52	2,183.94	41.12	0.00	12,868.37
	SCFD	52	0.00	0.00	0.00	0.00	0.00
Out District Non-Arts	TR	95	1,512.44	3,810.38	255.94	1.98	26,084.51
	PG	95	552.56	1,799.33	82.00	0.00	13,186.52
	GG	95	324.12	1,402.55	0.00	0.00	10,397.97
	ER	95	641.01	1,985.54	60.12	0.00	13,928.99
	SCFD	95	0.00	0.00	0.00	0.00	0.00

Source: Author's calculations from 2005 Form 990 tax filings.

a. TR = total revenue, PG = private giving, GG = government grants (less SCFD), ER = earned revenue, and SCFD = Scientific and Cultural Facilities District funding.

b. Thousands of dollars.

tion (organizations outside the SCFD were located in areas that had almost half the population of those in the district, on average) all four groups had similar levels of educational attainment, income, incidence of poverty, and Caucasians. Average TR, PG, ER, and GG (less SCFD funding) was comparable for in- and out-district organizations, although in-district organizations had higher average levels of TR and PG than out-district organizations.

The majority of variation in the sample is by organization type; arts organizations had lower levels of funding than non-arts organizations, which is not surprising given that social service organizations are generally larger than

Table 5-3. *Treatment and Comparison Group Variable Means, 2005*

Variable	In District (N = 379)	Out District (N = 147)	Arts (N = 203)	Non-Arts (N = 323)
Total revenue	1.502	1.366	1.064	1.715
(millions of dollars)	(5.014)	(3.570)	(3.788)	(5.112)
Private giving	0.700	0.487	0.360	0.817
(millions of dollars)	(3.754)	(1.636)	(1.220)	(4.094)
Earned revenue	0.548	0. 662	0.512	0.623
(millions of dollars)	(2.002)	(2.051)	(1.871)	(2.101)
Government grants (less SCFD)	0.187	0.220	0.062	0.281
(millions of dollars)	(0. 969)	(1.135)	(0.336)	(1.264)
Population	0.280	0.120	0.259	0.221
	(0.234)	(0.137)	(0.238)	(0.212)
Percent of population with	0 .865	0.899	0.871	0.877
a high school diploma	(0.073)	(0.071)	(0.078)	(0.072)
Percent of population with	0.421	0.399	0.429	0.406
a bachelor's degree	(0.150)	(0.173)	(0.155)	(0.158)
Income	0.047	0.045	0.046	0.047
(millions of dollars)	(0.010)	(0.010)	(0.010)	(0.01)
Percent in poverty	0.118	0.112	0.121	0.113
	(0 .048)	(0.046)	(0.046)	(0.049)
Percent Caucasian	0.781	0.859	0.795	0.808
	(0.121)	(0.078)	(0.122)	(0.112)

Source: Author's calculations from 2005 Form 990 tax filings and U.S. Census Bureau data. Standard deviations are in parentheses.

arts organizations. However, those differences are desirable if they help capture unobserved variations across comparison groups that are difficult to control for in a regression but that will bias results—for example, differences in donor behavior, which also may affect levels of funding.

Regression Results

In table 5-4, four variables of interest for each nonprofit organization—total revenue, private giving, earned revenue, and government grants (less funding from the SCFD)—are regressed on the following:

—whether the organization is inside the SCFD ("Inside District")

—whether the organization is an arts organization ("Arts")

—whether the organization is an arts organization inside the SCFD ("Inside District Arts")

—a number of control variables including city population, race, percent of population with a high school diploma, percent of population with a bachelor's degree, income, and percent of population living in poverty ("Controls"). Preliminary estimates indicated that some very large arts organizations (those making upward of $20 million a year) skewed the estimated impacts of the SCFD on a majority of organizations in the sample.[36] Moreover, there is no reason to assume that a "large" organization that receives SCFD funding will be confronted with the same outcome as a "small" organization. To accommodate differences in firm size, the following terms were added:

—whether the organization has total revenues of less than $700,000 per year ("Small")[37]

—interaction terms for all "small" variables: "Inside District Small"; "Small Arts"; and "Inside District Small Arts"

Finally, after each of the above individual treatment effects were estimated, the total effect of being a small or large arts organization inside the SCFD was calculated for each of the four funding streams ("Total Inside District Small/Large Effect"). The take-away results from table 5-4 are the estimated "total" effects of being inside the district for small and large organizations, shown in the last two rows of the table. These results combine all of the information contained in each of the marginal effects estimated separately above.

Results show that organizations experienced very different results depending on their size.[38] The results for small organizations are considered more robust because they made up the majority of the arts organizations in the sample (the sample included only twenty-two large organizations inside the district). For those organizations, there is no significant difference between the average amount of total revenue and earned revenue that they collected inside and outside the district, meaning that the SCFD did not crowd in or crowd out revenues. In fact, the coefficient on the "Inside District Small Arts" variable is positive and significant for earned revenue and total revenue, indicating that the effect of being a small arts organization inside the district—all else held constant—actually increases overall revenues (possible crowd in of funds). Last, small arts organizations received $210,000 less in average total contributions from individual donors. However, because there is no significant difference in total revenue between small organizations inside and outside the district, larger increases in earned revenue seem to be offsetting any losses in private giving.

On the other hand, large arts organizations inside the district had less total revenue and earned revenue than large arts and non-arts organizations inside and outside the district (possible crowd out of funds). Large organizations had

Table 5-4. Impact of SCFD Funding on Total Revenue, Earned Revenue, Private Giving, and Government Funding for Small and Large Organizations[a]

Independent variable	Total revenue	Earned revenue	Private giving	Government grants (less SCFD)
Inside District	0.125	-0.238	0.648*	0.119
	(0.701)	(0.219)	(0.265)	(0.102)
Small	-2.650***	-0.895***	-0.564***	-0.169*
	(0.560)	(0.181)	(0.136)	(0.0815)
Inside District Small	-0.0996	0.234	-0.766**	-0.135
	(0.685)	(0.226)	(0.278)	(0.105)
Arts	2.871**	3.614***	0.0390	-0.0993
	(0.936)	(0.316)	(0.369)	(0.0862)
Inside District Arts	-3.916***	-3.423***	-0.0942	-0.127
	(1.080)	(0.435)	(0.575)	(0.131)
Small Arts	-2.872**	-3.598***	-0.0635	0.0795
	(0.937)	(0.318)	(0.370)	(0.0886)
Inside District Small Arts	3.811***	3.384***	0.00266	0.126
	(1.077)	(0.435)	(0.571)	(0.133)
Constant	0.549	1.256	0.948	0.843
	(3.093)	(0.881)	(1.222)	(0.526)
Controls	Yes	Yes	Yes	Yes
Summary statistic				
N	507	508	517	515
R^2	0.437	0.388	0.299	0.187
Total Inside District	-0.079	-0.043	-0.210***	-0.018
Small Effect[b]	(0.118)	(0.038)	(0.060)	(0.020)
Total Inside District	-3.791***	-3.661***	0.554	-0.008
Large Effect	(0.847)	(0.362)	(0.496)	(0.086)

Source: Author's calculations based on data from 2005 Form 990 tax filings and U.S. Census Bureau data.

a. Each column of this table reports a separate ordinary least squares regression using data from 2005. The unit of analysis is a nonprofit firm. The dependent variables are measured in millions of dollars. Standard errors are in parentheses. The "Total Inside District Small Effect" and "Total Inside District Large Effect" are estimated by taking a post-estimation linear combination of all the individual treatment effects inside the district for small and large organizations, less those outside the district. Controls include population, race, percent of population with a high school diploma, percent of population with a bachelor's degree, income, and percent of population in poverty. ***$p < 0.001$; **$p < 0.01$; *$p < 0.05$.

b. The total effect is estimated by adding all the individual treatment effects for small arts organizations inside the district ("Inside District" + "Small" + "Inside District Small" + "Arts" + "Inside District Arts" + "Small Arts" + "Inside District Small Arts") and subtracting them from the individual effects that also apply to organizations outside the district ("Small" + "Arts" + "Small Arts"), isolating the combined total effect of being a small organization inside the district—that is, "Inside District" + "Inside District Small" + "Inside District Arts" + "Inside District Small Arts". To ensure the accuracy of the standard errors, this is done using a post-estimation linear combination. The same technique is used to estimate the impact on large arts organizations.

on average $3.79 million less in total revenue than control groups, largely due to an average of $3.66 million less in earned revenues. Losses in earned revenue may occur because in order to receive SCFD funds, larger organizations must provide a certain number of free days to the general public. In 2009 alone, 7.1 million visitors took advantage of free or reduced-rate visits to arts and cultural activities, while only 4 million paid full price for visits.[39] However, any immediate losses in earned revenue from the substantial volume of free visits made to these large institutions need to be balanced against potential long-term gains in community support. SCFD funding did not influence the amount of contributions that large organizations received from individuals. Finally, residing inside the district did not have any effect on the amount of other government grants that either small or large firms received.

Encouraging Results for the Future of Cultural Tax Districts

The results from this study indicate that there was no significant difference in the average amount of revenues that the majority of organizations inside the SCFD collected and the amount collected by organizations located outside the district, indicating that SCFD grants to those organizations can be taken purely at face value—that is, that SCFD grants neither crowd in or crowd out other funds. Smaller organizations in particular may want to leverage the possible crowd-in effect of public funds on earned revenues by spending their awards more on programming, advertising, and fundraising to increase private donations and enhance their future standing in the community. More data are needed to assess the impact that SCFD funds have on larger organizations, although estimates suggest that crowd out in earned and total revenues may be due in part to the large number of free or reduced-rate visits that the organizations provide to the general public.

Given the current paucity of research on the effect that cultural tax districts have on the fiscal health and future growth of participating organizations, additional research on similar tax policies would contribute to our understanding of the effects of government transfers on private giving in the United States. One approach would involve looking at spending on fundraising by the organizations themselves to see whether any interesting patterns emerge.[40] In particular, studies that analyze data from the period before and the period after the creation of a cultural tax district would be ideal.

Notes

1. Jane Hansberry, "Denver's Scientific and Cultural Facilities District: A Case Study in Regionalism," *Government Finance Review* (December 2000), pp. 13–16. See also chapter 4 in this volume for a discussion of the statewide Massachusetts program that awards grants to communities for local cultural economic development initiatives.

2. National Endowment for the Arts, "How the United States Funds the Arts" (January 2007), p. 1.

3. Ibid, p. vii.

4. Quoted in Patricia Cohen, "Suburban Taxpayers Vote to Support Detroit Museum," *New York Times*, August 8, 2012.

5. Scientific and Cultural Facilities District, "About SCFD," 2012 (http://scfd.org/?page=about&sub=1).

6. Ibid.

7. Ibid.

8. Information obtained from the Scientific and Cultural Facilities District by special request, August 13, 2012.

9. Scientific and Cultural Facilities District, "SCFD 2010 Annual Report" (August 2011) (http://scfd.org/downloads/ar/2010%20AR.pdf), p. 2.

10. Scientific and Cultural Facilities District, "About SCFD."

11. Ibid.

12. Hansberry, "Denver's Scientific and Cultural Facilities District," p. 15.

13. Ibid.; Scientific and Cultural Facilities District, "SCFD 2010 Annual Report," p. 4.

14. Hansberry, "Denver's Scientific and Cultural Facilities District," p. 15. See also chapter 6 in this volume for a more in-depth discussion of the role that arts education plays in the development of STEM professionals.

15. See Peter G. Warr, "Pareto Optimal Redistribution and Private Charity," *Journal of Public Economics*, vol. 19 (1982), pp. 131–38; and Russell D. Roberts, "A Positive Model of Private Charity and Public Transfers," *Journal of Political Economy*, vol. 92 (1984), pp. 136–48. For a more in-depth literature review, see Richard Steinberg, "Does Government Spending Crowd Out Donations? Interpreting the Evidence," *Annals of Public and Cooperative Economics*, vol. 65 (1991), pp. 519–617.

16. If donors are motivated by the public goods model, they view their donation as a perfect substitute for a government-financed or -taxed donation, leading to "perfect crowd out" (Warr, "Pareto Optimal Redistribution and Private Charity"; Roberts, "A Positive Model of Private Charity and Public Transfers"). On the other hand, the "impure altruist model" assumes partial crowd out. Here, agents receive utility from personal consumption, their individual contribution, and the overall supply of a given charity but treat the contributions of others and government funds as perfect substitutes. This model is explored in Burton A. Abrams and Mark A. Schmitz, "The 'Crowding-Out' Effect of Government Transfers on Private Charitable Contributions," *Public Choice*, vol. 33, no. 1 (1978), pp. 28–40, and developed in Martin Feldstein, "A

Contribution to the Theory of Tax Expenditures: The Case of Charitable Giving," in *The Economics of Taxation*, edited by Henry J. Aaron and Michael J. Boskin (Brookings, 1980), pp. 99–122; Richard Cornes and Todd Sandler, "Easy Riders, Joint Production, and Public Goods," *Economic Journal*, vol. 94 (1984), pp. 580–98; and Richard Steinberg, "Voluntary Donations and Public Expenditures in a Federalist System," *American Economic Review*, vol. 77 (March 1987), pp. 24–36.

17. The warm-glow theory holds that people give because they enjoy the gratification and/or recognition and prestige that results—not, as in altruistic giving, because they want solely to benefit others or society. See James Andreoni, "Philanthropy," in *Handbook of Giving, Reciprocity and Altruism*, edited by L. A. Gerard-Varet, Serge-Christophe Kolm, and Jean Mercier Ythier (North-Holland Elsevier, 2004), pp. 1201–1269.

18. Bruce R. Kingma, "An Accurate Measurement of the Crowd Out Effect and Price Effect for Charitable Contributions," *Journal of Political Economy*, vol. 97 (1989), pp. 1197–207.

19. Cagla Okten and Burton A. Weisbrod, "Determinants of Donations in Private Nonprofit Markets," *Journal of Public Economics*, vol. 75 (2000), pp. 255–72.

20. Arthur C. Brooks, "Public Subsidies and Charitable Giving: Crowding Out, Crowding In, or Both?" *Journal of Policy Analysis and Management*, vol. 19, no. 3 (2000), pp. 451–64, and Arthur C. Brooks "Taxes, Subsidies, and Listeners Like You: Public Policy and Contributions to Public Radio," *Public Administration Review*, vol. 63, no. 5 (2003), pp. 554–61.

21. Francesca Borgonovi, "Do Public Grants to American Theatres Crowd Out Private Donations?" *Public Choice*, vol. 126, no. 3-4 (2006), pp. 429–51.

22. Arthur C. Brooks, "Do Public Subsidies Leverage Private Philanthropy for the Arts? Empirical Evidence on Symphony Orchestras," *Nonprofit and Voluntary Sector Quarterly*, vol. 28, no. 1 (1999), pp. 32–45.

23. Thomas M. Smith, "The Effect of NEA Grants on the Contributions to Nonprofit Dance Companies," *Journal of Arts Management, Law, and Society*, vol. 33 (2003), pp. 98–114.

24. Thomas M. Smith, "The Impact of Government Funding on Private Contributions to Nonprofit Performing Arts Organizations," *Annals of Public and Cooperative Economics*, vol. 78, no. 1 (2007), pp. 137–60.

25. James Andreoni and Abigail Payne, "Do Government Grants to Private Charities Crowd Out Giving or Fund-Raising?" *American Economic Review*, vol. 93 (2003), pp. 792–812.

26. Jane K. Dokko, "Does the NEA Crowd Out Private Charitable Contributions to the Arts?" Working Paper 2008-10 (Washington: Federal Reserve Board, November 2007).

27. Counties within the SCFD included Adams, Arapahoe, Boulder, Broomfield, Denver, Douglas, and Jefferson counties. Out-district counties included Eagle, El Paso, Larimer, Pitkin, Pueblo, and San Miguel.

28. For a discussion on the selection of control groups when examining the incidence of endogenous policies, see Timothy J. Besley and Anne Case, "Unnatural Experiments? Estimating the Incidence of Endogenous Policies," *Economic Journal*, vol. 110 (2000), pp. 672–94.

29. Ibid.

30. If organizations outside the district moved inside the district to take advantage of SCFD funds, then any gains in revenue inside the district actually occurred because resources were being transferred from outside the district to inside the district. While this analysis does not deal directly with any potential problems of spatial autocorrelation, SCFD did not report having any strong evidence of organizations outside the district moving inside the district to take advantage of SCFD funds.

31. GuideStar uses the National Taxonomy of Exempt Entities (NTEE) coding system to classify organizations.

32. Sonia H. Manzoor and John D. Straub, "The Robustness of Kingma's Crowd Out Estimate: Evidence from New Data on Contributions to Public Radio," *Public Choice*, vol. 123 (2005), pp. 463–76.

33. Arts organizations inside the district may not receive funding from SCFD because they do not meet eligibility criteria, or, in the case of Tier 3 organizations, local county cultural councils may deny funding to an organization in a given year even if it is eligible. The presence of organizations that did not receive funding inside the district also introduces more variability into the in-district subsample.

34. Hansberry, "Denver's Scientific and Cultural Facilities District: A Case Study in Regionalism," p. 15.

35. Percentages may not add up due to rounding.

36. In the final regression, observations were dropped if the value of their Cook's Distance—a commonly used estimate of the influence of a data point when performing regression analysis—was greater than 4/N, or greater than 0.0076 (4/526). Doing so reduced the sample size from 526 to 507, 511, 519, or 517 for regressions on total revenue, earned revenue, private giving, and other government funding, respectively.

37. The cut-off point between small and large organizations was set at $700,000 because the majority of Tier 3 organizations—the SCFD tier containing small to midsize organizations—reported earnings below $700,000 in 2005; $700,000 also was the original threshold that organizations had to meet to qualify for Tier 2.

38. The results for small organizations are more robust because of their larger sample size.

39. Scientific and Cultural Facilities District, "SCFD 2010 Annual Report," p. 3.

40. For more research on the demand side of fundraising market, see Andreoni and Payne, "Do Government Grants to Private Charities Crowd Out Giving or Fund-Raising?"

ROBERT ROOT-BERNSTEIN, REX LAMORE, JAMES LAWTON,
JOHN SCHWEITZER, MICHELE ROOT-BERNSTEIN, EILEEN
RORABACK, AMBER PERUSKI, *and* MEGAN VANDYKE

6

Arts, Crafts, and STEM Innovation: A Network Approach to Understanding the Creative Knowledge Economy

Emerging research suggests that arts education in childhood and ongoing participation in the arts in adulthood may help individuals to develop the kinds of skills and knowledge that foster innovation in sciences and technologies. Since 1988 a number of scholars have noted the presence of indirect relationships between arts-rich communities and high-tech entrepreneurship.[1] These scholars have identified a so-called "creative class" of individuals—innovators, artists, and craftspeople—who tend to congregate in the same geographical locales, giving rise to new industries where arts support is strong. One reason that innovators and artists may co-localize is that an arts-enriched environment may also stimulate the *creative capacity* of current and future generations of workers.[2] Child development studies suggest that exposing children to the arts contributes to their creative potential.[3]

The observation that the people who constitute the creative class appear to congregate in geographical locales that bring together arts organizations and technology companies needs explanation. Correlations are not, of course, causation, and misconstruing the meaning of such correlations can result in misapprehensions and failure. If, for example, the relationship between arts and innovation can be reduced to a simple causal statement—"Arts drive innovation," as some people have interpreted Richard Florida to argue[4]— then investing in the arts should stimulate high-tech entrepreneurship in a community. However, such stand-alone investments have not, thus far, paid off in the kinds of returns expected from such a simple causal model. Moreover, it is not clear that that is what Florida is arguing, as his definition of the "creative class" is oddly dependent on the density of advanced degrees rather than on the measures of creativity preferred by Howkins, such as patents, copyrights, trademarks, designs, or new companies.[5] Another problem is that using advanced degrees as a measure of the creative class excludes most practicing artists, musicians, and craftspeople.[6] In contrast, many studies of centers of creativity define the "creative industries" as consisting solely of arts, architectural, and cultural organizations, ignoring innovators and entrepreneurs in the sciences and high-tech industries.[7] The reality is that not all Ph.D.s are creative, nor are all artists and craftspeople innovative. So the problem becomes one of teasing out the possible functional links that might exist between disciplines as disparate as arts and sciences or music and technology and between people who actually produce innovations (that is, ideas or products that are successfully brought to market) and act in entrepreneurial ways (that is, novel ways to deliver ideas or products to market).

If there truly is some connection between arts-rich communities and the presence of high-tech innovation that goes beyond the simple fact that some geographical locations are more population dense than others, a more nuanced set of interconnections needs to be considered. A high level of ongoing support of the arts in a community may require the economic stimulus provided by entrepreneurial activity accompanied by the presence of a highly educated, technologically literate audience devoted to the arts. Where these entrepreneurial and education requirements are lacking, mere investment in arts—or in new high-tech startup companies for that matter—appears not to suffice. The interaction between arts and entrepreneurship, in other words, may not be causal, but relational, best described as a complex network of mutually reinforcing interactions. As Reich has argued, any knowledge economy model must include elements such as the formal educational system (K–12, college, and professional studies) and the informal educational system (community programs, availability of private lessons, museums, mentoring, and so forth), both of which are essential to training entrepreneurial individuals.[8] In addition, established businesses (which provide a secure economic base and a trained workforce) are likely to be a prerequisite to successful development, as is availability of venture capital (to provide entrepreneurial opportunities) and a sufficient industrial base to provide a trained workforce to participate in startup ventures. At the center of this network, binding it together, lie the innovators and entrepreneurs who establish high-tech startup companies located in arts-rich communities. These individuals and their links to all the other economic, educational, and cultural aspects of the system must be our focus if we are to understand how arts, community development, and the knowledge economy are related.

One way of testing relational models is by looking at the intersections, or nodes, in networks that should be present but that have not yet been examined. For example, one may hypothesize that in order for arts to be supported in a community of entrepreneurial innovators, innovators must value the arts sufficiently to support them. One must then ask why such support would be forthcoming. What might make entrepreneurial innovators sufficiently interested in the arts to locate their businesses in arts-rich communities or even to develop such communities? We hypothesize that innovative and entrepreneurial professionals in the science, technology, engineering, and mathematics (STEM) fields are more likely than the typical American to have had an unusually high level of exposure to formal and informal arts education, to be engaged actively in arts and crafts as adults, to recognize that the skills and knowledge that they acquire from arts and crafts participation are valuable to their innovative capacity, and therefore to place an unusually high degree of value on arts and crafts that leads them to locate in, or to help to build, arts-rich communities. Arts and crafts, in short, may help to build an individual's innovative and entrepreneurial capacity; entrepreneurial innovators therefore may find it valuable to support arts and crafts education, businesses, and institutions.

This chapter focuses on three testable hypotheses:

—STEM entrepreneurial innovators engage in arts and crafts across their lifetimes at a rate significantly higher than that of the general population and therefore may have an unexpectedly large impact on the arts economy.

—The arts have an economic impact on science and technology by increasing measures of innovation, such as scientific breakthroughs, patents, and the founding of new high-tech companies.

—STEM professionals understand and value the connections between their arts and crafts avocations and their professional vocations. Taken together, these three hypotheses suggest that arts and crafts stimulate STEM innovation through indirect, geographically delocalized, and long-term mechanisms and that STEM entrepreneurial innovators may play an unrecognized role in supporting the arts economy.

Participation by STEM Professionals in Arts and Crafts

The hypothesis that entrepreneurial innovators are more likely to be personally engaged in arts and crafts than the average scientist or member of the public comes from studies of eminent scientists. The thesis that scientific creativity is correlated with creative avocations such as arts and crafts was first put

Figure 6-1. *Comparison of Participation in Arts and Crafts by Scientists as Adults*[a]

Percent

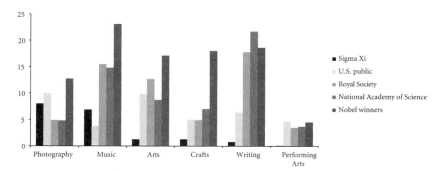

Source: Authors' analysis.

a. Comparing Nobel Prize winners in the sciences (n = 510); members of Sigma Xi (the Research Society) (n = 42,525) and the Royal Society (n = 1,634); U.S. National Academy of Science biographees (1,266); and the U. S. public (from the 1976 National Endowment for the Arts survey) (n = 4,250). See Robert Root-Bernstein and others, "Arts Foster Success: Comparison of Nobel Prizewinners, Royal Society, National Academy, and Sigma Xi Members," *Journal of the Psychology of Science and Technology*, vol. 1, no. 2 (2008), pp. 51–63.

forward by J. H. van't Hoff, the first Nobel laureate in chemistry, based on his observations of his colleagues.[9] Subsequent psychological studies of eminent individuals from many fields substantiated van't Hoff's hypothesis, providing evidence that the more successful people are, regardless of discipline, the more likely they are to engage in one or more long-term creative avocations.[10] Indeed, a variety of studies demonstrate that participation in arts and crafts strongly correlates with scientific success.[11] Nobel Prize winners, for example, have about three times as many adult avocations as the average scientist or a typical member of the American public.[12] In particular, these eminent scientists are between 15 and 25 times as likely as the average scientist to engage as an adult in fine arts such as painting, sculpting, and printmaking; crafts such as wood- and metalworking; performance arts such as acting and dancing; and creative writing or poetry (figure 6-1). In addition to the statistical correlations, many eminent scientists describe specific ways in which their scientific work benefits from their avocations through skill development, knowledge, concepts, methods, and understanding of the creative process.[13] These studies provided the impetus for us to investigate whether a similar link exists between arts and crafts participation and economic measures of entrepreneurial innovation, such as patent production and founding new companies, among science, technology, engineering, and mathematics professionals.

In order to investigate whether arts and crafts participation is related to STEM innovation and, if so, what the nature of that relationship might be, we developed a survey entitled "Survey on Problem Solving Related to Arts and Crafts Training," which was administered to four STEM populations. The first population was a convenience sample of engineering faculty at three institutions: Michigan State University, Michigan Technological University, and Princeton University. The second population consisted of STEM professionals in Michigan who had been awarded Michigan Economic Development Corporation (MEDC) funding through a competitive process to develop startup companies. The third population drew from STEM majors of the Michigan State University (MSU) Honors College who had graduated between 1990 and 1995 and were thus in mid-career. This group consisted of 90 percent scientists and 10 percent engineers. Finally, for our fourth population, contact information for as many members of the National Academy of Engineering (NAE) as could be found through public sources was gathered and those individuals were sent e-mails and letters requesting their participation in our study. Despite repeated invitations to fill out our survey, only 10 percent of the engineering population (45 respondents) and MEDC group (44 respondents) responded. About 15 percent of the MSU Honors College STEM graduates (74 respondents) and NAE members (72 respondents) returned surveys. Comparisons between the groups were made by using a chi squared analysis for larger populations and an exact binomial (nonparametric) test for smaller ones. Because of the low rates of response (unfortunately typical for surveys of scientists and engineers), some bias toward arts-active individuals may be present among those choosing to complete the survey instrument and due care should be taken in interpreting our results. The results presented here, however, generally use controls internal to the dataset so that any respondent biases are self-canceling. The nature of the bias canceling will be discussed in presenting the results of each comparison below.

Our survey asked participants to provide information about what arts and crafts they participated in at three stages of their lives: youth (through age 14); young adult (15–25); and mature adult (26 and older). At each stage of life, participants were requested to check boxes indicating whether they participated in each art or craft as part of their formal education in school or through private lessons or whether they were mentored informally or were self-taught. Mature adults were asked whether they performed, exhibited, or sold their work instead of being asked the question about formal school education. In addition, data were gathered about economic indicators of productivity, including number of patents filed, licensed patents held, companies founded, copyrights filed, articles published, and books published. Free-response questions asked participants whether knowledge, skills, processes, or other aspects of arts and crafts avocations played any role in their vocational work; how they were introduced to arts and crafts and what their most important experience in arts and crafts was; whether they believed that arts and crafts education should be a required part of STEM education; and how arts and crafts could best be introduced into STEM education, if that was a viable goal. While all respondents answered the questions concerning arts and crafts participation, only about 80 percent answered the free response questions.

One subset of our data regarding the MSU Honors College STEM graduates has already been published;[14] the remainder of our data is still being processed. What follows here are the highlights of our ongoing study thus far. Interpretation of these data may require some modification as we systematically investigate all of the control variables.

To begin, as predicted by our first hypothesis, our data demonstrate that successful professionals in STEM disciplines are more likely than the average American to participate in arts and crafts avocations as adults and across their lifetimes. Results of our survey of MSU Honors College STEM graduates mimic the results from the Nobel Prize study: the honors graduates were three to ten times more likely than the average American to be engaged in any given art or craft. While one might expect that the high rate of participation in arts and crafts by STEM graduates was a function of their extraordinary socioeconomic backgrounds, that was not the case, as we demonstrate below.

Our data also reveal that engineers in general were much more likely than the average member of the public to participate in various arts, especially photography and music, and especially in crafts such as wood- and metalworking. Figure 6-2 compares the reported lifetime participation in various arts and crafts by members of the National Academy of Engineering, Michigan engineering faculty, and MEDC-funded entrepreneurs with that of the U. S. public as determined by a 2008 National Endowment for the Arts survey.[15] The NEA survey was administered by telephone to 12,518 individuals 18 years old or older and to 5,925 spouses/partners; the sample was balanced by gender, age, income, and geography to reflect the U.S. population. The respondents undoubtedly included some STEM professionals, but no data concerning profession were recorded. The probability that those surveyed included individuals from any of our groups is negligible.

Figure 6-2. *Comparison of Participation in Various Arts and Crafts by Adults in the U.S. General Public and by Engineers*[a]

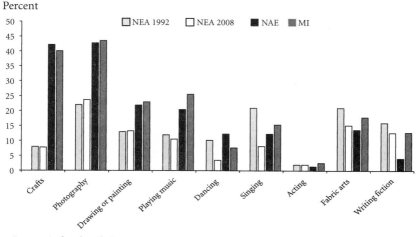

Percent

Source: Authors' analysis.

a. Adult general public participation, as measured by two NEA studies—National Endowment for the Arts, "2008 Survey of Public Participation in the Arts," Research Report 49 (Washington: National Endowment for the Arts, 2008) (www.nea.gov/research/2008-SPPA.pdf), and John P. Robinson, "NEA Survey of Arts Participation in America, 1982–1992," Research Division Report 27 (Washington: National Endowment for the Arts, 1992)—compared with participation of members of the National Academy of Engineering (NAE) and engineering faculty from Michigan universities (MI). Engineers are significantly more likely (chi squared analysis) to have an adult avocation in crafts, arts, music, or photography than is the typical American adult.

Members of the National Academy of Engineering had arts and crafts participation profiles that were similar but not identical to those of the Nobel Prize winners and MSU Honors College STEM professionals described above. NAE members were much more likely than the average American to participate as an adult in photography; to have crafts avocations such as woodworking, metalworking, glassblowing, and mechanics; to draw and paint; and to play music. Participation in photography and crafts was significantly higher among engineers than among the scientists profiled above, while participation in writing and arts avocations was significantly lower. Taken in aggregate, our studies of scientists and engineers suggest an unusual degree of participation by engineers in a variety of arts and crafts starting in childhood and lasting through maturity. That finding lends credence to the hypothesis that STEM innovators may be attracted to and help to build arts-rich communities because of their personal proclivities, values, and experiences.

The Impact of Arts and Crafts on STEM Innovation

Our second hypothesis is that participation in arts and crafts may have value to scientists and engineers for very practical reasons, such as its ability to build their personal entrepreneurial and innovative capacity. Our studies support this conjecture also. Arts and crafts participation by MSU Honors College STEM graduates correlates well with the production of intellectual property (IP) such as patents and companies (figure 6-3). While there was a general trend at every stage of life toward more participation in all arts and crafts (except music) among those who produced patents and founded new companies than among those who did not, sustained participation from childhood through mature adulthood in five arts and crafts was especially significant: photography, woodworking, mechanics, electronics, and dancing.[16] These data suggest that inventors tend to be people who enjoy working with their hands. It is important to note that the data are especially compelling because the comparisons here were done solely within the group of respondents so that any bias caused by self-selection among respondents to our survey could have no effect on the results.

National Academy of Engineering respondents who produced the most intellectual property were also found to have significantly greater participation in arts and crafts avocations than those who produced less intellectual property. National Academy respondents were divided into those with five or less patents and those with more than five patents. This process naturally eliminated any respondent bias since respondents were compared with respondents. Statistically significant positive correlations with IP production were found (figure 6-4) for sustained participation from childhood through mature adulthood in photography, music (playing an instrument, composing, or singing), crafts (woodwork, metalwork, mechanics, and glassblowing), electronics and computing, and writing (creative and nonfiction). Negative correlations were found for fabric arts (sewing, knitting, weaving) and performing arts (acting, dancing, theater)—which, interestingly enough, were practiced in the main by women members of the NAE, who also had the least production of IP. Hypothesizing that these negative correlations may reflect the difficulties that women engineers have in getting recognition for their work and their ability to attract venture capital, we examined the effects of practicing fabric arts and performing arts on production of IP within the group of women only. Within the group of women that we studied, the practice of fabric arts and/or performing had no significant effect on their probability of producing valuable IP.

Figure 6-3. *Sustained Arts and Crafts Participation and Patent Production by MSU Honors College STEM Graduates, 1990–95*[a]

Percent

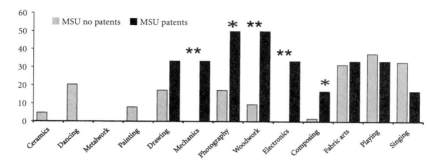

Source: Authors' analysis.

a. Comparing Michigan State University Honors College STEM graduates who report having filed patents with those who have not. Sustained practice of photography, woodwork, mechanics, electronics, and dancing correlated at a statistically significant level ($*p < 0.05$; $**p < 0.005$) with producing patents. "Playing" refers to playing an instrument.

Figure 6-4. *Impact of Persistent Arts and Crafts Participation on Patent Output among NAE Members*[a]

Percent

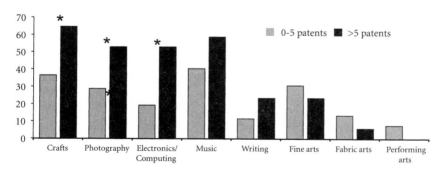

Source: Authors' analysis.

a. Sustained participation in arts and crafts from childhood through maturity generally correlated significantly and positively with producing more patents among National Academy of Engineering members ($n = 72$). Having a sustained avocation in photography, music, crafts, electronics and computing, or writing all correlated positively ($*p < 0.05$, by chi squared analysis). Fabric arts and performing arts correlated negatively, which may be an artifact of female NAE members filing significantly fewer patents than male members overall.

Figure 6-5. *Effect of Sustained Participation in Arts and Crafts on Entrepreneurial Innovation*[a]

Percent

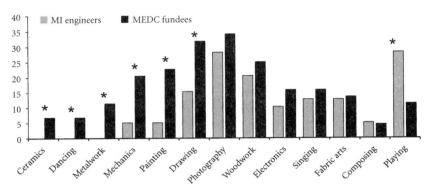

Source: Authors' analysis.

a. Entrepreneurial innovation was measured by respondents' having founded a company and/or having filed a patent. Michigan engineering faculty (MI engineers) (n = 44) were compared with Michigan STEM professionals awarded competitive Michigan Economic Development Corporation funding to support entrepreneurial activity (MEDC fundees) (n = 45). MEDC fundees were statistically significantly more likely that engineering faculty (*$p < 0.05$, by chi squared analysis) to have sustained participation in ceramics, drawing, painting, metalwork, mechanics, and dancing, but music was negatively correlated.

An additional comparison also suggests that sustained participation from childhood through mature adulthood in arts and crafts is strongly associated with production of intellectual property in the form of patents filed and companies founded. We compared the sustained avocations of Michigan engineering faculty, none of whom had helped to found companies, with awardees of Michigan Economic Development Corporation funds, all of whom had helped to found new companies (figure 6-5). Like the previous comparison within the NAE survey group, the comparison of the engineering faculty with the MEDC fundees was especially well-controlled because the same percentage of responses was received from both sets of surveys. Any bias toward arts-active respondents would be equal in each group and therefore cancel out in the comparisons. Positive significant differences ($p < 0.05$) correlate sustained participation in fine arts (drawing, painting, printmaking), crafts (woodwork, metalwork, mechanics, glassblowing), and performing arts (dancing, acting, magic) with founding new high-tech companies. A slight but not statistically significant negative correlation was found for sustained participation in music. Thus, successful entrepreneurs once again were shown to engage in significantly more arts and crafts activities throughout their lives than their less entrepreneurial peers.

Given the positive correlation between many arts and crafts and STEM innovation and entrepreneurship measures, one might posit that the most successful people in STEM fields simply had an educational and economic advantage from the outset. Perhaps children of more highly educated parents went to arts-rich schools and had more private lessons in the arts than other children and also got a better STEM education, catapulting them to future success in their chosen field. That turns out not to be the case. We surveyed our participants about their parent's educational attainments and then divided the parents into three groups: those with at most a high school degree (78 mothers, 67 fathers), those with some college or a college degree (102 mothers, 96 fathers), and those with an advanced degree of some type (43 mothers, 61 fathers). As might be expected, participants whose parents had more education were significantly more likely than those whose parents had less education to participate in music (playing an instrument, singing, or composing), writing (creative writing and nonfiction), and fabric arts (sewing, knitting, weaving). But participation in fabric arts did not correlate with any of our measures of STEM innovation or entrepreneurship, and music and writing did so only weakly for some measures in some groups. So simply having more arts and crafts opportunities due to parental education does not explain the arts-STEM productivity correlations reported above.

The conclusion that parental education did not provide a clear advantage for future entrepreneurial innovators is strengthened by the fact that we found no significant correlations (and often no correlation at all: $p > 0.9$) between parental education and participation by STEM professionals in visual arts (photography, drawing), fine arts (painting, printmaking, and sculpting), performing arts (acting, dancing, theater, magic), or electronics and computer programming. In fact, there is a significant ($p < 0.05$) *negative* correlation between parental educational attainment and participation by STEM professionals in crafts (wood- and metalworking, mechanics, and glassblowing). Those engineers and scientists who were raised by parents (particularly fathers) with the least education were significantly *more* likely to learn and practice a craft than those whose parents had high levels of education (table 6-1). In light of our finding that crafts, fine arts, performing arts, electronics, and computing were the most significant and persistent correlates of STEM entrepreneurship and innovation across all groups surveyed, our surprising conclusion is that higher parental education did not improve access to arts and crafts education (formal or informal) among STEM entrepreneurs and innovators.

Table 6-1. *Effects of Parental Education*[a]

Level	Mother's	Father's	Parents'
High school at most	78	67	56
College (some or graduate)	102	96	111
Postgraduate degree	43	61	56
Correlations between parental education and child's arts and crafts experience (chi square p values)			
Visual arts	NS	NS	NS
Fine arts	NS	NS	NS
Photography	NS	NS	NS
Music	$p < 0.05 +$	$p < 0.005 +$	$p < 0.005+$
Crafts	NS	$p < 0.05 -$	NS
Fabric arts	$p < 0.005 +$	$p < 0.05 +$	$p < 0.005 +$
Performing arts	NS	NS	NS
Writing	NS	$p < 0.05 +$	NS
Electronics/computers	NS	NS	NS
Correlations between parental education and child's economic productivity (chi square p values)			
Patents filed	NS	NS	$p < 0.05 -$
Patents licensed	NS	$p < 0.05 -$	NS
Companies founded	NS	NS	NS
Copyrights	NS	$p < 0.05 -$	$p < 0.05 -$
Books	NS	NS	$p < 0.05 -$
Articles (80/20)	$p < 0.05 -$	NS	NS

Source: Authors' analysis.

a. Table shows the effects of parental education (top section), a surrogate for economic status, on the likelihood that the STEM professionals that we surveyed were exposed to arts and crafts (middle section) and on the probability that they would produce some type of intellectual property (bottom section). NS = not significant. A positive sign after the p value denotes a positive correlation; a negative sign denotes a negative correlation.

In addition, we examined whether parental education correlated with the economic productivity of the 225 scientists and engineers in our survey, independent of their arts and crafts participation. Did parents with higher levels of education provide educational or other opportunities that improved the probability that their children would become entrepreneurs or innovators? In no case did we find a positive correlation between maternal, paternal, or combined parental education on number of patents filed, patents licensed, companies founded, articles or books published, or copyrights filed. In fact, higher combined parental education was significantly ($p < 0.05$) *negatively* correlated with three productivity measures: number of patents filed, books published, and copyrights filed. STEM entrepreneurship and innovation do not appear to be stimulated by childhood privilege; quite the opposite.[17]

In sum, our studies demonstrate that sustained participation across a lifetime in arts and crafts—most notably fine arts, photography, woodworking, metalworking, mechanics, and dancing—repeatedly correlated with patents filed and issued and the founding of new companies across diverse STEM groups. The data consistently demonstrate that scientists and engineers were much more likely than the general public to engage in arts and crafts and that their inclination for the arts was not a result of coming from better-educated families. Perhaps STEM professionals come from families that value arts and crafts or education in general to a greater degree than does the public as a whole, and perhaps they therefore seek places to live and work that support those values.

How STEM Professionals Value the Arts and Crafts

The speculation that STEM professionals value arts and crafts to a greater degree than the general public raises our third hypothesis, which is that arts and crafts avocations help them develop innovative and entrepreneurial skills. That possibility is supported by the results of the free-response portion of our survey, which moved the connection between arts, crafts, and innovation beyond mere correlations.

All of the groups surveyed were asked the following question: "Does your avocation or hobby—or the skills, knowledge, esthetic, social contacts, creative practices, or just plain perseverance that you have gained from it—play any role in your current vocation? If so, please explain how." An average of 65 percent of the surveyed scientists and engineers stated that there were direct links between their avocations and their vocations. Typical responses included the following:

—*I use some of my skills from drawing for creating stimuli for experiments. Experience with visual composition helps to create good diagrams and presentations.*

—*Quilting is a great way to use creativity and analytical thinking to solve problems and create something that is aesthetically appealing. It helps me lower my stress level, and likely improves my creativity in my current vocation.*

—*Certainly. These hobbies have assisted with problem solving when resources are scarce or different. In cooking, for example, we often encounter the need to improvise when ingredients are scarce or unavailable.*

—I work in lasers and photonics, which has an indirect, coincidental link to photography hobby.

—Playing with a Meccano set as a boy developed mechanical skills. Construction of a crystal set radio spurred my interest in electronics.

—Mechanical and material properties I learn in my hobbies can often relate to mechanical and material issues in microelectronics, especially in my specific discipline.

—Paper-folding, wood blocks gave me early insight into 3-D geometry.

All of the groups surveyed also were asked this question: "Would you recommend arts and crafts education as a useful or even essential background for a scientific innovator? Why or why not?" Surprisingly, 82 percent of the surveyed scientists and engineers responded "Yes." Again, typical responses provide insight into the varied reasons:

—Yes. Ability to make simple prototypes and models with own hands vital for creativity in product design.

—Mechanical skills are important for constructing experimental apparatus. Pattern visualization is very important, and is developed by arts and crafts.

—Yes—helps creativity.

—Yes, because it is relaxing and frees the mind. I think moving around—dancing, playing on the playground, helps one get a visceral feeling for physics.

—Hands-on experience with tools, materials, etc., whether for arts and crafts or more practical pursuits (carpentry, home repair, auto mechanics, etc.), represents a very important experience for practical problem solving.

—Yes, expands horizons and helps to think outside the box.

—Yes, allows you to explore materials in a different way, figure out how to put things together, try to do things differently.

—Yes. Not necessarily a "curriculum," but the chance to dabble and see how things work together. After these many years in the classroom, I see those that have music and arts background seem to do very well in physics and oftentimes head to engineering careers.

It is important to put these free responses in the context of existing literature concerning the value of arts and crafts for STEM education. To our knowledge, only one previous survey of STEM professionals has asked about the importance of arts and crafts for their vocations. In 1947, the 5 percent of scientists listed in *American Men of Science* who were considered to be the most eminent were queried regarding their arts training: 26 percent reported significant training; 35 percent, a little; and 39 percent, no arts training. Crafts training and experience was not, unfortunately, surveyed. Despite the relative lack of arts training, 80 percent—almost identical to the percentage found in our study—strongly recommended fine arts training as an essential component of a scientific education.[18] So recognition of the relationship between arts and STEM success is long-standing.

One explanation for the high regard that successful STEM professionals have for the arts and crafts can be found in the validation of their anecdotal evidence of utility by formal, controlled studies. Significant correlations have been found by many investigators between visual thinking ability and success in STEM subjects as measured by standardized test scores, classroom grades, and graduation rates. More important, intervention studies have demonstrated that classes in drawing or painting can significantly improve visual thinking ability among poor visualizers and that such training transferred into increases in classroom grades of STEM subjects as well as improved graduation rates among STEM majors.[19] Another skill used by many scientists is kinesthetic or body thinking.[20] Dance is an especially effective way of learning of body thinking within a STEM environment.[21] Similarly, most scientists report making mental and physical models a part of their problem-solving process, and a variety of studies demonstrate that formal exercises that involve making objects in three dimensions (that is, by using sculptural and crafts skills) improves STEM teaching and learning outcomes.[22] In addition, the ability to perform abstraction is a significant correlate of engineering ability,[23] and one of the best ways of teaching abstracting to STEM students is by means of the visual arts.[24]

In short, some of the connections between arts and crafts and STEM ability asserted on the basis of personal experience and observation by our respondents have a basis in formal scientific studies. What may be more important is that some of these connections have not yet been studied and may yield equally compelling results when formally tested. For example, many STEM professionals report that participating in arts and crafts develops the manipulative skills essential for setting up and performing scientific experiments and for inventing new apparatuses, yet there appear to be no formal studies of that assertion. Can learning how to bow and finger a violin, draw an accurate portrait, or do fine needlework also train the mind and hands for doing the best experimental work? We need to know, for such studies will be essential to understanding the economic value of arts-and-crafts participation for innovation in the STEM fields and how best to tailor arts and crafts experiences to the needs of an innovative knowledge economy.

The Complex Relationship between STEM and the Arts

We have drawn a number of tentative conclusions from our studies thus far. The most important is that the connections between arts and entrepreneurial innovation form a complex web of interactions that cannot be modeled using any simple cause-and-effect methodology. Included in this web are arts, crafts, formal educational systems, informal educational systems, private individuals and their mentors, cultural institutions, established businesses, entrepreneurs, venture capitalists, the intellectual property that STEM professionals invent and invest in and the new companies that they found. This system is centered on and mediated by individual STEM professionals and the interests and values that they develop through their educational, professional, and avocational experiences. Our results suggest that arts and crafts knowledge, whether acquired through formal or informal education, is important to STEM innovators and that persistent experience with arts and crafts correlates with economically important measures of STEM entrepreneurship, such as filing patents and founding companies. Participation in arts and crafts is therefore valuable in the development and training of STEM innovators. Our results suggest equally that because STEM innovators highly value arts and crafts, the system of interactions is likely to be reciprocal, with STEM innovators supporting arts and crafts in return.

What is perhaps most important and least obvious about our model of arts and crafts and STEM businesses within an emerging knowledge economy is that these reciprocal interactions take place over decades and may be manifested in geographically remote places rather than in localized clusters. The arts experiences that a child has in school, at home, or in a cultural institution determine to a large extent whether that child will become and stay engaged with an art or craft long enough to master its lessons and to apply them to the innovative and entrepreneurial work that she or he does as a STEM professional many years later. The arts programming in a school system in Omaha, Nebraska, or a community crafts program in Wichita, Kansas, might be the catalyst for an innovative company in Silicon Valley or the Research Triangle. So the focus on geographical clustering that has typified much research into the new economy may not identify some of the most important economic impacts of arts and crafts on STEM innovation, particularly those that are education- and avocation-mediated.[25] Tracking such geographically and temporally delocalized economic impacts will challenge standard modes of economic analysis. The value added to specific inventions and products by an arts and crafts sense and sensibility may not be measurable in terms of dollars and cents alone.

Thus far, current research supports four conclusions regarding the relationships between the arts economy and STEM entrepreneurship. First, STEM entrepreneurial innovators are far more likely to participate in arts and crafts across their lifetimes than are members of the general public. This finding suggests that STEM professionals may play more important roles in the arts economy as both participants and consumers than has previously been suspected. Second, and conversely, the arts economy appears to have a significant positive impact on STEM entrepreneurship: within the group of STEM professionals, successful entrepreneurial innovators participated in arts and crafts education and activities at significantly higher rates than non-entrepreneurs. Third, STEM professionals generally regard arts and crafts education and participation as a valuable or even essential component of their professional STEM work. Taken in combination, these three findings suggest that the arts economy is positively linked to STEM entrepreneurship through a diverse set of connections that run in both directions and involve interactions over the lifetimes of the participants. Fourth, arts and crafts participation by STEM professionals is likely be spread out across both time and place, beginning at home or with primary education and extending through university education into maturity. Investments in formal and informal arts or crafts education and cultural institutions that cater to children may pay off only decades later.

The policy implications of these findings are clear. Investing in arts and crafts professionals, institutions, and educational programs is critical to building a knowledge economy capable of STEM entrepreneurship and innovation. Such investments cannot, however, be evaluated in terms of immediate or local returns because education and avocation development are lengthy processes and individuals will take their knowledge and skills wherever they can best develop and use them. Arts and crafts must therefore be perceived not just as luxuries or forms of entertainment bought and sold for immediate pleasure—or even as repositories of culture to be guarded and valued—but also as essential components of the knowledge and skill infrastructure underpinning entrepreneurial innovation. Only when we recognize the value of this skill and knowledge infrastructure will arts and crafts regain their rightful place as contributors to the knowledge economy, which they held in eighteenth- and nineteenth-century Europe.

In conclusion, we can make a number of new, testable predictions based on our model regarding unexpected links between arts and crafts and entrepreneurial innovation. One set of predictions results from the finding in our sample that successful STEM innovators were themselves much more likely than the general public to be artists, musicians, performers, and craftspeople.

It follows that STEM innovators are likely to be unusually active supporters of community arts and crafts businesses and cultural institutions. This support, we conjecture, will be manifested in at least three ways: first, by spending an unusual amount on arts and crafts supplies, equipment, and materials; second, by attending arts, crafts, and other cultural events such as concerts and art exhibitions in unusually high numbers; and third, by personally supporting arts, crafts, and cultural institutions by volunteering and making charitable donations at a rate far exceeding that of the general public. All of these forms of participation help to explain the observation that high-tech innovators seem to cluster in arts-rich communities. While some of the predictions may be testable using data from the Center on Philanthropy Panel Study (COPPS), most of the tests will require the development of new databases. We also predict that companies founded by high-tech innovators will be unusually likely to support arts, crafts, and other cultural institutions in their communities, which would also help explain the geographical co-localization of high-tech industries and arts-rich communities. We know of no datasets that currently make it possible to test these predictions.

Our model posits, in sum, a much more nuanced view of the interactions that exist between arts and crafts and innovative entrepreneurship than previous studies such as Florida's have provided. These interactions go far beyond the direct-return-on-investment models that are typically used to evaluate the value of arts investment within a community. The model purposely includes formal and informal education; the long-term impacts of arts and crafts training on the skills and knowledge necessary to train entrepreneurial STEM professionals; economic returns in the form of patents, companies, and other intellectual property that derive from such skills and knowledge; the returns that skilled professionals make to the arts community through their varied forms of support; and the economic benefits to the arts community of the high-tech companies that skilled professionals found and the innovations that they produce. The range of benefits may be difficult to measure in typical economic terms because their effects may be divorced in time and place from the sites of investment, but such individually mediated, transferred benefits seem to us to represent a type of value that we need to learn how to measure and then invest in to optimize growth in a knowledge economy.

Notes

1. Franco Bianchini and others, *City Centres, City Cultures: The Role of the Arts in the Revitalisation of Towns and Cities* (Manchester, U.K.: Centre for Local Economic Development Strategies, 1988); Michael Parkinson and Franco Bianchini, *Cultural Policy and Urban Regeneration* (Manchester University Press, 1993); Charles Landry and others, *The Creative City in Britain and Germany* (London: Anglo-German Foundation for the Study of Industrial Society, 1996); Charles Landry, *The Creative City: A Toolkit for Urban Innovators* (London: Earthscan, 2003); Klaus Kunzmann, "Culture, Creativity, and Spatial Planning: The Abercrombie Lecture," *Town Planning Review*, vol. 75, no. 4 (2004), pp. 383–404.

2. Robert Root-Bernstein and Michele Root-Bernstein, *Sparks of Genius* (Boston: Houghton Mifflin, 1999); Daniel Pink, *A Whole New Mind* (New York: Berkley Publishing Group/Penguin Group, 2005).

3. Western Michigan University Foundation, *New Economy Progress Report* (Lansing, Mich.: EPIC-MRA, 2005).

4. Richard Florida, *The Rise of the Creative Class* (New York: Basic Books, 2002).

5. John Howkins, *The Creative Economy: How People Make Money from Ideas* (London: Allen Lane, 2001).

6. Ann Markusen, "Urban Development and the Politics of a Creative Class: Evidence from the Study of Artists," *Environment and Planning A*, vol. 38, no. 10 (2006), pp. 1921–40.

7. For example, Richard E. Caves, *Creative Industries: Contracts between Art and Commerce* (Harvard University Press, 2000); UK Creative Industries (www.creative-industries.co.uk/); United Kingdom, Department for Culture, Media, and Sport, "Creative Industries Economic Estimates" (2011) (www.culture.gov.uk/what_we_do/creative_industries/default.aspx); National Assembly of State Arts Agencies, "Economic Impact Studies" (2012) (www.nasaa-arts.org/Research/Key-Topics/Creative-Economic-Development/Economic-Impact-Studies.php).

8. Robert Reich. *The Future of Success: Working and Living in the New Economy* (New York: Vintage, 2001).

9. J. H. Van't Hoff, "Imagination in Science," translated by G. F. Springer, *Molecular Biology, Biochemistry, and Biophysics,* vol. 1 (1967), pp. 1–18.

10. Catherine Cox, *The Early Mental Traits of Three Hundred Geniuses* (Stanford University Press, 1926); Ralph K. White, "The Versatility of Genius," *Journal of Social Psychology,* vol. 2 (1931), pp. 460–89; Mildred George Goertzel, Victor Goertzel, and Ted George Goertzel, *Three Hundred Eminent Personalities* (San Francisco: Jossey-Bass, 1978); Victor Goertzel and Mildred George Goertzel, *Cradles of Eminence* (Boston: Little, Brown, 1962); Roberta Milgram and E. Hong, "Creative Thinking and Creative Performance in Adolescents as Predictors of Creative Attainments in Adults: A Follow-Up Study after 18 Years," in *Beyond Terman: Longitudinal Studies in Contemporary Gifted Education,* edited by Rena Subotnik and Karen Arnold (Norwood,

N. J.: Ablex, 1993), pp. 173–95; Roberta Milgram and others, "Out of School Activities in Gifted Adolescents as a Predictor of Vocational Choice and Work Accomplishment in Young Adults," *Journal of Secondary Gifted Education*, vol. 8 (1997), pp. 111–20; Robert Root-Bernstein and Michele Root-Bernstein, "Artistic Scientists and Scientific Artists: The Link between Polymathy and Creativity," in *Creativity: From Potential to Realization*, edited by Robert Sternberg, E. L. Grigorenko, and Jerome Singer (Washington: American Psychological Association, 2004), pp. 127–51.

11. Paul Cranefield, "The Philosophical and Cultural Interests of the Biophysics Movement of 1847," *Journal of the History of Medicine*, vol. 21 (1966), pp. 1–7; Louis M. Terman, "Scientists and Non-Scientists in a Group of 800 Gifted Men," *Pscyhological Monographs*, vol. 68, no. 378 (1954); Robert Root-Bernstein, Maurine Bernstein, and Helen Garnier, "Correlations between Avocations, Scientific Style, and Professional Impact of Thirty-Eight Scientists of the Eiduson Study," *Creativity Research Journal*, vol. 8 (1995), pp. 115–37.

12. Robert Root-Bernstein and others, "Arts Foster Success: Comparison of Nobel Prizewinners, Royal Society, National Academy, and Sigma Xi Members," *Journal of the Psychology of Science and Technology*, vol. 1, no. 2 (2008), pp. 51–63.

13. Robert Root-Bernstein, *Discovering* (Harvard University Press, 1989); Robert Root-Bernstein, "Art Advances Science," *Nature*, vol. 407 (2000), p. 134; Robert Root-Bernstein, "Music, Creativity, and Scientific Thinking," *Leonardo*, vol. 34 (2001), pp. 63–68; Robert Root-Bernstein, "Sensual Chemistry: Aesthetics as a Motivation for Research," *Hyle*, vol. 9 (2003), pp. 35–53; Root-Bernstein, Bernstein, and Garnier, "Correlations between Avocations, Scientific Style, and Professional Impact of Thirty-Eight Scientists of the Eiduson Study"; Root-Bernstein and others, "Arts Foster Success."

14. Rex LaMore and others, "ArtSmarts among Innovators in Science, Technology, Engineering, and Mathematics (STEM)" (Center for Community Economic Development, Michigan State University, 2011) (http://ced.msu.edu/upload/reports/ARTS-MART%20Report-FINAL.pdf); Rex LaMore and others, "Arts and Crafts: Critical to Economic Innovation," *Economic Development Quarterly* (forthcoming).

15. National Endowment for the Arts, "2008 Survey of Public Participation in the Arts," Research Report 49 (Washington: National Endowment for the Arts, 2008) (www.nea.gov/research/2008-SPPA.pdf).

16. John P. Robinson, "NEA Survey of Arts Participation in America, 1982–1992," Research Division Report 27 (Washington: National Endowment for the Arts, 1992).

17. Note that the opposite was found to be true in Nick Rabkin and E.C. Hedberg, "Arts Education in America: What the Declines Mean for Arts Participation," Research Report 52 (Washington: National Endowment for the Arts, 2011).

18. Stephen S. Visher, *Scientists Starred 1903–1943 in American Men of Science* (Johns Hopkins Press, 1947), pp. 106–07.

19. Eugene S. Ferguson, "The Mind's Eye: Nonverbal Thought in Technology," *Science*, vol. 197 (1977), pp. 827–36; Maizam Alias, Thomas R. Black, and David E. Grey, "Effect of Instructions on Spatial Visualization Ability in Civil Engineering Students,"

International Education Journal, vol. 3, no. 1 (2002), pp. 1–12; Thomas R. Lord, "Enhancing the Visuo-Spatial Aptitude of Students," *Journal for Research in Science Teaching,* vol. 22, no. 5 (1985), pp. 395–405; Sheryl A. Sorby and B. G. Baartmans, "A Course for the Development of 3D Spatial Visualization Skills," *Engineering Design and Graphics Journal,* vol. 60, no. 1 (1996), pp. 13–20; Sheryl A. Sorby, "Developing Spatial Cognitive Skills among Middle School Students," *Cognitive Process,* vol.10, supplement 2 (2009), pp. S312–S315.

20. Root-Bernstein, *Discovering;* Root-Bernstein, Bernstein, and Garnier, "Correlations between Avocations, Scientific Style, and Professional Impact of Thirty-Eight Scientists of the Eiduson Study"; Root-Bernstein and Root-Bernstein, *Sparks of Genius.*

21. Michele Root-Bernstein and Robert Root-Bernstein, "Body Thinking beyond Dance: A Tools for Thinking Approach," in *Dance: Current Selected Research,* vol. 5, edited by Lynette Overby and Billie Lepczyk (2005), pp. 173–202.

22. Holly Ewing and others, "The Role of Modeling in Undergraduate Education," in *Models in Ecosystem Science,* edited by Charles D. Canham, Jonathan J. Cole, and William K. Laurenroth (Princeton University Press, 2003), pp. 413–27; John K. Gilbert, Carolyn J. Boulter, and Roger Elmer, "Positioning Models in Science Education and in Design and Technology Education," in *Developing Models in Science Education,* edited by John K. Gilbert and Carolyn J. Boulter (Dordrecht, Netherlands: Kluwer Academic Publishers, 2000), pp. 3–17; Mike Stieff, Robert C. Bateman Jr., and David H. Uttal, "Teaching and Learning with Three-Dimensional Representations," in *Visualization in Science Education Book Series: Models and Modeling in Science Education,* vol. 1, edited by John K. Gilbert (Springer, 2005); Mike Stieff, "When Is a Molecule Three Dimensional? A Task-Specific Role for Imagistic Reasoning in Advanced Chemistry," *Science Education,* vol. 95, no. 2 (2011), pp. 310-36.

23. Jens Bennedsen and Michael E. Caspersen, "Abstraction Ability as an Indicator of Success for Learning Computing Science?" *Proceedings of the Fourth International Workshop on Computing Education Research,* Sydney, Australia, September 6–7, 2008; "ICER [International Computing Educational Research] '08," symposium proceedings (New York: Association for Computing Machinery, 2008), pp.15–26.

24. Robert Root-Bernstein, "Teaching Abstracting in an Integrated Art and Science Curriculum," *RoeperReview,* vol. 13, no. 2 (1991), pp. 85–90.

25. Michael Porter, *Clusters and the New Economics of Competition* (Harvard Business School Press, 2002); Allen J. Scott, *The Cultural Economy of Cities: Essays on the Geography of Image-Producing Industries* (Thousand Oaks, Calif.: Sage, 2000); Florida, *The Rise of the Creative Class.*

DOUGLAS S. NOONAN *and* SHIRI M. BREZNITZ

7

Arts Districts, Universities, and the Rise of Media Arts

On the surface, the expected relationship between indicators of economic growth and the presence of universities and arts districts might seem fairly straightforward. Universities are generally associated far more closely with innovation, at least the kinds of innovation measured in terms of patents and inventions, while arts districts are typically thought to promote or certify greater intensity of employment in artistic fields. Regardless of intuition, the relationship between these local clusters of investment and indicators of economic growth is ultimately an empirical one, and careful data analysis shows that a casual intuition is not supported. Arts- and media arts–related employment seems to follow universities, while innovation in media arts follows arts districts.

The empirical evidence presented in this chapter reveals the impact of arts districts and universities in select metropolitan areas on the development of the media arts subsector in terms of employment shares and patenting rates. By overlapping the two types of clusters, the quantitative analysis teases out the roles of different approaches to promoting economic growth. The analysis emphasizes new media arts because their high profile attracts attention from regional economic development advocates and because they bridge the gap between the arts and new technology and patented inventions. The findings highlight the role of public investments and policy in crafting successful and sustained development and point to the critical role of selective sorting (migration of people and jobs) and other indirect impacts. The conclusion highlights some policy implications of the findings.

Arts, Universities, and Economic Development: What Do We Know?

To examine the impact of major universities and arts districts on local economic development in terms of both jobs and innovation, especially in the media arts sector, several strands of literature must be woven together. Research on the direct impact of arts institutions and artists themselves on local economies, their export bases, and the general composition of the economy is discussed in other chapters in this volume.

Culture and the Arts in Economic Development

The idea that culture affects economic development is not new.[1] Investment in the arts can help revitalize communities,[2] and investment in large cultural institutions and facilities has become central to cities' strategies to attract and retain certain types of companies and the highly skilled, creative workers that they employ.[3] Over the past decade, a large literature has developed around "the creative class" and the creative economy more generally.[4] In short, much of this literature divides the impacts of arts and culture on local economies into two components: direct income from local cultural institutions and arts production; and indirect impacts of arts and creative activities in attracting particular types of (high human capital) employees and (high-technology, progressive) firms to a region. Arts and cultural production can enhance a region's export base, and cultural institutions can attract outside funding and visitors.[5] Yet the sustainability and relative economic performance of cities' cultural investments remain in doubt.[6] This chapter emphasizes the more indirect processes through which arts affect growth.

A region's arts and culture can be seen as a strong promoter of amenity-driven rather than traditional productivity-led growth in a region[7] by helping to shape the local environment or "scene" in which firms and households choose to work and live.[8] The superior performance of urban areas in adding jobs over time might result from concentrated cultural industries and the diversified economic base that they bring. The direction of the causal arrow in this relationship, however, is disputed.[9]

Whether or not a region or city attracts new resources, its ability to make use of existing resources and amenities in new and different ways can be a recipe for economic growth. The endogenous growth theory of Paul Romer emphasizes that knowledge generation comes from within the economic system.[10] The cultural and arts sectors of the economy may contribute much to new growth by fostering creativity and new combinations of local resources—

some of which surely include individuals with high human capital and creative talents.

Universities in Economic Development

Another strand of literature, quite distinct from the arts policy and creative economy literature, looks at the economic development impacts of universities, particularly university spillovers into local economic activity. While some of this literature on university spillovers obviously connects directly with labor markets—both as a major employer and as a training center for other firms' employees—a great deal of work examines how universities impact their surrounding communities through research and development and technology transfer.[11] Universities produce new knowledge and disseminate it partly through "tech transfer" mechanisms like patents, licenses, and spinout firms.[12] The rise of the knowledge economy has increased the economy's reliance on academic research generated by universities to support economic development.[13] Further, a geographic cost to transmitting their knowledge at least partly localizes universities' economic impact.[14] Many leading technological regions have at their center an innovative university that specializes in research on the technology that defines the region.

Despite the emphasis on supporting local communities through tech transfer via patenting and commercialization of technology, universities have other powerful local economic impacts,[15] including less quantifiable impacts on policy, real estate, and neighborhood revitalization. Universities also can play a major although less recognized role through their community work and influence in economic initiatives.[16] These roles may be of even greater importance to local economic growth than commercialization of technology. Recently, universities have come under increasing pressure to contribute to their surrounding communities through more than just tech-transfer relationships with industry.[17]

Yet nearly all of the research on universities' impact on local economic development and stimulation of new ideas and innovation has focused on technologies with a scientific emphasis or industrial or commercial applications. This chapter takes the investigation into universities' impact on economic development and innovation in another direction—the arts—thereby enriching the understanding of broader university roles and informing new growth theory concerning creative industries. Much of universities' innovations and new knowledge may apply only minimally to most art forms, with the exception of the more technology-intensive media arts sector. Nonetheless, previous work has linked universities and the "creative class." Florida argues that universities provide the "3 Ts"—technology, talent, and tolerance—pointing to more indirect pathways than traditional tech transfer whereby universities can foster stronger creative economies locally. Universities may draw talented students and faculty, cultivate a skilled workforce with heightened demand for arts and culture (see chapter 6 in this volume), and support environments with greater diversity and tolerance. As major cultural and economic institutions, universities may catalyze changes in the existing economic landscape by influencing existing residents and firms as well as selectively attracting newcomers.

New Media Arts

This chapter highlights the impacts of universities and arts districts on economic development in media arts–related areas. New media arts include artistic and creative content in new, especially digital, formats and media, such as digital art, computerized animation, and Internet and interactive art. Closely related high-profile industries include video games, motion pictures and television, Internet publishing, and a host of online entertainment services (for example, streaming content and music and video downloads). Investment in media-related artwork accounts for a substantial component of the broader economy. The National Alliance for Media Arts and Culture (NAMAC) recently conducted a survey of 1,170 media arts organizations and found, for the 37 percent of organizations responding, an average operating budget of $668,000 and a total audience exceeding 33 million people.[18]

Why Focus on New Media Arts?

New media arts were the focus of our research because they bridge the gap between universities and arts districts. The genre of new media arts contrasts with more conventional forms of art in its use of media technologies, especially digital and emerging technologies, to create the art. Media arts often employ new technologies, which makes their applications more relevant for patenting (a common metric for innovation) than conventional art forms. New media arts often utilize or create inventions for which patents, in addition to copyrights for artwork, matter. Hence, in order to detect where more innovation occurs in the creative economy in conventional terms (that is, in terms of patenting), the analysis emphasizes media arts.

Media arts also exhibit a stronger connection to the arts sector and much of the "rest of campus," which can still directly participate in new media arts through disciplines outside of the fine arts like science, technology, engineering, and mathematics (STEM). The new media arts genre integrates the arts sector into different disciplines common to universities.

While media arts nicely bridge conventional universities, conventional measures of innovation, and the broader arts and cultural sector of the economy, they also attract a good deal of attention from policymakers and economic development experts. Many media arts organizations produce high-profile media, often highly visible by their nature as broadcast media, that leverage mass media and telecommunications technologies. NAMAC reports that media arts organizations create media primarily in television (36 percent), video (18 percent), radio (12 percent), film (9 percent), and multimedia (8 percent). Economic development policies often seek to promote media arts activities like filmmaking[19] or to incubate and support startup firms in this area (for example, the Pave Program in Arts Entrepreneurship at Arizona State University and Creative Capital in New York City). Beyond specific cases, little is known about how universities and arts districts contribute to economic growth in media arts.

How Cultural Districts and Universities Might Impact Jobs and Innovation in Media Arts

One way to connect universities and arts districts in economic development is to view them as alternative ongoing local development projects or concentrated investments. A city's arts district and its college campuses are both clusters of local amenities that affect economic development. Arts and cultural districts might directly affect employment in arts-related industries as any industrial cluster would. This concentration could spill over into related media arts work. District amenities might also indirectly attract different firms and talent to the city. A more "creative" region, perhaps with more diversity or larger concentrations of media arts activity, might engender more innovation and knowledge generation than other regions.[20] Similarly, universities might directly contribute to media arts innovation and tech transfer through their research activities. They can also directly influence employment in arts-related jobs by either hiring employees directly or training them to improve their productivity.[21] Even ostensibly nonartistic STEM fields demonstrate important links with the arts. University impacts might be stronger in new media arts, where the overlaps between technology and creative arts are stronger.

Research Design

With respect to direct effects, the expected relationship between universities and arts innovation should be primarily positive, as should the expected relationship between cultural districts and arts employment. To identify the impact of local clusters of investment like universities and arts districts on economic development, a sort of "natural experiment" was performed. The idea behind this approach is that there is a "treatment," say the establishment of an arts district, that only some cities receive; the experiment is "natural" in the sense that the researcher does not control the treatment. Treatment variables include the presence of arts districts and universities. Some cities receive the arts district treatment, some receive the university treatment, some receive both, and some receive neither. The central question here is how economic growth indicators, employment growth and patenting in this case, differ systematically for U.S. cities across those different treatments.

The Data

To assess patterns of growth, data for U.S. cities were collected from several sources. The sample of cities uses the 100 largest U.S. cities today as the starting point and adds the 89 cities with cultural districts identified by Frost-Kumpf in her inventory of cultural districts around the United States.[22] Without double-counting cities, that brings the total number of cities in the sample to 148, with cultural districts in 60 percent of them in 1998. The other form of "treatment," the presence of a major university, was measured by the number of "research extensive," or "R1," universities in a city.[23] The count of postsecondary schools with art departments or art degree programs in each city was also used to test the extent to which a university's impacts were driven by the direct arts education provided.[24]

Two primary datasets were matched to these cities for numerous years. Employment indicators came from the Current Population Survey (CPS), a major national survey jointly sponsored by the U.S. Census Bureau and the Bureau of Labor Statistics. The strength of the CPS as a data source lies in its high-quality, excellent detail on employment characteristics and the frequency of sampling (monthly since 1962). For instance, recent waves of the CPS obtained information on occupation and industry of respondents' first and second jobs. The CPS is more limited regarding geographic identifiers because of the sensitive nature of the survey questions and privacy concerns, so residence of respondents is identified only by metropolitan area, unfortunately a less precise indicator than city of residence.[25] For 1999 and earlier, employment was measured for the metropolitan statistical area (MSA); for later years, it was measured for a core based statistical area (CBSA). This switch follows a change in reporting in the CPS public use data files. MSAs include larger urban areas with populations exceeding 50,000, while CBSAs include urban centers exceeding 10,000 residents and nearby areas from which residents commute to the center. The CBSA includes micropolitan areas and thus covers more urban areas than the MSA measure. Accordingly, a few smaller cities that have cultural districts in the Frost-Kumpf inventory might escape matching with the CPS. (Respondents outside of MSAs can be assigned only to a state, not to a particular metro area.) Employment for a city in the sample is measured as the share of CPS respondents in that city's metro area that report employment in a first (or second) job of a particular type.[26]

The second major data source joined to this dataset is the U.S. patent database, maintained by the National Bureau of Economic Research. Patents represent a form of intellectual property commonly used to measure "innovation" in an economy. While patent counts are not necessarily the best match with artistic innovation, using this limited measure does facilitate linking our research to the large volume of research on university impacts and innovative economies in general. While the CPS data extend to 2011, the patent dataset extends only up to the year 2006, but it is otherwise rich in terms of comprehensiveness and level of detail about U.S. patents. Only "utility" (not "design") patents are used.[27] Each patent assigned to an individual or organization for a particular year is matched to a city from the sample based on the assignee's address. Care was taken to correctly match by city despite misspellings in the raw patent data files ("Milwaukee" has thirteen alternate spellings in the patent data). Patents are classified following a detailed classification scheme, enabling the identification of patents in media arts–related technology categories. The share of all patents in media arts–related technologies assigned in a particular city in a particular year serves as the basic measure of media arts innovation.

The general categories of "the arts" and "media arts" do not match up especially well with the classification schemes used for employment in the CPS or for technologies in the patent data. Even if they did, complications would arise because the CPS's employment classification schemes changed after 1999.[28] The creative economy literature has defined arts-related employment so inconsistently that comparability across studies cannot be assumed. To be transparent, appendix 7A lists the classification categories used in the CPS to characterize employment by industry type (tables 7A-1 and 7A-2) and by occupation type (tables 7A-3 and 7A-4), before and after the coding change, and for arts-related jobs and for media arts–related jobs. Altogether, eight different employment definitions are used here. Markusen and her colleagues argue that categorizing arts-related employment by industry or by occupation can greatly influence a study, so this analysis uses both definitions and shows them side by side.[29] Further, employment definitions based on jobs that are included in both arts-related industries and arts-related occupations are considered in extensions to the basic analysis. As other arts activity rarely gets patented and likely conforms to usual patent classifications more poorly, no attempt was made to measure arts-related patents. Only media arts–related patents were tracked.

Once compiled, the data reveal several interesting patterns. Table 7-1 shows how rare arts-related employment is across all measures (around 1 to 1.5 percent). Employment in media arts–related industries was twice as common as in arts-related industries in 1998, but otherwise arts- and media arts–related employment shares are similar in magnitude. On average, arts employment shares have not changed much since 1999, although employment shares in media arts–related industries fell as shares in media arts–related occupations rose. More restrictive definitions, of course, have smaller shares and trends in employment shares. Employment shares are small on average, but considerable inter-city variation is observed (consistent with findings in chapter 3 in this volume). Patenting rates are small for media arts (approximately 2 percent of all patents), but they rose even faster than the climbing rates of overall patenting in the United States between 1998 and 2006. On average, cities produced two and one-third more media arts–related patents in 2006 than in 1998. Most cities in the sample had no R1 universities, and only thirteen cities had more than two R1s. At first glance, R1s appear roughly evenly distributed among cities with and without cultural districts. Still, further analysis is needed to detect the impact of arts and cultural districts and R1 universities—the treatment variables in this context—on local economic conditions.

Statistically Identifying the Impacts

The statistical models estimated here specify the economic growth indicator (that is, media arts innovation and media arts employment) as a linear function of *district*, the number of R1s, and the number of art schools in town. There are two alternative measures for arts-related employment (for arts industries and arts occupations) and two alternative measures for media arts–related employment (for media arts industries and media arts occupations). The innovation measure has just one construction: media arts patenting rate. The simplest and most direct modeling approach predicts these

Table 7-1. *Variable Definitions and Descriptive Statistics*[a]

Variable	Definition	Observations	Mean	Standard deviation	Minimum	Maximum
District	1 if city listed in Frost-Kumpf's catalog of cultural districts; 0 otherwise	148	0.601	0.491	0	1
R1s in city	Count of R1 universities in the city	148	0.554	0.950	0	6
R1s in CBSA	Count of R1 universities in city's CBSA	148	1.459	2.094	0	9
Art schools	Count of schools in city with art department or art degree program	148	6.365	6.013	0	36
Arts industry$_{98}$	Percent employed in arts industry in 1998	133	0.015	0.009	0	0.052
Arts occupation$_{98}$	Percent employed in arts occupation in 1998	133	0.011	0.007	0	0.040
MA industry$_{98}$	Percent employed in MA industry in 1998	133	0.028	0.015	0	0.093
MA occupation$_{98}$	Percent employed in MA occupation in 1998	133	0.011	0.007	0	0.046
Arts industry$_{9811}$	Percent employed in arts industry in 2011 minus percent in 1998	121	-0.001	0.011	-0.047	0.028
Arts occupation$_{9811}$	Percent employed in arts occupation in 2011 minus percent in 1998	121	0.003	0.008	-0.021	0.033
MA industry$_{9811}$	Percent employed in MA industry in 2011 minus percent in 1998	121	-0.010	0.013	-0.077	0.015
MA occupation$_{9811}$	Percent employed in MA occupation in 2011 minus percent in 1998	121	0.010	0.011	-0.019	0.049

Table 7-1 (continued). *Variable Definitions and Descriptive Statistics*[a]

Variable	Definition	Observations	Mean	Standard deviation	Minimum	Maximum
Arts industry and occupation$_{9811}$	Percent employed in arts industry and arts occupation in 2011 minus percent in 1998	121	0.002	0.004	-0.012	0.020
MA industry and occupation$_{9811}$	Percent employed in MA industry and arts occupation in 2011 minus percent in 1998	121	0.003	0.006	-0.019	0.018
Arts and media arts industry and occupation$_{9811}$	Percent employed in arts and MA industries and arts and MA occupations in 2011 minus percent in 1998	121	0.0001	0.003	-0.013	0.008
Arts (or MA) occupation in MA (or arts) industry$_{9811}$	Percent employed in Arts occupation in an MA industry or in an MA occupation in an arts industry in 2011 minus percent in 1998	121	0.002	0.005	-0.019	0.019
MA patent share$_{98}$	Percent of patents in MA in 1998	140	0.014	0.030	0	0.25
MA patent count$_{98}$	Count of MA patents in 1998	148	3.020	9.227	0	73
MA patent share$_{9806}$	Percent of MA patents in 2006 minus percent in 1998	136	0.008	0.040	-0.154	0.2
MA patent share$_{9806}$	Count of MA patents in 2006 minus count in 1998	148	2.345	14.087	-35	145

Source: Authors' calculations.

a. "MA" represents "media arts–related."

economic indicators for a city using variables capturing the presence of universities and arts and cultural districts. This simple linear model is esti-mated with ordinary least squares (OLS) regression using Huber-White heteroskedasticity-robust standard errors.

Two modifications to this straightforward approach help to obtain unbi-ased estimates of the average impact of districts and universities. First, there may be other factors that affect the economic indicators that also are corre-lated with the location of universities or districts. This kind of spurious cor-relation, if not controlled for, could skew the estimated impacts by making the effect of, say, universities on patents seem rather large when it is due simply to patents and R1 universities separately tending to accrue to larger cities. This is ultimately a problem of universities and districts not being randomly distributed across cities.[30]

To mitigate the problem, the statistical analysis uses several important design features. First, the dependent variables in the regressions—the indica-tors for economic growth (employment, innovation)—are measured as "shares" or "rates." By predicting a city's share of jobs in the arts rather than the gross number of arts jobs, the analysis implicitly controls for scale effects. This is critical for a period—like the Great Recession—during which arts activity contracts to the same degree that other sectors in the city's economy shrink, even if cities endure the era with varying levels of success. Shocks that diminish employment prospects in some cities more than others, even if they are correlated with the presence of universities or districts, will affect total employment, not *relative* employment. The same goes for patenting rates or the share of patents in media arts–related technologies. Measuring everything in terms of the relative size of the arts sub-area (employment or innovations) sidesteps factors that influence overall employment and innovation in favor of only those forces that differentially influence the arts and media arts sec-tors. Thus, if universities bring more media arts patents because they bring more patenting overall, that kind of impact will not be detected here.

Second, a "first-differences" approach is taken to analyze *trends* in employ-ment and innovation rather than their levels at any particular moment. Look-ing at the trajectory of employment and innovation for cities with and without universities and districts bypasses the potential problem that some latent factors that cause both different economic conditions and the presence of a local cluster cannot be observed and controlled for in the regression (chapter 3 identifies several such factors in its cross-sectional analysis of the distribution of arts and cultural activity in California cities). Their omission might bias the results and attribute too much influence to the universities or districts, but looking for differential trajectories for cities with and without local cluster "treatments" justifies ignoring unobserved latent factors influencing the size of cities' creative economies in 1998. It is not the size that matters in this construction, but the change in size.[31] The results here measure the differences in trends in employment or innovation rates from 1998 to the most recent period between cities with and without "treatment," regardless of their starting point or initial level of media arts activity.

Ultimately, the basic OLS regressions predict the changes in the share of arts-related employment or patenting by using the presence of R1 universities or cultural districts as of 1998. Of course, many of the cities that were not on Frost-Kumpf's 1998 inventory of cities with cultural districts (that is, the control cities) subsequently designated an arts district of some sort. Many of them even established their arts district prior to the 2006 or 2011 end-dates in this analysis. Thus, some of the control cities can be expected to have received *some* treatment from the new districts, even if only for a few years. If the economic impact of districts takes time to manifest, the estimated impact of districts in this analysis should be understating the true impact because some of the control group cities actually received a small dose of treatment. This conservative approach, which acknowledges that the *district* measure is imperfect and that some measurement error is associated with it, also has the advantage of being simpler to interpret than a more complicated metric for timing of establishment.

Another important concern about the *district* variable is that a binary indicator for the existence of an arts district obscures the great variety in the kinds of cultural districts that exist in cities today.[32] Some are "reactive," formed around existing arts strengths of a city. Others are more "proactive," formed to guide future arts activity into that district and cultivate a new cluster. Some are districts on paper or in marketing only, while others involve zoning changes, subsidies, or other significant changes in rules and incentives (see chapter 5 for an example from Colorado). Some are thematic (for example, theater and museum districts), while others promote artists' housing or subsidize local start-ups. All of this heterogeneity is condensed here to a signal binary indicator. The results revealed are simply the average impact of cultural districts, regardless of their type. Of course, some types of districts may have bigger or smaller impacts than other types (chapter 5 details one district's impacts.)

Testing the Robustness of the Results

Robustness is embedded in the analysis by design, as discussed above, but additional robustness checks are performed. Alternative classifications of arts-related and media arts–related employment might yield different sorts of results.[33] Several different definitions are tested in each of the analyses reported here. Moreover, alternative timeframes are used in measuring the economic trends. Typically the main findings are unchanged, except as noted below.

It should be reiterated that this approach, measuring the economic development indicators as shares and in trends, has important implications for robustly interpreting the results. Only differential effects in trends are identified here. The impacts measured exclude impacts on non-arts patenting or employment; they also exclude any one-time "bump" or shock to the initial level of media arts–related patenting or employment that is due to establishment of the university or cultural district. The approach taken here cannot identify those kinds of impacts. That is the statistical price paid to avoid contaminating the results with possible bias from other correlated external shocks to cities or some latent (and static) attributes of cities that also just happen to have arts districts or R1 universities. As robust as these results are to various forms of bias, they are still susceptible to bias if there was a factor that affected media arts–related employment (or innovation) disproportionately, *and* its influence changed over time, *and* it was systematically correlated with cities that had cultural districts or more universities. If all three conditions hold, the results presented here will be biased.

The Findings: Impacts on Employment

The regression results for the employment models are presented first in table 7-2. The most striking result is that the presence of cultural districts and R1 universities in a city has little or no explanatory power across the various definitions of arts- and media arts–related employment. It simply does not explain the variation in the growth of the intensity of arts-related employment in these 121 U.S. cities. This is consistent with Markusen and Gadwa's skepticism about the relative efficacy of encouraging clustering of cultural capital. The number of postsecondary schools offering arts degrees, most of which are not major research universities, does consistently have a modest and positive effect on the intensity of arts-related employment growth. The *art schools* variable does less to predict growth in the employment share for media arts–related jobs in table 7-2 (positive for media arts occupations, insignificant for media arts industries). To put these impacts in perspective, a city with ten art schools could be expected to see the intensity of its arts occupations rise an additional 0.1 percentage point faster than that of a city with five art schools. Although small, this 0.1 percentage point increase is substantial

Table 7-2. *Employment Trends, 1998–2011*[a]
Coefficient (*t* statistic)

Independent variable	Arts industry$_{9811}$	Arts occupation$_{9811}$	Media arts industry$_{9811}$	Media arts occupation$_{9811}$
District	0.0027	-0.0023	0.0001	-0.0008
	(1.36)	(-1.54)	(0.06)	(-0.40)
R1s in CBSA	0.0003	-0.00004	0.0005	-0.0006
	(1.54)	(-0.10)	(0.76)	(-1.35)
Art schools	0.0002*	0.0002**	-0.00007	0.0002*
	(1.82)	(2.30)	(-0.45)	(1.90)
Constant	-0.0049***	0.0026*	-0.0101***	0.0084***
	(-3.02)	(1.87)	(-5.70)	(4.87)
N	121	121	121	121
R^2	0.0441	0.0439	0.0044	0.0333

Source: Authors' calculations.

a. See table 7-1 for variable definitions. Dependent variables (columns) are changes in percent employment; independent variables (rows) are static count variables. *$p < .10$, **$p < 0.05$, ***$p < 0.01$.

relative to the small base rate of change (0.3 percentage point, on average) and the baseline share of employment (1.1 percent).

This initial analysis gives us two simple takeaway results concerning the hypothesized relationship between local clusters of investment and economic growth. Cultural districts and R1 universities did very little in terms of promoting employment growth (disproportionately) in the arts and media arts. Their presence was not associated with significantly higher or lower growth rates in creative class sorts of jobs. The number of art schools in town, however, was positively associated with disproportionate employment growth in these arts sectors. That suggests that, insofar as postsecondary education fosters more growth in arts-related sectors, it does so by attracting and training workers in these fields fairly directly rather than through more indirect pathways by promoting more wealth, cultural demand, and so forth.

Mindful of concerns that researchers' definitional choices for employment categories may drive these results, regressions are estimated using alternative, more restrictive constructions.[34] Specifically, jobs that are classified in both the arts industry and arts occupation categories are used to create a more restrictive employment category. A parallel construction also is used for media arts jobs. Table 7-3 reports on the results of regressions for these employment growth indicators. Also, jobs that are classified as both an arts and a media arts occupation in both an arts and a media arts industry are used in a regression

Table 7-3. *Employment Trends (1998–2011), Other Employment Definitions*[a]
Coefficient (*t* statistic)

Independent variable	Arts industry and occupation$_{9811}$	Media arts industry and occupation$_{9811}$	Arts and media arts industry and occupation$_{9811}$	Arts (or media arts) occupation in media arts (or arts) industry$_{9811}$
District	0.0001	0.0005	-0.0003	0.0001
	(0.10)	(0.48)	(-0.52)	(0.09)
R1s in CBSA	0.0003	0.0004*	0.0002*	0.0003
	(1.48)	(1.78)	(1.69)	(1.18)
Art schools	0.0002***	0.0001*	0.0001*	0.0002***
	(3.05)	(1.71)	(1.89)	(2.76)
Constant	-0.0001	0.0009	-0.0006	0.0001
	(-0.08)	(0.97)	(-1.10)	(0.13)
N	121	121	121	121
R^2	0.0974	0.0431	0.0495	0.0698

Source: Authors' calculations.

a. See table 7-1 for variable definitions. Dependent variables (columns) are percent changes in employment; independent variables (rows) are static count variables. *$p < .10$, **$p < 0.05$, ***$p < 0.01$.

model. A final alternative definition, including jobs that are classified as arts-related occupations in media arts–related industries *or* as media arts–related occupations in arts-related industries, also is used.

The results show that the more restrictive notions of arts-related jobs are better predicted in these models. In each case, the number of art schools is positively and significantly related to growth in the share of arts-related employment between 1998 and 2011. What is more, given the number of art schools in town, the growth rate for media arts–related jobs is even higher in metro areas with more R1 universities. Here is the first evidence of some impact of R1 research universities on local media arts employment above and beyond the more direct impact of local art schools. Perhaps most important, there is no significant impact of *district* on growth in the share of arts employment regardless of how the arts or media arts sectors are defined. Simply put, there is no evidence that cultural districts promote employment growth in the arts or media arts on average.

The ineffectiveness of cultural districts in promoting more growth in arts-related employment is maintained over longer and shorter time spans. Cities with cultural districts in 1998 did not experience significantly higher or lower arts-related (as defined in the various ways used in tables 7-2 and 7-3) employment growth from 1990 to 2011. Likewise, looking at just growth from 1998 to 2006 and avoiding the period of the Great Recession, the presence of a cultural district in 1998 appears to be unrelated to arts employment growth in the metro area no matter how it is defined. The evidence for universities' role in fostering arts employment differs somewhat when using longer or shorter time spans. From 1990 to 2011, having more R1 universities does predict a rise in the employment shares for arts industry jobs, broadly or narrowly defined. From 1998 to 2006, neither R1 universities nor art schools had any power in explaining variation in arts employment share trajectories.

The Findings: Impacts on Patenting

Turning to innovation as measured by patenting, the results in table 7-4 offer some insight into the role of local clusters of investment in promoting innovation in media arts. The results are, again, somewhat unexpected: cities with cultural districts in 1998 experienced much faster increases in the rate of media arts patenting in subsequent years, while more R1 universities or more art schools did not have a positive impact on innovation in media arts technologies. Major research universities simply did not promote innovation in media arts–related technologies more than they did innovation in other technology classes over this period. That universities did not favor this type of innovation is perhaps unsurprising, but it is surprising that cities with cultural districts had a steeper trajectory in media arts patenting.

The positive impact of cultural districts on media arts patenting is quite substantial. The first set of results in table 7-4 indicates that the *district* effect amounts to a 2 percentage point increase in all patents for media arts–related technology classes (over a baseline level of roughly 2 percent), effectively doubling the media arts patenting rate.[35] The second column of results in table 7-4—in which the patenting variable is measured as the change in the raw count of patents for media arts–related technology classes for assignees in a given city—gives another perspective on this impact. The growth rate in media arts–related patents of cities with cultural districts in 1998 increased by four additional patents over the rate in other cities. The more innovative cities in the media arts sector appear to be those with an arts and cultural district.

Reconciling the Unexpected

The bottom line from this analysis is twofold: universities foster some employment growth in media arts–related jobs but do nothing special to promote

Table 7-4. *Trends in Media Arts Patenting, Shares and Counts, 1998–2006*[a]
Coefficient (*t* statistic)

Independent variable	Media arts patent share$_{9806}$	Media arts patent count$_{9806}$
District	0.0196***	4.2660**
	(2.97)	(2.08)
R1s in City	−0.0044	−1.9112
	(−1.32)	(−1.06)
Art schools	0.0006	0.5741
	(1.07)	(1.19)
Constant	−0.0046	−2.8163
	(−1.11)	(−0.95)
N	136	148
R^2	0.0601	0.0504

Source: Authors' calculation.

a. See table 7-1 for variable definitions. Dependent variables (columns) are changes in patent trends (percent and counts); independent variables (rows) are static count variables. *$p < .10$, **$p < 0.05$, ***$p < 0.01$.

patenting in this area; and cultural districts coincide with more media arts innovation but do not appear to generate more arts- or media arts–related employment. These results are at odds with a naïve expectation that links universities to patenting and arts districts to arts employment. This raises some questions about why conventional wisdom misaligns with the evidence.

The first explanation for these unexpected results follows from how the statistical analysis is designed. The results speak to relative intensity of economic growth in the media arts, not absolute amounts. The patent data clearly indicate that having more R1 major research universities in a city is associated with more patenting—overall *and* in media arts–related technologies. Yet just because research universities promote more patenting in general and also in media arts does not mean that they disproportionately favor media arts technologies. The results here suggest that universities are neutral to developing media arts technologies. That alone might be somewhat heartening, in that universities are not leaving behind arts-related technology in their quest for innovation. Similarly, that metro areas with arts districts do not experience more growth in arts jobs is not to say that they do not have more arts jobs, just that the *share* of residents working in the arts is not growing. The evidence here is about arts intensity and the relative growth of the arts sector, and many casual observations rely more on absolute growth.

A second and related explanation is that these local institutions (universities and districts) may already have generated higher levels of employment or innovation, while this analysis looks at whether they alter the trajectory of economic development going forward. Even if cities with arts districts started off with large clusters of artists and universities began with pools of talented inventors, the question here is whether universities and districts promote faster growth and more economic development regardless of their starting point. And here the intuition is not so clear, because the starting point may already represent an equilibrium. Additional artists or inventors may seek greener, less crowded pastures if a local market is already saturated. New districts may have a novelty that wears off over time, and footloose entrepreneurs and innovators may be less and less geographically tied to college campuses as telecommunication and travel costs fall. The trajectory of the "creative economy" in cities with research universities or cultural districts is ultimately an open empirical question without much theoretical guidance.

A third explanation builds on a better understanding of the various pathways by which local economies develop. Many rely on indirect impacts, and some rely on intercity migration or "sorting" of people and firms. Local clusters of investment can be very powerful amenities that indirectly shape the economic growth of their host city by attracting particular types of households, firms, innovators, and jobs from elsewhere. Concentrated cultural capital can attract more innovative firms and individuals in the media arts field. This pathway to growing the arts sector essentially relies on relocating or redistributing resources.[36] One city's growing arts economy may not imply a growing arts economy for the nation as a whole. The patenting evidence is consistent with this sorting explanation.

Some indirect impacts of local clusters of investment may also yield dividends by generating economic growth from within the cluster. The setting of a district or a college campus might enhance arts-related productivity for those in or near it. There may be important economies of scale in the production of media arts innovations, and having a cultural district can serve as a focal point around which the necessary "critical mass" of relationships can develop. Beyond recruiting certain types of students and employees, universities can also support and cultivate tastes for the arts among non-artists, which in turn leads to growth in arts-related work. If research universities bring prosperity to a region and the arts are luxury goods, then their arts-related growth should outstrip growth of the metro economy as a whole. The evidence here, that art schools better predict arts employment growth than R1 universities, seems to favor a more direct explanation, although the demand for artists' skills may come from universities' promoting the city's media arts sector.

Finally, the indicators for local clusters of investment, be they universities or cultural districts, may be proxies for some other factor or signal something "special" about the city. It might not actually be the district or the schools that even indirectly drive economic growth. For instance, cities with increasingly innovative entertainment industries might also tend to establish arts districts. Schuetz shows how art galleries concentrate in neighborhoods with particular exogenous amenities; similarly, arts districts might follow types of infrastructure that, after 1998, also promoted media arts innovation. Cities with more art schools may have developed a more arts-friendly atmosphere or arts-friendly nonprofits that explain the rise in arts-related employment. Chapter 3 in this volume argues that these sorts of community characteristics explain the location of arts activity. At this early stage of research, these sorts of explanations are difficult to disentangle from the fuzzier, indirect pathways that link these local amenities to economic growth.

Cautious Implications

Understanding of the connection between regional economic growth and arts-related industries is still in its early days. Policymakers would do well to enter into this fray with some caution. Policy experimentation may yield the best social dividends in the long run. The evidence here casts doubt on the merits of cultural districts as engines for arts employment growth and on the value of research (and other) universities in promoting new media arts technologies. Instead, policymakers might look for less obvious impacts of these focal points that arise because of their appeal as amenities that attract and create particular kinds of residents and firms. Universities and art schools help create an arts workforce, including for media arts. Cultural districts may cultivate entrepreneurship and foster technological innovation in media arts. The obvious and direct connections (universities and patenting; districts and employment) are not especially strong for a host of reasons; nonetheless, communities with these arts-related institutions have seen their media arts sector grow faster in terms of innovation and employment. So while policymakers ought to be skeptical of bold promises of the positive direct effects of these kinds of investments, they should also be aware of the potentially significant indirect effects that supporting these kinds of local amenities can have.

Appendix 7A. Industry and Occupation Categories

Table 7A-1. Industry Categories in the Current Population Survey, 1998 and Earlier

Category	Arts related	Media arts related
Printing, publishing, and allied industries	No	Yes
Pottery and related products	Yes	No
Photographic equipment and supplies	Yes	Yes
Radio and television broadcasting and cable	Yes	Yes
Radio, television, and computer stores	No	Yes
Music stores	Yes	Yes
Jewelry stores	Yes	No
Video tape rental	Yes	Yes
Advertising	Yes	Yes
Computer and data processing services	No	Yes
Theater and motion pictures	Yes	Yes
Miscellaneous entertainment	Yes	Yes
Museums, galleries, and zoos	Yes	No

Table 7A-2. *Industry Categories in the Current Population Survey, 2011*

Category	Arts related	Media arts related
Pottery, ceramics, and related product manufacturing	Yes	No
Radio, television, and computer stores	No	Yes
Jewelry, luggage, and leather goods stores	Yes	No
Music stores	Yes	Yes
Book stores and news dealers	Yes	No
Publishing (except newspapers)	No	Yes
Software publishing	No	Yes
Motion pictures and video industries	Yes	Yes
Sound recording industries	Yes	Yes
Radio and television broadcasting and cable	Yes	Yes
Internet publishing and broadcasting	No	Yes
Video tape and disk rental	Yes	Yes
Specialized design services	Yes	Yes
Computer system design and related services	No	Yes
Advertising and related services	Yes	Yes
Independent artists, performing arts, spectator sports, and related industries	Yes	Yes
Museums, art galleries, and similar institutions	Yes	Yes

Table 7A-3. *Occupation Categories in the Current Population Survey, 1998 and Earlier*

Category	Arts related	Media arts related
Architects	Yes	No
Art, drama, and music teachers	Yes	No
Authors	Yes	Yes
Technical writers	Yes	Yes
Designers	Yes	Yes
Musicians and composers	Yes	Yes
Actors and directors	Yes	Yes
Painters, sculptors, craft-artists, and artist printmakers	Yes	No
Photographers	Yes	Yes
Dancers	Yes	Yes
Artists, performers, and related workers	Yes	Yes
Editors and reporters	Yes	Yes
Computer programmers	No	Yes
Camera, watch, and musical instrument repairers	Yes	Yes
Jewelers	Yes	Yes
Patternmakers and model makers, wood	Yes	Yes

Table 7A-4. *Occupation Categories in the Current Population Survey, 2011*

Category	Arts related	Media arts related
Advertising and promotions managers	Yes	Yes
Computer and information systems managers	No	Yes
Agents and business managers of artists, performers, and athletes	Yes	No
Computer programmers	No	Yes
Computer software engineers	No	Yes
Computer support specialists	No	Yes
Architects	Yes	No
Artists and related workers	Yes	Yes
Designers	Yes	Yes
Producers and directors	Yes	Yes
Dancers and choreographers	Yes	No
Musicians, singers, and related workers	Yes	Yes
Entertainers and performers	Yes	Yes
Announcers	Yes	Yes
Editors	Yes	Yes

Table 7A-4 (continued). *Occupation Categories in the Current Population Survey, 2011*

Category	Arts related	Media arts related
Technical writers	Yes	Yes
Writers and authors	Yes	Yes
Miscellaneous media and communications workers	No	Yes
Broadcast and sound engineering technicians	No	Yes
Photographers	Yes	Yes
Television, video, and motion picture camera operators	Yes	Yes
Media and communication equipment workers	Yes	Yes
Motion picture projectionists	Yes	Yes
Hairdressers/hairstylists	Yes	Yes
Miscellaneous personal appearance workers	Yes	Yes
Radio and telecommunications equipment installers and repairers	No	Yes
Model makers and patternmakers, wood	Yes	No
Jewelers and precious stone and metal workers	Yes	No
Painting workers	Yes	No
Photographic process workers	Yes	Yes

Notes

1. Ann Markusen and Anne Gadwa, "Arts and Culture in Urban or Regional Planning: A Review and Research Agenda," *Journal of Planning Education and Research*, vol. 29, no. 3 (2010), pp. 379–91. Also see chapter 9 in this volume.

2. Franco Bianchini and others, *City Centres, City Cultures: The Role of the Arts in the Revitalization of Towns and Cities* (Manchester, U.K.: Centre for Local Economic Development Strategies, 1988).

3. Elizabeth Strom, "Converting Pork into Porcelain: Cultural Institutions and Downtown Development," *Urban Affairs Review*, vol. 38, no. 1 (2002).

4. Richard Florida, *The Rise of the Creative Class* (New York: Basic Books, 2002).

5. Ann Markusen and David King, "The Artistic Dividend: The Arts' Hidden Contributions to Regional Development," *Arts Research Monitor*, vol. 2, no. 5 (November 2003) (http://www.hhh.umn.edu/img/assets/6158/artistic_dividend.pdf); Ann Markusen and Greg Schrock, "The Artistic Dividend: Urban Artistic Specialization and Economic Development Implication," *Urban Studies*, vol. 43, no. 10 (2006), pp. 1661–86. Also see chapter 3 in this volume.

6. Markusen and Gadwa, "Arts and Culture in Urban or Regional Planning: A Review and Research Agenda," pp. 379–91. Also see chapter 9 in this volume.

7. Chapter 10 in this volume offers evidence on productivity impacts of cultural clusters as well as support for cultural clusters that have high amenity value.

8. Andy Pratt, "The Cultural Industries Production System: A Case Study of Employment Change in Britain: 1984–1991," *Environment and Planning A*, vol. 29 (1997), pp. 1953–74; Susan C. Eaton and Lotte Bailyn, "Work and Life Strategies of Professionals in Biotechnology Firms," *Annals of the American Academy of Political and Social Science*, vol. 562, no. 1 (1999), pp. 159–73.

9. Edward Glaeser, *Review of The Rise of the Creative Class by Richard Florida* (2004) (www.economics.harvard.edu/faculty/glaeser/files/Review_Florida.pdf); Ann Markusen, "Urban Development and the Politics of a Creative Class: Evidence from the Study of Artists," *Environment and Planning A,* vol. 38, no. 10 (2006), pp. 1921–40. Also see chapter 2 in this volume, which investigates the causality issue and the impacts of concentrations of art galleries in New York.

10. Paul M. Romer, "The Origins of Endogenous Growth," *Journal of Economic Perspectives,* vol. 8, no. 1 (1994), pp. 3–22.

11. Henry Etzkowitz and Loet Leydesdorff, *Universities and the Global Knowledge Economy: A Triple Helix of University-Industry-Government Relations* (London: Pinter, 1997); Maryann P. Feldman and Shiri M. Breznitz, "The American Experience in University Technology Transfer," in *European Universities Learning to Compete: From Social Institutions to Knowledge Business,* edited by M. McKelvey and M. Holmén (Edward Elgar, 2009); Donald S. Siegel and others, "Toward a Model of the Effective Transfer of Scientific Knowledge from Academicians to Practitioners: Qualitative Evidence from the Commercialization of University Technologies," *Journal of Engineering and Technology Management,* vol. 21, no. 1-2 (2004), pp. 115–42; Gideon D. Markman and others, "Innovation Speed: Transferring University Technology to Market," *Research Policy,* vol. 34, no. 7 (2005), pp. 1058–75.

12. Dante Di Gregorio and Scott Shane, "Why Do Some Universities Generate More Startups than Others?" *Research Policy,* vol. 32, no. 2 (2003), pp. 209–27; Donald S. Siegel, David Waldman, and Albert Link, "Assessing the Impact of Organizational Practices on the Relative Productivity of University Technology Transfer Offices: An Exploratory Study," *Research Policy,* vol. 32, no. 1 (2003), pp. 27–48; Jerry G. Thursby, Richard Jensen, and Marie C. Thursby, "Objectives, Characteristics, and Outcomes of University Licensing: A Survey of Major U.S. Universities," *Journal of Technology Transfer,* vol. 26, no. 1 (2001), pp. 59–72.

13. Etzkowitz and Leydesdorff, *Universities and the Global Knowledge Economy;* John Goddard and Paul Chatterton, "Regional Development Agencies and the Knowledge Economy: Harnessing the Potential of Universities," *Environment and Planning C: Government and Policy,* vol. 17 (1999), pp. 685–99.

14. Maryann P. Feldman, *The Geography of Innovation* (Dordrecht, Netherlands: Kluwer Academic Publishers, 1994); Adam B. Jaffe, Manuel Trajtenberg, and Rebecca

Henderson, "Geographic Localization of Knowledge Spillovers as Evidenced by Patent Citations," *Quarterly Journal of Economics*, vol. 108, no. 3 (1993), pp. 577–98.

15. Tim Minshall, Celine Druilhe, and David Probert, "The Evolution of 'Third Mission' Activities at the University of Cambridge: Balancing Strategic and Operational Considerations," paper presented at the 12th Annual High-Technology Small Firms Conference, May 24–25, 2004, University of Twente, Netherlands.

16. Robert Forrant and others, *Approaches to Sustainable Regional Development: The Public University in the Regional Economy* (University of Massachusetts Press, 2001); David J. Maurrasse, *Beyond the Campus: How Colleges and Universities Form Partnerships with Their Communities* (New York: Routledge, 2001); Shiri M. Breznitz and Maryann P. Feldman, "The Engaged University," *Journal of Technology Transfer*, vol. 37, no. 2 (2012), pp. 139–57.

17. Tim Minshall, Céline Druilhe, and David Probert, "The Evolution of 'Third Mission' Activities at the University of Cambridge" (2007) (www.econbiz.de/en/search/detailed-view/doc/all/the-evolution-of-third-mission-activities-at-the-university-of-cambridge-balancing-strategic-and-operational-considerations-minshall-tim/10003499985/?no_cache=1).

18. NAMAC, *Mapping the Field* (2012) (www.namac.org/mapping).

19. National Governors Association, *Promoting Film and Media to Enhance State Economic Development* (Washington: NGA Center for Best Practices, 2008) (www.nga.org/files/live/sites/NGA/files/pdf/0807PROMOTINGFILMMEDIA.PDF); Susan Christopherson and Ned Rightor, "The Creative Economy as 'Big Business': Evaluating State Strategies to Lure Filmmakers," *Journal of Planning Education and Research*, vol. 29 (2010), pp. 336–52.

20. Chapter 8 in this volume delves deeper into the connection between the arts and entrepreneurial innovation in communities.

21. Chapter 6 outlines more links between universities, arts, and innovation.

22. Hillary A. Frost-Kumpf, *Cultural Districts: The Arts As a Strategy for Revitalizing Our Cities* (Washington: Americans for the Arts, 1998).

23. Carnegie Foundation for the Advancement of Teaching, "1994 Edition Data File" (http://classifications.carnegiefoundation.org/resources/).

24. An alternative measure, the number of art departments and programs (across all schools) in a city, is also available. The count of programs did not provide a better fit to the data, however, so the count of schools was used instead.

25. Future research would do well to explore other data sources, such as the American Community Survey, to see whether larger samples and different geographic measures alter the results.

26. For employment analyses, because employment is measured for the city's larger metro area, the presence of universities is measured as the count of R1 schools in the CBSA rather than just in the city.

27. Patents are typically categorized as either utility or design patents. (A third type, plant patents, covers asexually reproduced plant varieties.) Utility patents, which

are the most common, cover novel processes, machines, materials, manufactured articles, or improvements to them. Design patents are the rarest and protect only the appearance or ornamental design rather than the functional features of inventions.

28. Because the re-categorization affects all cities or observations equally and simultaneously, the problems caused when the CPS changed its coding scheme should be mitigated by examining trends.

29. Ann Markusen and others, "Defining the Creative Economy: Industry and Occupational Approaches," *Economic Development Quarterly,* vol. 22, no. 1 (2008), pp. 24–45.

30. Cultural districts may be endogenous to local economic development. The OLS results will be inconsistent if there is reverse causality, where the chicken of the cultural district is the result of the egg of arts employment trends and not just the other way around. To test for this, instrumental variables models were estimated, with 1989 levels of arts- and media arts–related employment and 1989 media arts–related patent rates used as instruments for *district.* This approach should purge the model of endogeneity in *district* establishment under the assumptions that 1989 levels of arts activity do not belong in the main model (which predicts 1998–2011 trends in arts employment) and that they do help predict which cities had cultural districts as of 1998. Estimating these models revealed that the instruments were validly excluded from the main regression equations—they did not predict arts employment trends—and that they also were very weak in predicting which cities had arts districts by 1998. The evidence that cultural district designation in 1998 is uncorrelated with the earlier size of the "creative economy" in a city suggests that the incidence of the *district* variable may be sufficiently idiosyncratic that it functions as an exogenous treatment variable.

31. Of course, there might still be some factors that are correlated with trends in the size of the creative economy in a city that are also correlated with whether the city had a university or district by 1998. Failing to control for these correlated latent trends could yet bias the estimated impacts.

32. Markusen and Gadwa, "Arts and Culture in Urban or Regional Planning."

33. Ann Markusen and others, "Defining the Creative Economy," pp. 24–45.

34. Ibid.; Elisa Barbour and Ann Markusen, "Regional Occupational and Industrial Structure: Does One Imply the Other?" *International Regional Science Review,* vol. 30, no. 1 (2007).

35. For further context, consider that the share of patents in media arts–related classes for cities in this sample was 1.4 percent in 1998, or 1.6 percent in cities with cultural districts at that point and 1.2 percent in other cities. The difference is not statistically significant. By 2006, the share of patents in media arts technologies had fallen to under 1 percent in cities without districts and climbed to almost 3 percent in cities that had districts. This increase of 2 percentage points thus represents more than a doubling of the previous intensity of media arts patenting in cities with arts districts

and leaves them with triple the patenting rate of the control group cities. That the control group cities' patenting rates fell suggests the possibility that arts districts merely redistributed innovation rather than generating additional innovation. This possibility merits further research.

36. See chapter 4 in this volume for further discussion of redistributing scarce cultural resources.

ROLAND J. KUSHNER

8

Cultural Enterprise Formation and
Cultural Participation in America's Counties

"Is this a good place to start my arts venture?" Arts entrepreneurs invariably consider that question as part of their overall development. Entrepreneurship, like labor and capital, is mobile, but a new arts enterprise is most likely to emerge from a particular locale. As seen from other chapters in this volume, the particular characteristics of American communities affect the kinds of arts entities and activities that locate in them, just as the arts affect communities in a reciprocal relationship.

New growth theory (NGT), a unifying theme of this volume, suggests that economic growth is a function of endogenous activity such as investments in human capital or innovation and that it is new ideas and new energy, not choices made in the face of scarcity or the constraints of existing production functions, that primarily drive economic development.[1] In this view, growth is more a function of entrepreneurial energy than of population scale or capital concentration, the mainstays of economic success in neoclassical economics. The potential application to entrepreneurship in arts and culture is unmistakable: what better for new energy and innovation than the arts? Yet the causal direction is not immediately clear: are the arts a consequence of

Thanks to Randy Cohen, Americans for the Arts; Martin Cohen, Cultural Planning Group; Ariel Fogel, Muhlenberg College 2011; Ryan Lindsay, Muhlenberg College 2012; Paul Larson, archivist of the Bach Choir of Bethlehem; Sunil Iyengar and Ellen Grantham of the National Endowment for the Arts; and Heekyung Sung. Thanks also to Ann Markusen, Bob Root-Bernstein, Lauren Schmitz, and especially Michael Rushton for their thoughtful reviews of earlier drafts. This research was conducted within the Local Arts Index project of Americans for the Arts, funded by the Kresge Foundation, the Paul G. Allen Family Foundation, the Rhode Island Foundation, and the Morris and Gwendolyn Cafritz Foundation.

144

economic growth or a precursor? That is, do the arts promote community growth and development, or do vigorous communities support the arts? To address these questions, this chapter examines the relationships between selected community characteristics and arts enterprise formation in American communities. In subsequent sections, I describe an entrepreneurial arts episode from the early twentieth century in one American community. Considering the initial question ("Is this a good place to start my arts venture?"), I proceed with a broad cross-sectional analysis of early twenty-first-century arts enterprise in 281 American communities. This analysis considers how environmental characteristics, including overall demand for culture, as well as the strength of competition affected the presence and performance of new and small arts enterprises in both the commercial and nonprofit sectors.

Arts Entrepreneurship: A Centennial Anecdote

In 1912, the Bach Choir of Bethlehem, Pennsylvania, renewed its festival after a hiatus of several years. Its renewal was a markedly entrepreneurial saga of invention, determination, and calculation. The effort was led by savvy Gilded Age business leaders who had dominant market positions in borax mining, railroads, steel mills, and banking. They shared a passion for the choral music of J. S. Bach, and they were determined to make Bethlehem a center for the performance of his music. As leaders of the largest businesses in the area (Bethlehem Steel, especially), they wanted the choir and festival to have a profound impact on the community. They were crafty in their pursuit of a highly regarded musical leader, adept at grassroots work to develop a base of volunteers and supporters, and efficient in their development of a durable organizational structure—all in the service of Bach.[2]

Their work laid the foundation for a century-old institution that still maintains a vibrant musical presence. Yet their initial entrepreneurial vigor and energy at that pivotal time also sparks enduring interest. It is clear that throughout history and into the present, the arts and entrepreneurship have grown and evolved together. As manifestations of the human spirit, coincident adventures, and pro-social services, both intertwine excitement and progress. Artists and entrepreneurs interact as impresarios, investors, conveners, presenters, and producers of the collective body of aesthetic work in the neighborhood and around the globe. Bach in Bethlehem is only one example, but an instructive one.

From its inception, the founders of the Bach Choir devised and built a sustainable organization and festival. They employed a thoughtful financing scheme, asking supporters, before they had heard the music, to guarantee that they would cover anticipated deficits from a top-quality musical program. They used best practices borrowed from their friend Andrew Carnegie, and they found (then lost and then regained) J. Fred Wolle, a musical leader par excellence (whose father had invented the paper bag). They and their wives planned a sales network to finance the costs of the event, in an era when tickets cost one or two dollars. While the choir's founders might have been robber barons by day, they were unquestionably arts patrons on the weekend, and their domain was a small town in what was then rural Pennsylvania. Their entrepreneurial moves in finance and sales may have been informed by their day jobs, but the moves were successful because the founders understood the characteristics of their environment.

This basic scenario has been repeated tens of thousands of times in the century since 1912 in all manner of American communities, from the largest to the smallest. The twenty-first century, so far, has been a time of especially rapid growth. From 2000 to 2009, there was a net addition of 37,000 arts nonprofits, an increase of 48 percent.[3] In the aggregate, workforce and business commitment to the arts is significant. In 2010 there were 2.2 million workers who identified themselves as artists, more than 113,000 nonprofit arts organizations, and more than 700,000 arts businesses in "Creative Industries," defined by Americans for the Arts using 644 Standard Industrial Classification (SIC) codes.[4] An especially entrepreneurial mode of organizing in the arts is illustrated by the steadily increasing number of Americans who are independent non-employer artists, categorized in North American Industrial Classification (NAICS) code 7115 (independent artists, writers, and performers).[5]

Many arts organizations have serendipitous founding events like that of the Bach Choir in Bethlehem. These episodes create stories that often are inspiring and constitute a wellspring of cultural strength within the organization that supplements shared aesthetic principles and interests. The fact that these stories are so often seen in modern as well as historic times attests to the steady attraction not only of the arts but also of new ways to present, preserve, and organize them. But founding is only one step: once under way, arts organizations begin their organizational life cycle subject to the same possibilities of success and failure as other early-stage enterprises. They carry the same needs for sufficient capital, a friendly environment, and adequate cash flow. Their artistic appeal does not make them any less vulnerable in their early years, making them like any startup company whose leaders believe in its mission, cause, and way of creating value.

Bach in Bethlehem shows that the composition of the leadership team is an irreplaceable internal component of early-stage entrepreneurial success. But many factors affecting the ability of early-stage arts enterprises to succeed are external, part of the organization's environment. New artists and arts organizations first see the light of day at the community level, which might mean "around the corner," "in town," or within some radius that is considered "community" or "local" in a particular place. Bethlehem in the early twentieth century was dominated by two major institutional forces, the Moravian Church and Bethlehem Steel. As influence in the community shifted from the sacred to the secular and from a communitarian structure to a commercial one, Bethlehem's entrepreneurial business leaders were ready to start their quest for a great Bach festival. Among the key assets that they brought to their endeavor was their knowledge of the market: they sensed that there was an eagerness to hear the music, a sufficiently large group of ticket buyers, and a segment of willing donors. They recognized both the broad social changes and arts market factors present in the environment into which they re-launched the festival.

This chapter is concerned primarily with the external environment of arts enterprises. It addresses the initial question that almost all arts entrepreneurs— in the commercial, nonprofit, or public sector—must answer: "Is this a place where my arts venture can succeed?" It models arts entrepreneurship in the twenty-first century as a consequence of the same elements present in Bethlehem in 1912: a willing audience, a philanthropic community ethic, and an environment of economic growth. Using cross-sectional data from 281 American counties in the early decades of this century, it examines elements of the support or strain that environments place on new arts enterprises. Regression analysis is used to measure the presence and strength of these effects. The hypotheses, data, and results are presented after a brief discussion of underlying concepts and theories related to the initial question. The chapter concludes with a description of how arts entrepreneurship continues to be a vital force in Bethlehem in the late twentieth and early twenty-first centuries.

Conceptual Underpinnings for Examining Arts Entrepreneurship

As noted above, the arts and communities are inseparable. They have a reciprocal relationship: the arts help communities, and communities help the arts. Cultural capital is a source of definition and identity,[6] and some places specialize in particular forms of culture.[7] Florida made his well-known argument for community cultural vitality based on occupations; Pratt argued that cultural industries, more than cultural workers, fuel economic growth.[8] The ability to fuse entrepreneurial and artistic capabilities is an element of artistic longevity and success.[9]

To the extent that it involves bringing something new to market, entrepreneurship needs to be considered as a process of market entry. In any industry, adept innovators may threaten incumbent competitors, but entrants inevitably confront barriers to entry of varying heights. An arts venture that succeeds must climb through and past the introduction and rapid growth phases of an organizational life cycle. Some (not a majority) of new ventures in many industries fail to accomplish this climb, and they expire early. To last longer, an entrepreneur's evolution might include expansion to achieve favorable economies of scale or scope. That is, entrepreneurs may use more capital, expand their product lines to widen their scope, or otherwise compete for new revenues. New arts nonprofits, like nonprofits in any service area, are especially likely to compete by trying to generate both contributed and earned revenues, which constitute, in effect, two different product lines, each helping to finance arts activity. The fact that customers for tickets may also be donors facilitates that expansion of scope, because of lower-cost cross-marketing and selling possibilities. But they are essentially like two product lines in a company's portfolio.[10]

In strategic management, environmental analysis typically assesses both the proximity and impact of external forces as they relate to a specific firm. A common framework describes factors affecting every firm in a particular industry as the "micro" or "competitive" forces; forces that tend to act on all industries are described as "macro" or "general." Figure 8-1 shows them in a concentric relationship to a particular focal firm. In Porter's well-known "five forces" model, which is especially effective for characterizing competitive forces, rivalry and the threat of entry are of special concern to entrepreneurs, who are the new entrants that existing competitors hope to deter. On the other hand, evidence that market demand can be expected to grow can encourage entry regardless of current rivals. Because nonprofit arts entrepreneurs may pursue both customers and donors, they assess market demand in both segments.[11] Large market size, scarcity of powerful competitors, and low price elasticity can all be positive indicators of entrepreneurial opportunity, especially when barriers to entry from existing competitors are low. By extension, if market power is held by large incumbents, that could retard growth for early-stage firms in the arts, as in other industries.

These environmental and competitive forces are at the micro level, because they address a single market's specific customers, competitors, and entrants. But the arts are sensitive to broader environmental forces, including community demographic and socioeconomic patterns. The macro or general environmental factors are the tides that may lift or sink all boats in a community.

Figure 8-1. *Competitive and General Environments of a Company*

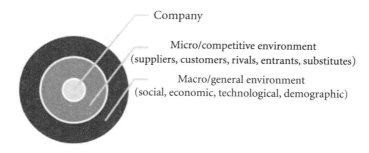

Company

Micro/competitive environment
(suppliers, customers, rivals, entrants, substitutes)

Macro/general environment
(social, economic, technological, demographic)

Source: Author's illustration.

Some environments provide greater capacity and opportunity: the arts are traditionally associated with increased income and with better educated and older patrons, as has been shown repeatedly in studies such as the National Endowment for the Arts Survey of Public Participation in the Arts.[12]

The ability of a new arts enterprise to grow and survive over time derives from other community environmental factors, too. Does arts enterprise need the density of urban centers to thrive? Or alternately, is it a phenomenon that is invariant to urban or rural settings? More crowded communities could invite entry into the arts because they provide lower-cost access to a greater concentration of potential audience members. So too could other community factors that typically correlate with economic development: population growth, level of educational attainment, age distribution of the population, and the like. Just like the competitive environment factors, these indicators of community capacity are visible to both prospective and current arts entrepreneurs. Jane Jacobs, in various writings, described local economies as open systems that evolve in response to internal and external change; in an early work, she observed that "Shakespeare's theater found room in a city economy that had grown room for it. This does not explain Shakespeare's genius, but does explain why there was scope for that genius in the local economy of London rather than in Newcastle, or, for that matter, in the local economy of Stratford-on-Avon."[13]

Jacobs's observation is a reminder that arts entrepreneurs have choices of organizational form, too. Shakespeare, a writer seeking patronage and pitching his work to theater ensembles, collaborated with an institution, the Globe Theater. The Bach Choir of Bethlehem formed a charitable nonprofit, an evergreen model for early-stage arts organizing. Many paths are viable options for arts entrepreneurs and enterprises—such as proprietorship as a solo artist, collaboration in a formal or informal ensemble, or formation of an institution—as are many other structural configurations and hybrids, such as cooperatives and other new tax-exempt forms.[14]

Regardless of form, all enterprises face the quest for revenue. Solo arts entrepreneurs face a potentially narrower range of revenue options, but they still must consider the opportunities: How many galleries might exhibit my work? What clubs might hire me to play? Which theaters might produce my plays? A key planning question for solo artists as well as for solo entrepreneurs in other fields is "Is this my full-time job?" While artists have these concerns, galleries, clubs, and theaters exercise a curatorial role as buyers and gatekeepers, and they have concerns about the availability of desirable artistic "product" that they can offer.

Recalling the stylized research question, "Is this a place where my arts venture can succeed?" the empirical portion of this chapter addresses the emergence and survival of arts enterprises in diverse American communities as a function of key community characteristics. Using data illustrating the nature of communities where entrepreneurial nonprofits have emerged and survived at least into the early stages helps to further the quest for insight into the effect of location. One may hope that arts entrepreneurs may pass through the introduction and growth phases of the organizational life cycle. But whether they actually reach maturity at an economically sustainable level is an empirical question. County-level data point the way to at least partially answering the research question, with the understanding that any answer has to span the range of organizational forms that make up arts entrepreneurship.[15]

Empirical Analysis

Here I present exploratory hypotheses regarding the relationship between community-level environmental factors and the presence of arts entrepreneurs in both the commercial and nonprofit sectors at the county level. I then test them with a set of data describing 281 U.S. counties in the first years of the twenty-first century and analyze and discuss the results.

The ideal model here would be sequential: community variables at time t lead to new cultural enterprise at time $t + 1$. The "first years" range from 2000 to 2011. However, the data on cultural consumption and participation described below were available only from years late in the decade (2009–11), while the data on new enterprise formation pertain to the years from 2000 to 2009. Thus they reflect both early and late decade activity. However, the results can still be informative. First, while it would be a mistake to be complacent about the pace of change, many environmental factors display long-running stable trends that are comparatively slow to evolve; the passage of a few years does not radically alter all of a community's measured characteristics. Second, entrepreneurs are likely to proceed on the basis of their expectations as well as their understanding of the past, although the quality of their expectations is recognizable only in hindsight (a test that the Bach organizers did meet). The year 2013 provides some evidence of how relatively young organizations were able to survive, thus ratifying—or not—their founders' understanding of the world around them.

The relationships that I expected to see show the phenomenon of interest—entry into the arts marketplace—supported or deterred by specific environmental factors, listed here with some supporting notes in the form of hypotheses (H):

—H1: Community philanthropic practice supports entry, measured by relating levels of arts enterprise to levels of private giving.

—H2: Cultural expenditures support entry, measured by relating levels of arts enterprise to levels of personal consumption of arts goods and services.

—H3: Cultural participation supports entry, measured by relating levels of arts enterprise to levels of overall community participation in artistic activities.

—H4: High concentration of market share held by competitors deters entry, measured by relating levels of arts enterprise to the share of the market held by the top competitors. Communities with cultural activity concentrated in a small set of organizations exhibit less arts enterprise. In such settings, large incumbent competitors may have brand identity, large and well-known facilities, and strong community stature. This hypothesis is limited to the non-profit arts sector.

—H5: Community capacity supports entry, measured by relating levels of arts enterprise to levels of community household income, residents' ages, and population density. Numerous studies have shown the positive relationship between income and age as predictors of arts participation; this hypothesis adds the degree of crowding.

Data on Arts Enterprise and Community Characteristics

This chapter emerged from the Local Arts Index project of Americans for the Arts in 2011 and 2012. The following empirical analysis uses part of a county-level dataset assembled for that project, which features dozens of different indicators of county-level arts activity and performance; the data presented here were initially gathered to use on the Local Arts Index website (www.artsindexusa.org). The following paragraphs specify the measures of arts entry and the various community factors that are theorized to support or deter them. Choices to incorporate some datasets and measurement schemes in this analysis necessarily exclude others. What is used here is one approach, but it is not the only one; other researchers may approach these issues with different questions, methods, and measures.

The overall phenomenon of interest—entrepreneurial activity in the arts—cannot be captured in only one measure. Instead of a single unique dependent variable, three separate indicators of the particular phenomenon of interest, two in the nonprofit domain and one in the commercial, are used.

Two measures of nonprofit arts entrepreneurship are the share of arts nonprofit organizations that have been founded since the beginning of the new millennium and the share of community arts nonprofit revenues received by millennial (post-1999) nonprofits. One cannot assume that an entrepreneurial attitude is restricted to new organizations, but neither can one ignore the likelihood of a strong correlation between an organization's youth and its entrepreneurial spirit. Some arts entrepreneurs may want new organizations to do the same old thing, but that is a less plausible scenario than the arts entrepreneur who wants to do something different. A young age (from recent founding) supports a behavioral assumption of a more entre-preneurial spirit.

"Recent," for the purposes of this chapter, is "since 2000." The change of centuries[16] is a convenient designation in 2012, when the references to the "new century" and its differences from the old are present in many settings and much discourse. For example, the label "millennial" is used to distinguish the things of the new century as qualitatively different from the things of the old. "Millennial" is applied as an adjective to population cohorts much as the term "baby boomer" has been. Just as those labels aggregate multiple years into a single labeled cohort, this measure aggregates the founding of new arts nonprofits from 2000 until the last dataset year of 2009 as evidence of recent arts enterprise formation on the nonprofit side.

The fact that millennial organizations are present in a community does not ensure their longevity over a longer time period—that usually takes money. Relatively few arts organizations last very long without boosting revenues and capturing some sustainable portion of overall arts spending in a community. So a second indicator of nonprofit arts entrepreneurship is the economic scale that these millennial organizations achieve. What revenues can they raise? What is the scale of their arts spending? And critically, do new organizations build market share?

These two markers (of presence and market share) view organizations and their revenue in the context of the larger populations in which they reside. New organizations emerge, but does their creation lead to significant activity?[17] It is not only the number of new arts organizations but also their share of the total population of arts organizations that points to the sustainability of an arts enterprise, and economic heft is needed as well as presence. So the revenues of these new organizations are best evaluated in the context of the overall arts nonprofit market.

Data on new nonprofit arts organizations were obtained from the 2009 Core Files of the National Center for Charitable Statistics at the Urban Institute and aggregated at the county level. Arts nonprofits were defined as those classified in the National Taxonomy of Exempt Enterprises (NTEE) major group "A," plus four in other NTEE codes for libraries, zoos and aquariums, fairs and festivals, and botanical gardens/arboreta.[18] Using IRS ruling dates of January 2000 or later to separate millennials and others makes it possible to measure millennials' percentage share of all (filing) county arts nonprofits and millennials' share of all (filing) county arts nonprofit revenues and expenses.

Nonprofit organizations represent one paradigm for the arts, while independent artists are another. This leads to a third marker for arts entrepreneurship, one that captures the role of individuals who are non-employer, independent solo artists in a community. Data for this indicator, expressed in terms of solo artists per 100,000 population, are from the 2009 "Nonemployer Statistics" from the U.S. Bureau of the Census. Nonprofits are subject to disclosure requirements that make it possible to calculate their arts market share, but proprietor revenue data are confidential, and it is possible to measure only the county-level presence of solo artists—not their revenues or when they first operated as arts entrepreneurs.[19]

Given the three dependent variables, the independent variables measure elements of the community environment for arts enterprise at two levels: competitive market factors affecting arts organizations in particular and broader environmental forces affecting whole communities (figure 8-1). Data are available to measure four of these competitive forces, three relating to market demand and one relating to barriers to entry:

—expenditures on arts and cultural products, services, and experiences
—participation in cultural activities
—philanthropic support of arts and cultural nonprofit organizations
—concentration of market share activity among few competitors.

Data on expenditures were obtained from Claritas/Neilsen, which estimates potential expenditures on various consumer products at the county level for all but a handful of very sparsely populated counties. The expenditure measure is based on Claritas/Neilsen's 2009 estimates for expenditures on reading material, recorded music and video, admission fees, and musical instrument purchases, rental, and accessories. These were summed into a per capita county-level figure of expenditures on arts and culture.

Data on participation in arts and culture activities and on arts and culture philanthropy were obtained from Scarborough Research.[20] Scarborough gathers information from 200,000 interviews each year with adults in 81 "designated market areas," which include almost half of the nation's 3,143 counties. Data used in this study were gathered in three separate waves, in 2009, 2010, and 2011, and averaged over those years. The three-year averaging smoothes out year-to-year variation, resulting in a better estimate of a county's arts participation in the medium term. In keeping with guidance from Scarborough, the analysis was limited to counties where there were at least 180 responses in total over the three years. Ultimately, 525 counties had that many responses or more; in some counties, the total responses numbered in the thousands.

Scarborough's survey, similar to the National Endowment for the Art's *Survey of Public Participation in the Arts*, asks adult respondents whether they had participated in the prior twelve months in a set of target activities including attendance at movies, pop music concerts, the symphony, the opera, the theater, ballet productions, or art museums; purchase of recorded music; and contribution to arts and culture organizations and public broadcasting. The data are reported as percentages of adult respondents (or households in the case of contributions).

Because these participation activities are non-rivalrous (respondents can participate in more than one activity), the percentages can be summed into an overall index of participation in arts and culture activities. To eliminate double counting, Scarborough aggregated the data into measures of broader cultural engagement. One, focusing on popular entertainment, is the percentage of adult respondents who had attended a country music *or* rap/R&B/Hip-Hop *or* rock music concert. A second measure, on the live performing arts, is the percentage of adult respondents who had attended a symphony concert or a theater or an opera or a dance performance. The third was the percentage of adult respondents who had visited an art museum. To capture broad-based participation by arts "omnivores," an index of participation was developed. The three percentages (for popular music, live performing arts, and museums) were added together, then normalized to a scale of 0 to 100, with a score of zero for the lowest index value among those counties and

100 for the highest (perhaps not surprisingly, that was New York County— that is, Manhattan).[21] This index score serves as independent variable measuring overall community cultural participation.

The Scarborough and Claritas data each capture a different dimension of cultural participation. The Scarborough data estimate the *number of people* engaged in one or another kind of arts-related activity. The Claritas data estimate *how much money people spend* on different arts-related activities. A consumer may participate in more than one arts activity over a period of time, but each dollar is spent only once. The two together help to triangulate estimates of the scale and scope of the market: How many customers are there? How much do they spend? These are the inquiries that a prospective arts entrepreneur might make regardless of whether the ultimate aim is a nonprofit or a for-profit arts venture.

While new arts proprietors would worry about whether a community had a large enough pool of potential paying customers, nonprofits would also inquire into the generosity of the community in order to assess the possibility of competing for contributed as well as earned income. A final measure of community cultural engagement is Scarborough's measure of the percentage of households that gave to an arts and culture organization or to public radio or to public television in those three years.

Together, these competitive and community characteristics are necessary components of an arts entrepreneur's knowledge base. But knowledge of demand has to be matched by an understanding of how to convert competitive opportunity into success. Entrepreneurs might shy away from markets where barriers to entry are high, especially where existing competitors have the market wrapped up. In this study, barriers to entry were modeled as a function of the power of large competitors. A four-firm concentration ratio for arts expenditures was calculated by dividing the sum of expenditures of the largest four arts nonprofits in a county by total county arts nonprofit expenditures.[22] This was limited to counties with at least twenty arts nonprofits.

Other independent variables measure broader environmental factors, including five specific demographic and socioeconomic characteristics, measured with data from 2005–09 American Community Survey five-year estimates (available from the U.S. Census Bureau):

—population density per square mile in 2010
—total population growth in percent terms for 2000–09
—median age of the population for 2005–09
—percent of the population with a bachelor's degree
—median household income in current dollars in 2009.

These characteristics are only one set of possible community factors affecting the emergence, scale, and scope of arts enterprise, but they nonetheless provide meaningful insight into community factors that are supportive of cultural enterprise formation.

Two limitations were placed on the data for construct validity purposes. First, data came from only those counties with at least 180 adult respondents to the Scarborough Research surveys in 2009, 2010, and 2011. Second, there had to be twenty or more filing arts nonprofit organizations in each county in 2009. The Scarborough threshold was met in 525 counties, and 426 counties had sufficient arts nonprofits. The final overlapping dataset was of 281 counties with a total population of 186.1 million people. While those counties represent only 9 percent of all 3,143 U.S. counties, they are home to about 60 percent of the total U.S. population. The largest county (by population) is Los Angeles County, the smallest is Kauai County, Hawaii.

Descriptive statistics for the sample of 281 counties are shown in table 8-1. In the median county, 32 percent of the arts nonprofits had emerged since the millennium, but they obtained only 14 percent of the total revenue of arts organizations in the median county (which is not necessarily the same place for both measures). In the county with the smallest share of millennial arts organizations (Cumberland County, Pennsylvania), they made up only 12 percent of all arts nonprofits; in Douglas County, Colorado, the county with the largest share, seven of ten of the nonprofits were new. Solo artists, however, were plentiful, with more than 1,800 catering to every 100,000 residents of the most artistically entrepreneurial county. The average across the country for all counties is 254 solo artists per 100,000 population, while the median county had 219 such performers per 100,000 population.

For the median county, 2009 per capita cultural expenditures were approximately $314 and 21 percent of households contributed to arts and culture and/or public broadcasting organizations. The cultural participation index ranges from 12 to 100, signifying that the participation rate in the least culturally active county in the dataset was 12 percent of the participation rate for the most active county. Adults in the average county participated at a rate of 45 percent of the rate of the most active county; in the median county, the rate was 44 percent. Table 8-2 shows that compared with the United States as a whole, the median county in this sample was more crowded, had slightly slower growth, was slightly older and better educated, and had a higher 2009 median household income.

Table 8-1. *Descriptive Statistics*[a]

Measure	Minimum	Maximum	Mean	Standard deviation	Median
Arts entrepreneurship					
Millennial share of nonprofits (percent)	11.6	70.0	33.0	9.1	32.1
Millennial share of revenue (percent)	-0.5	76.9	18.6	15.0	14.3
Solo artists per 100,000 population (number)	61.06	1,826.69	253.60	168.51	215.18
Competitive market environment					
Consumer expenditure per capita (dollars)	58.97	515.79	316.02	62.93	313.46
Cultural participation index	12.2	100.0	45.5	14.1	44.0
Arts philanthropy (percent)	5.5	45.8	21.9	5.8	21.1
Four-firm concentration ratio (percent)	15.7	97.1	56.7	16.2	56.8
General community environment					
Population density	21.3	69,468.4	1882.2	5440.3	699.5
Population growth (percent)	-29.1	84.1	11.5	13.9	8.7
Median age (years)	23.2	50.7	37.2	3.8	37.1
Percent with bachelor's degree	8.4	36.5	19.6	5.4	19.2
Median household income (dollars)	30,034	112,021	58,331	14,562	55,350

Source: Author's calculations.

a. N = 281.

Table 8-2. *Comparison of U.S. National Statistics with Those of the Median Sample County*

Measure	United States	Median county
Population density per square mile, 2010[a]	87.4	699.5
Total population percentage growth, 2000–09[b]	9.0	8.7
Median age of the population, 2005–09[c]	36.8	37.1
Percent of the population with bachelor's degree[d]	17.6	19.2
Median household income in current dollars, 2009[e]	51,914	55,530

Source: Author's compilation.

a. Chris Middleton, "U.S. Population Density: People per Square Mile, U.S. Census 1930 to 2010," December 21, 2010 (www.bloomberg.com/news/2010-12-21/u-s-population-density-people-per-square-mile-u-s-census-1930-to-2010.html).

b. Data from Population Estimates Program, U.S. Bureau of the Census (www.census.gov/popest/data/historical/2000s/vintage_2009/index.html).

c. Data from "Median Age, by State," *USA Today*, July 1, 2009 (www.usatoday.com/ news/nation/census/median-age-by-state.htm).

d. Data from "Educational Attainment in the United States: 2009," table 1, U.S. Bureau of the Census (www.census.gov/prod/2012pubs/p20-566.pdf).

e. Data from "State and County QuickFacts," U.S. Bureau of the Census (http://quickfacts.census.gov/qfd/states/00000.html).

Results

The results are shown in tables 8-3 and 8-4, with the three dependent variables (millennial share of organizations, millennial share of revenue, and solo artists per 100,000 population) regressed against the competitive market factors alone in table 8-3 and then against the competitive and general environmental environment factors together in table 8-4.

The first hypothesis, that cultural expenditures support entry, is generally supported: millennial nonprofit organizations in counties with a higher level of arts and culture expenditures did have a slightly larger share of overall arts nonprofit revenues. However, that was in the context of a regression with very low explanatory power. The second hypothesis (cultural participation supports entry) is supported when considering competitive market conditions as the main drivers of cultural enterprises; counties with higher levels of cultural participation had higher shares of millennial arts nonprofits and more solo artists per capita. The coefficients for solo artists per capita are strengthened by a moderate degree of explanatory power (adjusted R^2 is 37.6 percent). The third hypothesis (community philanthropic practice supports entry) is generally not supported: arts and culture philanthropy does not correlate positively with nonprofit enterprise formation, but somewhat surprisingly, it is associated with higher per capita levels of individual arts entrepreneurship.

Hypothesis 4, which specifically addresses competitive market barriers to entry, is supported, too: counties with low nonprofit arts concentration/oligopoly power were those with higher levels of solo artists per capita. That may be a reflection of county density. The last hypothesis, regarding community factors, is largely supported when those factors are looked at in tandem with specific arts market independent variables. Table 8-4 features these main findings:

—There were more solo artists per capita where counties were more crowded.

—Counties with older populations had fewer millennial nonprofits (perhaps a mark of cultural conservatism?) but more solo artists.

—Better-educated counties had more millennial nonprofits and more solo artists per capita, but counties with lower incomes had fewer solo artists per capita.

—Counties with more competition/less concentration in the nonprofit arts sector had more solo artists per capita.

—Faster-growing counties supported entrepreneurial development in nonprofits but not the revenue that they need to grow.

Table 8-3. *Effects of Competitive Environment Variables on Arts Entrepreneurship*[a]

Dependent variable	Millennial share of nonprofits	Millennial share of revenue	Solo artists per capita
Model	1	2	3
Cultural expenditure per capita		+0.279***	
Cultural participation	+0.145*		+0.239***
Arts and culture philanthropy		-0.0183**	+0.340***
Four-firm concentration ratio			-0.177***
F statistic (significance)	1.848 (.120)	4.634 (.001)	43.269 (.000)
Adjusted R^2		.049	.376

Source: Author's calculations.
a. Results are reported as standardized beta coefficients; $*p < .10$, $**p < 0.05$, $*** p < 0.01$.

Table 8-4. *Competitive and General Environment Effects on Arts Entrepreneurship*[a]

Dependent variable	Millennial share of nonprofits	Millennial share of revenue	Solo artists per capita
Model	4	5	6
Arts and culture philanthropy		-0.173 **	+0.244***
Cultural expenditure per capita		+0.236 **	+0.259***
Cultural participation			
Four-firm concentration ratio			-0.169***
Population density, 2010	+0.138**		+0.446***
Population growth, 2000–09	+0.336***		
Median age, ACS 2005–09			
Percent with bachelor's degree, ACS 2005–09	+0.413***		+0.218***
Median household income, ACS 2005–09			-0.314***
F statistic (significance)	10.509 (.000)	2.272 (.018)	4.520 (.000)
R^2	.234	.039	.577

Source: Author's calculations.
a. Results are reported as standardized beta coefficients; $* p < .10$, $**p < 0.05$, $***p < 0.01$.

The relationship between millennial share of organizations and general environmental factors shows that counties that experienced faster population growth, that were more crowded, and that had a well-educated population were more likely to have experienced growth in the population of nonprofit arts organizations. An additional effect on organization formation, median age, is also (barely) significant: counties with younger populations had more new arts organizations.

Formation is one stage of entrepreneurship; successful competitive operation is another. Millennial share of revenues, a marker for whether that cohort of organizations is reaching economic scale, in general does not behave as predicted in the hypotheses. Model 2 in table 8-3, with a very small R^2 coefficient of 4.9 percent, shows cultural philanthropy and cultural expenditures working in opposite directions. In counties where people spent more money on arts experiences, newer organizations had a higher share of revenues, but where people spent more on arts donations, newer organizations had a smaller share of revenues. Organizations with higher revenues must be generating them in ways other than philanthropy, such as through earned revenue. That would be consistent with the positive correlation with participation in arts experiences and spending on arts goods and services, but it is speculative given the low R^2.

Overall, variance in the general environmental factors is not systematically associated with variance in revenues in newer organizations. No specific characteristic from these socioeconomic and demographic variables tended to attract or suppress the ability of new arts organizations to fill their coffers from earned or contributed income. This result is instructive in its own way: it implies that the ability of new nonprofit arts organizations to build their revenues—which typically is critical to their durability—does not have one specific set of predictors from those hypothesized here. The grass was effectively no more or less green than in other places that had different levels of education and income or that had grown faster or more slowly; organizations everywhere were having very similar experiences in raising money.

The presence of individual artists in a community is the aspect of entrepreneurship most strongly correlated with the expected signs, especially for the independent variables measuring the community market and general characteristics. Interestingly, while arts and culture philanthropy and participation are strong and positive correlates of solo arts entrepreneurship, arts and culture expenditures are not significantly related. Perhaps that can be explained by the comparatively lower prices that local artists may charge. Local residents will go out to hear local musicians, but they won't spend a lot of money on them! While some community factors are favorable for solo artists—notably higher population density, older age, and greater educational attainment—household income has a negative relationship. Perhaps that signifies that well-off communities shift their preferences from local solo artists to better-known artists from out of town.

Examining the results on these two dimensions helps to distinguish the various strands of arts entrepreneurship and makes it possible to make some plausible overall observations that can help artists, entrepreneurs, communities, and policymakers. While some of the hypotheses may not have been supported in many of the empirical tests, it still remains the case that the selected vector of explanatory variables correlates strongly—and as expected—with two of the three different specifications of arts entrepreneurship.

The imbalance between the share of millennial arts organizations in the population and their share of total revenues highlights the economic struggle faced by early-stage arts organizations. They are mighty in numbers and overflowing with artistic and entrepreneurial spirit and vigor, but collectively they do not generate revenue in proportion to their weight in the population. A too-rapid pace of entry into the nonprofit arts sector becomes untenable for early-stage organizations that do not compete effectively from the start. However, the regression models for the effect of competitive and community factors on millennial share of revenues had quite low explanatory power. That supports Hager's notion that arts organizations were especially vulnerable to closure (compared with other nonprofits), the root causes being that the organizations were young, small, and dependent on too few revenue streams.[23] On the other hand, relationships between community variables and the third measure of arts enterprise show that the presence of solo artists is strongly affected by those competitive and community factors.

Discussion and Conclusion

"Is this a good place to start my arts venture?" is the stylized question that launches this chapter. The rampant scale of entry into the arts nonprofit arena shows that the dream of community arts organizing, illustrated a century ago by the enthusiasts for J. S. Bach in Bethlehem, Pennsylvania, has remained attractive. On the individual level, the steadily increasing number of individual artists shows that the opportunity to be a solo artist in a community continues to have wide appeal to many people. It should also be made clear that neither new arts nonprofits nor solo artists are the full expression of arts entrepreneurship. Many small organizations are too small to be required to fill out IRS Form 990, but they have great and positive impacts in their communities. Select environmental characteristics have been shown to have a measurable and meaningful effect on the presence of all of those nascent artistic enterprises, although the broad community factors have a greater impact than the competitive market factors. Where expected findings were not supported by the data, it is possible to learn from the alternative results and to recognize that differences between places might not be critical in every element of arts formation. The dream of starting an arts enterprise is national, but it is most likely to take visible form locally. On the other hand, while local artistic traditions and an arts entrepreneur's distinctly local viewpoint might help create identity and serve to differentiate communities, the actual experiences of new and small arts ventures exhibit similarity from place to place.

It remains to ask what other factors contribute positively to building scale in early-stage nonprofit arts organizations. A plausible set of factors affecting early-stage revenues would certainly include the character and capability of organizational leadership, both artistic and strategic. An early-stage visionary would detect the need for a cultural center for an ethnic group, an artistic genre, or a community; ongoing artistic leadership would deliver excellent programs that are self-supporting, with an appropriate mix of earned and contributed revenues. But needs assessment, leadership, and financial planning are managerial activities that organizations actually undertake, not environmental factors over which they have no control. Additional exploration is also needed to uncover how an arts nonprofit environment dominated by the biggest players in a community relates to the presence of local arts entrepreneurs.

Another question that remains is whether and how artists and arts entrepreneurs assess demand. Do they dive in before they see how deep the water is? Perhaps some share of their business planning revolves around rational, trend-based forecasting. Its complement, though, might be a sense of certainty from within the artist/entrepreneur that making the startup move is just the right thing to do. Overall, new growth theory is validated as an appropriate means of examining local entrepreneurship in the arts by the fact that even when entrepreneurs know that there is a rocky path ahead, they set out on it just the same. It is in fact their inherent capabilities and spirit that animate their artistic drive—just as NGT proposes.

A coda to this chapter returns to Bethlehem, to see how arts entrepreneurship has flourished there. During the last decades of the twentieth century and the first years of the twenty-first, Bethlehem has remained a setting for vigorous arts entrepreneurship. Art education, festivals, and cultural venues and programs now operate in new facilities, built in the shadows of the shuttered Bethlehem Steel blast furnaces, which now serve as a backdrop and visual brand. Bethlehem's arts programs draw large, enthusiastic, and supportive audiences. Local entrepreneurs began these programs in the 1980s, a time of unusual economic stress for the community because its mainstay employer closed up shop. In the intervening years, those local leaders have modified and expanded the programs to reach a sufficient economic scale to accompany their artistic and social impact.

Bethlehem's experience has shown, for more than a century, that being a good place to start an arts enterprise is not a result of a uniform set of predictors, save one: the imagination of artists in their roles as visionaries, innovators, and leaders who bring arts to market with successful and dynamic program offerings. Fortunately, Bethlehem is not unique—there are similar great stories around the United States, strong evidence that new growth theory provides an appropriate and healthy lens for examining arts entrepreneurship.

Notes

1. See Paul M. Romer, "The Origins of Endogenous Growth," *Journal of Economic Perspectives*, vol. 8, no. 1 (1990), p. 3, and Paul M. Romer, "Endogenous Technological Change," *Journal of Political Economy*, vol. 98, no. 5 (1990), p. 71.

2. This story is extracted from two works by Paul Larson, archivist of the Bach Choir. One is his book *Bach for a Hundred Years: A Social History of the Bach Choir of Bethlehem* (Lehigh University Press, 2011); the second is his lecture "Capitalizing the Bach Choir: Banks, Borax, and Steel," delivered at the Bach Choir, Bethlehem, April 14, 2012.

3. Roland J. Kushner and Randy Cohen, *National Arts Index 2012* (Washington: Americans for the Arts, 2012), p. 51 (www.artsindexusa.org).

4. Ibid., p. 50.

5. Ibid., p. 47.

6. Gary Paul Green and Anna Haines, *Asset Building and Community Development*, 3rd ed. (Thousand Oaks, Calif.: Sage Publications, 2012).

7. Judith R. Blau, *The Shape of Culture: A Study of Contemporary Cultural Patterns in the United States* (Cambridge University Press, 1989).

8. Richard C. Florida, *The Rise of The Creative Class* (New York: Basic Books, 2002), and Andy C. Pratt, "Creative Cities: The Cultural Industries and the Creative Class," *Geografiska Annaler*, Series B, Human Geography, vol. 90, no. 2 (2008), pp. 107–17.

9. Ann Markusen and others, *California's Arts and Cultural Ecology* (San Francisco: James Irvine Foundation, September 2011) (http://irvine.org/news-insights/publications/arts/arts-ecology-reports).

10. Henry B. Hansmann, "The Role of Nonprofit Enterprise," *Yale Law Journal*, vol. 89, no. 5 (April 1980), p. 835.

11. Michael Porter, *Competitive Strategy* (New York: Free Press, 1978), and Michael Porter, "The Five Competitive Forces That Shape Strategy," *Harvard Business Review* (January 2008), pp. 78–93. The *Harvard Business Review* article is a reprise of his work requested by the *Review*'s editors thirty years after the original publication—a tribute to its enduring influence and utility.

12. The survey results from 2008 and earlier years are available at National Endowment for the Arts, "Research Publications" (http://arts.gov/research).

13. Jane Jacobs, *The Economy of Cities* (New York: Vintage, 1970), p. 163.

14. Bonnie Nichols, "Artists and Art Workers in the United States: Findings from the American Community Survey (2005–2009)," NEA Research Note 105 (2011); and the Quarterly Census of Employment and Wages: 2010 (Washington: National Endowment for the Arts) (http://arts.gov/research/Notes/105.pdf).

15. I use "county" and "community" in a similar fashion in this chapter, an equivalency that might not sit easily for every reader. The county level of analysis is intermediate between nation- and state-level analyses, which may lead to broad social or policy considerations, and more micro-level (city- and neighborhood-level) analyses, which are difficult (or more accurately, expensive!) to examine systematically across multiple sites. While counties may be bigger than one might naturally suppose with a "community" level of analysis, they do provide analysts a broader set of secondary data, collected and made available by more institutions and data providers.

16. Which, for convenience, I will say occurred at the beginning of 2000.

17. Referring here to economic significance; their artistic importance and impact are inviting to explore but outside the scope of this chapter.

18. Specific NTEE codes besides those in major group "A" are B70 (libraries), C41 (botanical gardens), D50 (zoos and aquaria), and N52 (fairs and festivals).

19. See www.census.gov/econ/nonemployer/; note that the data used here are not affected by the error cited by the bureau on August 15, 2012, for 2009 data.

20. Scarborough data are used here courtesy of Americans for the Arts, which obtained them for the Local Arts Index.

21. They were normalized to avoid using a measure of total percentages greater than 100 percent, which is disconcerting.

22. Normally this ratio is calculated by using revenues rather than expenditures. Two factors indicated use of expenditures in this case. First, anomalous results emerged when some organizations reported negative total revenue (perhaps due to portfolio losses). When their negatives were subtracted from county totals, the four top revenue-

earning nonprofits had more revenue than all county arts organizations put together, resulting in ratios of more than 100 percent. Using expenditures as a substitute is consistent with the field of interest; what makes an organization an "arts" organization is determined more by how it spends money than by how it brings it in. Therefore, the spending of the top four organizations in a county is used as a proxy for their market power.

23. Mark A. Hager, "The Survivability Factor: Research on the Closure of Nonprofit Arts Organizations," *Monographs,* vol. 4, no. 1 (Washington: Americans for the Arts, 2000).

PETER PEDRONI *and* STEPHEN SHEPPARD

9

The Economic Consequences of Cultural Spending

Does increasing local arts and culture production have a positive impact on the local economy? In some sense the answer to that question is obvious. When arts and culture production occurs, inputs are purchased, artists and support staff are paid, and that activity, like other types of production activity, is part of the local economy. Increased arts and culture production adds to the local economy in the short run, but what is less obvious is whether its impact persists in the long run. The economy is a dynamic and complex system that responds to change. An increase in live performing arts programming may lead eventually to reduced attendance at carnivals or sporting events. More museums might eventually crowd out amusement parks or even shopping centers. Whether arts and culture production can generate a permanent increase in economic activity, or economic growth, is a question that is more subtle than the question of whether such production has a positive impact on the local economy.

Is there a relationship between local arts and culture production and local prosperity that is not transitory, but permanent? Given the thousands of pages that have been written on the economic impact of the arts or the creative economy, it might seem that finding a satisfactory answer to that question would be a matter of sorting through a bibliographic database to select the best of several analyses. However, we argue that despite the obvious public policy interest in the subject and the importance with which the question appears to be regarded, there has been no fully satisfactory empirical analysis of this question. In this chapter, we endeavor to provide a model that allows us to think systematically about the problem and we present an empirical methodology capable of testing hypotheses relevant to possible answers to the question. We identify data to which these methods can be applied and carry out the analysis using data for U.S. urban areas.

The idea of developing and supporting cultural sites and cultural organizations to promote economic prosperity is certainly not novel. Owen argues that the construction of cathedrals is an explanation for growth of the European economy during the thirteenth century.[1] Alternatively, Bercea, Ekelund, and Tollison see such activities as a device for limiting competition in culture markets and religion.[2]

During the 1930s and early 1940s, the Works Progress Administration included public support for the work of artists and writers along with support for constructing roads, bridges, and public buildings as activities worthy of funding. All of those activities were viewed as having a stimulative effect on the economy. While the artworks created through this program are highly prized today, there is little evidence concerning the contribution that their creation made to economic recovery.

More recently, the United Nations Conference on Trade and Development prepared a comprehensive report describing what the authors called a "new paradigm" in which culture and creativity are "powerful engines driving economic growth and promoting development in a globalizing world."[3] The report includes extensive data on international trade in cultural goods ranging from carpets to paintings and discusses the mechanisms for channeling public resources and investment into the cultural economy.

The writers for the UN report assert that culture "drives" economic growth, but the report itself offers scant evidence. The data provided demonstrate that arts and culture production is a significant economic sector that employs large numbers of workers and generates large amounts of economic output and export earnings; in that respect the report is similar to many studies of communities and regions in the United States. For example, Lawton and Colgan survey the size, growth, and distribution of arts and culture nonprofits and employment in the New England states in a report[4] that is part of a series of similar studies, sponsored by the New England Foundation for the Arts, beginning with Wassall.[5] These and other studies show that arts and culture production is a significant sector of the economy and that in many areas the size of this sector is growing. They do not, however, demonstrate that increasing the size of this sector leads to an increase in economic prosperity or per capita GDP in the urban area.

Much of the interest in the topic during the past decade has been encouraged and actively promoted by the work of Richard Florida and his coauthors, who have analyzed what they see as the basis for economic growth and development.[6] Florida's writing itself draws attention not to specific industries or economic sectors like arts and culture production but to specific occupational categories and types of workers that are part of what he characterizes as the "creative class." His writing goes out of its way to include "poets and novelists, artists, entertainers, actors" as being among the "super creative core" of workers that drive economic growth. His work has been interpreted as supporting the notion that communities that are culturally active and diverse and that provide a good environment for the arts will be economically successful.

Unfortunately, little evidence has been available to directly test that claim, and much of what has been put forward has been unpersuasive for several reasons. First, much of the evidence consists of demonstrating that culture production and the arts are a significant part of the economy. This line of inquiry concludes by showing that arts and culture production is a "multibillion" dollar industry or presenting some variation on that theme. Frequently, in an effort to improve the result, the definition of the industries that are part of the cultural economy is expanded to include production of ancillary inputs or services that are peripheral to the actual production of arts and cultural works and activities. Markusen, Wassall, DeNatale, and Cohen provide a useful comparison of such concepts and show that, depending on the definition used, the fraction of the local labor force engaged in cultural production or the creative economy can range from less than 1 percent to nearly half of the labor force.[7] Whatever the size of the cultural economy, such evidence cannot demonstrate that a change in the size or level of support for this sector will cause an increase in economic prosperity.

A second reason for such evidence being unpersuasive is that it fails to show that the impacts of culture production are persistent. As noted above, it is clear that arts and culture production must contribute to the economy; what is not clear is whether its impact is persistent. If arts and culture production generates a short-run impact that simply crowds out other economic activities over time, there may be zero long-run impact on the economy; if so, these impact studies are of very limited use. This point is not a new revelation; it was discussed by Seaman in 1987.[8]

If the evidence presented so far has been inconclusive about the causal connection between arts and culture production and local economic prosperity, why do scholars and policymakers continue to pursue such results? One reason is that a correlation between arts and culture production and local prosperity is readily apparent in analyses of cross-sectional data. The upper panel in figure 9-1 shows the simple bivariate relationship across U.S. metropolitan areas between per capita GDP and per capita cultural organization expenditures.

Figure 9-1. *Relation between Local GDP and Cultural Organization Expenditures and Automobile Dealer Payrolls*

Logarithm of 2006 dollars per capita

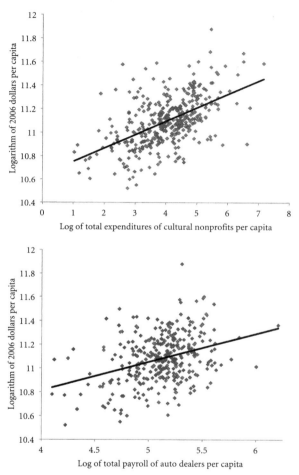

Source: Moody's Analytics Metro Forecast Database, Bureau of Economic Analysis, National Center for Charitable Statistics, and authors' calculations.

Even though this figure shows only the bivariate relation, there is a clear relationship suggesting that urban areas with higher levels of per capita spending by cultural organizations tend also to have higher levels of per capita GDP. If we couple that observation with arguments about how the arts and culture stimulate creativity or attract and retain creative and productive workers, it can be presented as an argument in support of the arts.

A similar relationship, however, can be seen between many different types of economic activity and per capita local GDP. The lower panel of figure 9-1 shows the apparent impact of increasing the activity of new car dealers (as measured by the per capita total payroll of new car dealers in the urban area). Here again we see a clear positive relationship in the cross-sectional data. In this case, the interpretation of the relationship that seems most reasonable is that communities with higher GDP purchase more automobiles and that results in a larger automobile dealer sector.[9]

Because the evidence put forward to date has not always been persuasive, public policies to support the arts have sometimes been controversial. The controversy is due in part to a variety of political issues; it is not based on serious criticism of the evidence advanced in favor of the policies. Nevertheless, when in the midst of the most severe recession in the United States since the 1930s members of Congress proposed and nearly passed a restriction prohibiting the use of stimulus funds for any art or cultural project, there must have been some who supported those restrictions because they believed that such spending would have zero stimulative effect on the economy or because they believed that any effects would not contribute to a permanent increase in output or employment. They may have believed that such programs are analogous to policies designed to increase the size and payroll of local automobile dealerships; while increasing automobile dealer payrolls would generate a short-term boost in the local economy (because automobile dealers are part of the economy), it would be unlikely to generate a long-term process of economic growth. Once the policy was implemented, other parts of the economy would adjust to dampen and likely eliminate the short-term gains.

A further concern about such policies is that they devote scarce resources to cultural facilities when the payoff would be greater from investing in education, public infrastructure, or private sector initiatives that are displaced by spending on arts and culture. In an influential treatise, McCarthy, Ondaatje, Zakaras, and Brooks raise objections to focusing attention on evaluation of the economic (or other "instrumental") benefits of the arts, fearing that such analysis "runs the risk of being discredited if other activities are better at generating the same effects."[10] They worry that failure to consider the opportunity costs of devoting scarce resources to culture and the arts weakens the arguments of arts advocates and recommend broadening the approach taken by arts advocates to devote more emphasis on the intrinsic benefits of the arts, which are more subjective and difficult to verify. While that might make sense as a strategy for arts advocacy, it begs the question of what the real relationship between the arts and local economic prosperity is.

To better inform policymaking, it is essential to answer two central questions. First, is there a causal connection running from arts and culture production to economic prosperity? That connection is to be distinguished from a connection that is merely a correlation and therefore unlikely to be useful for economic policy. Second, is the effect of arts and culture production on economic prosperity more than a simple transitory effect? The second question addresses the extent to which the arts and culture sector is capable of generating economic growth. In what follows we offer a novel approach to answering both of these questions. After discussing a model capable of providing a framework for formulating the questions, we analyze data for U.S. urban areas to determine the answers.

A Simple Model of Culture and Growth

Is there a model of economic growth that would suggest that there is or might be a causal link between arts and culture production and local economic output? It is a straightforward matter to adapt the stylized growth model presented in Canning and Pedroni,[11] which itself is adapted from Barro.[12] A thorough exposition with technical details may be found in Barro and Sala-i-Martin,[13] and readers who want a more complete mathematical presentation of the models should consult these sources. A more detailed version of this model with specific application to the impact of arts and culture on urban prosperity is presented in a recent paper by Pedroni and Sheppard.[14]

In a simple growth model, total economic output is a function of the capital and labor available to the economy. As discussed, we want to analyze the impact of arts and cultural activities on the local economy, particularly the possibility that increasing the provision of cultural activities in a local economy might generate a permanent increase in local economic activity—what economists refer to as an increase in *steady state* economic output.

The availability of cultural amenities might be thought of as an input to production that works in a way similar to the way that physical capital works. In a simple model for a representative urban area, we would identify aggregate income at time t, denoted as Y_t, as depending on the capital (K_t) and labor (L_t) available in the urban area and the total cultural resources (C_t). The relation between these is given by the aggregate production function

$$Y_t = A_t \cdot K_t^{\alpha} C_t^{\beta} L_t^{1-\alpha-\beta}.$$

The parameter A_t in the production function represents total factor productivity. Increases in total factor productivity result from processes of learning and technological change, and over time they make it possible to produce higher levels of local income with the same or reduced inputs of labor, capital, and culture. Note that the production relationship implies that labor, capital, and culture are all necessary for the local economy to function. Setting any of them equal to zero results in zero economic output for the local economy.

A local economy can be modeled as experiencing ongoing economic growth that comes from an outside (exogenous) process or as generating growth as result of internal (endogenous) processes that increase capital, culture, or labor available to the economy. In this framework, whether or not culture can have a permanent effect on output depends on the values of the production function. Specifically, if alpha and beta sum to one, then culture fulfills the conditions required for endogenous growth, whereby shocks or innovations in arts and culture production have the potential to lead to permanent increases in output. While the central focus of our inquiry is the capacity of spending on culture and the arts to generate long-run changes in economic prosperity, our model does not assume that this capacity exists, and it allows for economic growth to come from other sources.

While in most cities the total resources devoted to arts and culture are modest compared with those devoted to other sectors of the local economy, providing culture to the community is not costless. It competes for scarce investment resources that might otherwise be allocated to capital. A natural way to model this is to assume that there is a constant share s of local income that is available for investment in capital or for production of culture. Let $s \cdot Y_t$ equal private savings, the amount of income not used for consumption. We assume that culture claims a share τ_t of the local income that is not used for consumption. In actual economies, the share devoted to production of culture comes from many different sources: private production of culture (such as in the home or by firms), production of culture by the public sector, and production of culture by nonprofit organizations. These culture production activities are subject to random variation because of changes in resources available to culture producers. We assume that the share of savings devoted to culture production each year is given by $\tau_t = \bar{\tau} + \mu_t$, an average value of $\bar{\tau}$ plus random variation that averages out to zero. The amount of culture available to the local economy is then given by $C_{t+1} = (\bar{\tau} + \mu_t) \cdot s \cdot Y_t$.

The parameters $\bar{\tau}$ and μ_t are of central interest from a policy perspective. In the context of our model, asking whether cultural spending "causes" economic prosperity can be tested by determining whether the random changes in the share of savings devoted to culture production (μ_t) cause permanent changes in per capita Y_t.

Note that the link between culture and economic prosperity may be an adverse one. If too many resources are being devoted to culture production—if $\bar{\tau}$ is "too large"—then increases in local culture production $\mu_t > 0$ will have negative long-run impacts on per capita Y_t. That could happen because spending on culture takes away from the investment in capital required for the local economy. Intuitively, if support for culture production uses funds required for schools or roads, the impact on the local economy may be negative. That is represented in the simple economic model by requiring that the amount of capital available for the local economy be the share of local savings that is not devoted to culture production: $K_{t+1} = (1 - \tau_t) \cdot s \cdot Y_t$. This equality, combined with the previous expression showing culture production as a share of total economic output, implies that the economy must have savings ($s \cdot Y_t$) equal to investment (K_{t+1}) plus culture provision (C_{t+1}). This captures the reality that culture production uses valuable resources that have alternative uses in the economy.

There will be a particular value of $\bar{\tau}$ that provides a level of culture production that maximizes local per capita income. In general, the value of $\bar{\tau}$ that achieves this depends on the random fluctuations in cultural spending and produces a situation such as that illustrated in figure 9-2.[15] Here we see that if $\bar{\tau} < \tau^*$, a small positive shock to culture will have a positive long-run effect on per capita income. If $\bar{\tau} > \tau^*$, then a small positive shock to culture will reduce per capita income in the long run.[16] The methods that we describe and employ in this chapter do not permit us to directly estimate τ^*. However, once we have tested and accepted the hypothesis that there is a causal connection in which fluctuations in local culture production have a non-zero impact on long-run income, the methods that we employ do permit us to consider groups of urban areas and estimate whether, within each group, a positive shock to culture production generates a positive or negative long-run impact on local prosperity.

This model provides a useful framework for evaluating the causal impacts of providing arts and culture resources to a local economy, and it allows for several different potential cases of interest. It can accommodate either public sector support of the arts or private philanthropy. Depending on parameter values, it can represent the case in which increases in the production of culture might have a positive impact in the short run but no causal connection to economic prosperity in the long run.

Figure 9-2. *Steady-State Income and the Share of Savings Devoted to Culture (τ)*

Steady state income

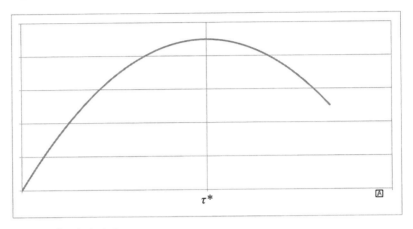

τ^*

Source: Authors' calculations.

Finally, the model allows for the possibility that there is a causal link between arts and culture provision and per capita income that is persistent in the long run, including both the case in which the link is a negative one (small increases in culture provision diminish per capita income) and the case in which the link is a positive one (small increases in culture increase per capita income). We discuss next our empirical strategy for testing hypotheses about the causal connections between cultural spending and local economic output.

The Data

We assembled a balanced panel dataset covering 384 metropolitan statistical areas (MSAs) or metropolitan statistical area divisions (MSADs) following the definitions put forward by the Office of Management and Budget.[17] Total metropolitan GDP is made available for all metropolitan areas in the United States by the Bureau of Economic Analysis (BEA), but only for years after 2000. Moody's Analytics has used the BEA methodology to produce a quarterly series of GDP estimates for all 384 metro areas as part of its U.S. Metropolitan Areas Forecast Database. We used these for our measure of total output, averaging the quarterly data to obtain amounts for each year from 1990 through 2006.

Measurement of culture production in each urban area is more difficult. Arts and culture production takes place in a variety of institutions and places: within the home, in public and private schools, in commercial enterprises ranging from film studios and cinemas to publishers and private galleries, and in not-for-profit enterprises such as museums, art schools, and centers for performing arts. For some of these venues (such as private art dealers) there are no data whatsoever or only data that are not specific to the urban area (such as the Survey of Public Participation in the Arts). For others (like public and private schools) there are annual data but the data do not distinguish between culture production and other types of activities unrelated to culture and the arts.

The most comprehensive data that are available over time and that provide national coverage at the local level are annual data on the operation of not-for-profit enterprises that are engaged in producing, supporting, presenting, and preserving culture and the arts. The data cover between 15,780 organizations in 1990 and 39,043 organizations in 2006, most of which were located within the boundaries of one of the 384 metropolitan areas that we study. The organizations themselves are engaged in a wide variety of arts and culture production activities. These data are available to researchers through the National Center for Charitable Statistics (NCCS), and we used the NCCS data as the basis for our analysis.

The NCCS data cover all 501(c)(3) organizations that have been certified by the IRS as not-for-profit organizations engaged in charitable activities. When the IRS accepts an application from such an organization, the application is reviewed and the organization is assigned a code from the National Taxonomy of Exempt Enterprises (NTEE) to designate the primary activity of the organization. All organizations with annual budgets exceeding $25,000 are required to file an annual return that provides a limited breakdown of total revenues, expenditures, and assets. While the returns themselves are rarely if ever audited and the details provided in the returns may be inconsistently reported, the total revenues and total expenditures of the organizations seem to be reasonably accurate and, for larger organizations, are generally drawn directly from audited annual financial reports.

The NCCS scans organization returns and descriptions of activities to correct and update the NTEE codes assigned to each organization. We therefore use the activity codes provided by NCCS and identify all organizations engaged in the broad category of "Arts, Culture, and the Humanities," which includes everything from "Arts Alliances and Advocacy Organizations" (A01) through "Organizers of Commemorative Events" (A84). It includes essentially every art museum, symphony, performing arts center, dance company, and arts advocacy organization in the United States.

The available NCCS data include at least the zip code and county in which the organization is located. We used that information to assign each organization to an urban area. While it is possible that such assignments do not always guarantee that the activities of the organization are exclusive to the assigned urban area, data are not available to determine the accuracy of the assignment or to improve it. For each urban area we summed the reported expenditures of all such organizations for each year and took that as a measure of (or proxy for) the total production of arts and culture within the urban area.

There is an arguable advantage, in addition to the availability of data, to focusing on the not-for-profit arts and culture producers. These organizations are supposed to be run with a charitable purpose, and they are certified as such in order to receive not-for-profit status. In this context "charitable" does not mean to operate in the service of the poor or to reduce income inequality; it means to operate so as to produce a general public benefit. In economic terms that can be interpreted as operating in a way that produces significant positive externalities. Those externalities might reasonably be thought to include educating and improving the creativity of the local labor force, which is one way in which a causal connection between local culture production and local GDP might arise.

Total population for each urban area was obtained from the Current Population Survey and was used to calculate the local GDP and local arts and culture production per capita. Our estimates are of the relationship between changes in the natural logarithm of per capita GDP and per capita culture production, so we used nominal dollar measures to avoid concern about which would be the appropriate price index to use for inflation adjustment. Table 9-1 provides some descriptive statistics for local GDP and culture production expenditures per capita.

The statistics presented in table 9-1 show that the expenditures on cultural production vary considerably more than local GDP across the sample. Within any given year, the magnitude of the coefficient of variation of per capita GDP is about one-sixth the magnitude of the coefficient of variation of per capita expenditures on culture production. Some of the individual urban areas that are at the extremes of the distribution can be surprising. Both in terms of local GDP and arts and culture production, the small MSA of Hinesville–Fort Stewart, Georgia, exhibits the lowest values. The urban areas with the highest values of local GDP per capita are San Francisco; Wilmington, Delaware; and Midland, Texas.

Table 9-1. *Descriptive Statistics for Sample: Local per Capita GDP (Y) and Culture Production (C)*

Variable	Mean	Standard deviation	Minimum	Maximum	Observations
All years					
Year	1998	4.9	1990	2006	6,528
Y_t	39693.12	15069.06	12235.75	144184.50	6,528
C_t	48.41	71.09	0.10	1276.11	6,528
1990					
Y_{1990}	24348.52	5343.82	12235.75	50591.52	384
C_{1990}	24.15	33.45	0.10	391.35	384
2006					
Y_{2006}	67434.08	14818.21	37095.49	144184.50	384
C_{2006}	89.13	116.63	2.79	1276.11	384

Source: Authors' calculations.

Figure 9-3 illustrates the variation among cities and over time in local culture production. The urban area with the highest value of arts and culture production expenditures is Washington-Arlington-Alexandria, which remains consistently the highest; over the past decade, Pittsfield, Massachusetts, and Santa Fe, New Mexico, have exchanged places for the next two positions. As noted above, the actual analysis involves estimating the dynamic relationship between the first differences of the natural logarithm of these two per capita variables within a given urban area over time. Before we present the results of our analysis, it is interesting to examine a few examples of these relationships for some specific cities. The relevant series for Honolulu, Santa Rosa–Petaluma, St. Louis, and Syracuse are presented in figure 9-4.

There are a couple of points worth mentioning with respect to the examples presented in figure 9-4. First, as would be consistent with time series with a unit root in the series of levels, the first-difference data appear to be stationary or nearly so. Second, there is some variability in the apparent dynamics present in the data. As might be expected from the descriptive statistics in table 9-1, the series of culture production expenditures exhibits greater volatility than the local GDP data. There also appears to be some variability in the timing of the dynamics, with St. Louis appearing to show movements in culture production that are more or less contemporaneous with movements in local GDP, while in Santa Rosa–Petaluma there is little contemporaneous

Figure 9-3. *Panel Data for Arts and Culture Expenditures per Capita*

Per capita arts expenditures, U.S. dollars

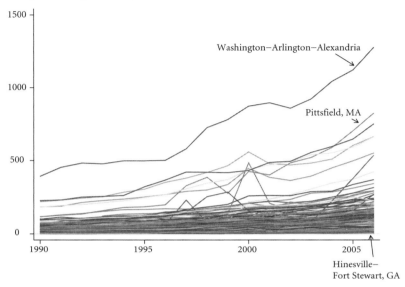

Source: Authors' calculations.

correlation in the first eight years of the data, although since the late 1990s changes in culture production seem to have come before similar changes in local GDP by a year or two.

Empirical Methodology

The information and comparison presented in figure 9-1 were intended to illustrate the need for caution in making inferences about the "causal" connection between variables based on observations of relationships between variables. Looking across U.S. metropolitan areas, we see a clear positive relationship between per capita income and cultural spending. Comparison with other industries suggests that we should be very cautious about inferring that a policy of increasing cultural spending will increase local economic prosperity. Inferences of this sort are propositions about dynamic behavior. If a change in policy or behavior occurs, then (in subsequent time periods) a particular economic result will occur. Discovery of such relationships is achieved most naturally by using data over time, which allows for observing changes in

Figure 9-4. *Four Examples of the Relationship between Proportionate Growth Rates in Per Capita Income (∆Log Y) and Per Capita Cultural Spending (∆Log Arts)*

Change in log income or log arts expenditures

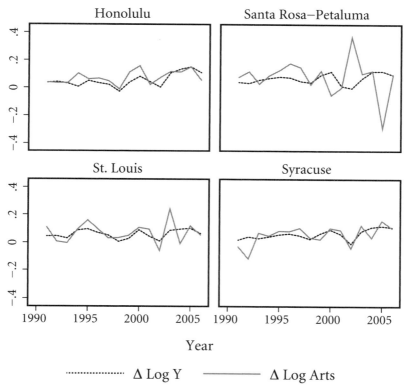

culture production and measuring the response of the economy to those changes over time.

In our analysis we focus on the relationship between the logarithm of local economic output per capita, which we denote y_t, and the logarithm of total per capita spending by cultural nonprofit organizations, which we designate c_t. The first step in our approach is to determine whether both of these data series have a unit root in each of the metropolitan areas that we study. An implication of such a finding is that there is at least something that is causing permanent changes in the data. Conceptually, this condition will be important if we want to establish that something can lead to permanent increases in per capita income or per capita spending by cultural organizations.

Passing this first step does not establish that there is a long-run relationship between culture and economic activity, nor does it establish the causal direction of any relationship that might exist. Testing for the existence of a long-run relationship, measuring the direction of causality if it exists, and avoiding spurious regressions require determination of the presence of *cointegration* between y_t and c_t. Two data series having a unit root are said to be cointegrated if there is a linear combination of the two variables that is stationary. This linear combination would define a *cointegrating relationship* in each city of the form $c_t = a + b \cdot y_t + \varepsilon_t$, where a and b are fixed parameters that can be estimated and ε_t is an error term that is stationary and has an expected value of zero. There are several tests that can be used to check whether two variables are cointegrated, and the application of those tests to data on culture production and local economic activity is the second step in our methodology.

Intuitively, if two variables are cointegrated, then they can still be subject to random fluctuations but over time they remain bound by the cointegrating relationship that ties them together. Since the error term ε_t has an expected value of zero and is stationary, as the data evolve over time there can be systematic departures from the relationship between y_t and c_t at any point in time, but in the long run changes in y_t and c_t will have to occur to restore $c_t = a + b \cdot y_t$. Testing for cointegration provides insight into the causal connection between y_t and c_t. If y_t and c_t are cointegrated, then we know that there is at least some long-run causal relationship between y_t and c_t, although cointegration alone does not tell us the direction of the causal relationship.

We note that this long-run causality is a much stronger notion than Granger causality, which is a causal relationship at *any* time horizon, including short time horizons. It should not be surprising to find a Granger causal relationship between the variables. What is central to our question is whether there is a *long-run* causal relationship. Furthermore, it would not be surprising if a long-run causal relationship exists running from y_t to c_t. If so, it would tell us that increases in local incomes and local prosperity eventually translate into increased support for local cultural organizations. A more important finding would be the converse finding—that c_t causes y_t in the long run. Such a finding would provide some support for the creative economy perspective.

There also are important limitations of the notion of Granger causality in evaluating economic development strategies. By itself, establishing that c_t Granger causes y_t will not establish the sign of the causal relationship nor the time horizon over which it occurs. As noted above, since culture production is a part of the local economy, it would not be surprising if an increase in the activity of cultural organizations generated an impact on local economic activity for a few or perhaps even several years afterward. Such an impact represents an ordinary multiplier effect in which other local enterprises expand to provide inputs to the organizations. The critical question for evaluating the validity of ideas about the creative economy is whether the effect is positive and is still present after all adjustments in the local economy have taken place. If an increase in the activity of cultural organizations crowds out other local economic activity so that there is no long-run impact, then increasing arts and cultural activities would not seem to be a good strategy for promoting economic growth. Even in such a case, however, it would be possible for c_t to Granger cause y_t because of the medium-term impact, which eventually fades away.

That brings us to the third step in our methodology. If c_t and y_t are cointegrated, then there exists an *error correction representation* of the relationship. The intuition behind this representation is not difficult to understand. Suppose, referring to the cointegrating relationship described above, that at some time period we observe a positive value of the error term ε_t. The positive error term means that at time t per capita culture provision c_t in the city is larger than would be expected for a place with the observed level of per capita income y_t. To maintain the cointegrating relationship, there will have to be adjustments in c_t and y_t, denoted Δc_t and Δy_t, that eventually restore the relationship. Those adjustments will depend on the adjustments that have already taken place in the economy and will be proportional to the magnitude of the error ε_t.

The observed year-on-year changes in c_t and y_t provide us with observations for Δc_t and Δy_t, and those changes are regressed on past values of Δc_t and Δy_t and the estimated error ε_t to provide estimates of the speed-of-adjustment parameters λ_1 and λ_2. The parameter λ_1 indicates the impact on the adjustment in cultural organization spending Δc_t that results from an increase in the estimated error ε_t; the parameter λ_2 indicates the impact on the adjustment in local per capita income Δy_t that results from the error ε_t.

The error correction process described in the preceding paragraphs provides a structure within which we can evaluate both the long-run impacts of the economy on culture production and also of culture production on the economy. We also can ascertain the sign of those impacts. Suppose that increasing local economic activity has a positive impact on culture production in the steady state of the local economy, after all adjustment has taken place. Then an increase in y_t will initially make culture production c_t smaller than expected for a city of this new level of affluence. Per capita culture production being smaller than expected implies a negative value for ε_t. The error correction process described above implies that the change in culture production in response to the negative value for ε_t will be $\lambda_1 \cdot \varepsilon_t$. So if culture production is to increase in response to growth in income, we expect that $\lambda_1 < 0$; if λ_1 is statistically significant, then we can be confident that a causal relationship exists.

In order to conclude that culture production has a long-run impact on local income, we focus on λ_2. Consider the hypothesis that increasing culture production has an impact on steady-state income levels in the economy. Then an increase in c_t will generate a positive value of ε_t and the adjustment Δy_t will change by $\lambda_2 \cdot \varepsilon_t$. If λ_2 is statistically significant, we can be confident that there is a causal connection between culture production and steady-state income. If the sign of λ_2 is the opposite of the sign of λ_1, then this steady-state causal connection is the one suggested by arguments presented in the creative economy literature and that would be expected if $\bar{\tau} < \tau^*$, as illustrated in figure 9-3.

Using the estimated dynamic adjustment parameters λ_1 and λ_2 from the error-correction models as a test for the existence of a long-run causal relation was first described by Canning and Pedroni. They derived two results that are central for our application.[18] They showed that the coefficient λ_2 is zero if, and only if, random fluctuations in per capita culture provision have no long-run effect on per capita income, and they showed that the ratio of the coefficients $-(\lambda_2/\lambda_1)$ has the same sign that an increase in culture provision has on steady-state income.

To summarize, the third step in our methodology is to estimate the cointegrating relationship between c_t and y_t that was tested for in the second step. Then, using the estimated errors ε_t from this relationship along with observed year-on-year changes in Δc_t and Δy_t, we estimate an error-correction model and obtain speed-of-adjustment parameters λ_1 and λ_2.

It is worth mentioning here that the tests for unit roots in the data, tests for and estimation of cointegrating relationships, and the estimation of the error-correction model and speed-of-adjustment parameters are all undertaken using techniques that take advantage of the panel structure of our data. Our analysis brings together similar data from all U.S. metropolitan areas over a seventeen-year time period. Such relatively short time series drawn from a single city considered in isolation can make it difficult to estimate relationships or to test for causality. The heterogeneity of the data—that is, the differences between the urban areas—and the time-series structure of the data make this ideal for application of the techniques developed and presented by Pedroni,[19] which increases the power of our statistical tests. Failure to use those techniques would lead us to accept more frequently a null hypothesis of no relationship when a relationship actually is present.

The final step in our methodology is to undertake statistical tests on the set of estimated dynamic adjustment parameters λ_1 and λ_2 from all of the metropolitan areas in the United States. Doing so involves five separate evaluations. The first two consider the average t statistic measure of the statistical significance of λ_1 and λ_2 over all U.S. cities. That average could be zero for two reasons: on average there is no dynamic causal relationship between the variables ($y_t \rightarrow c_t$ for λ_1 or $c_t \rightarrow y_t$ for λ_2), or alternatively, the heterogeneity across cities produces a situation in which some cities experience one direction of adjustment in response to ε_t, other cities experience the opposite direction of adjustment, and the average of all cities taken together is zero. The next two tests seek to separate the two possibilities by testing the separate hypotheses that λ_1 and λ_2 are *pervasively* zero. That is, we test the null hypothesis that all 384 values of the estimated λ_1 are zero. Rejection of this hypothesis implies that there is generally a causal connection between culture production and steady-state income. Combining these two tests with the first two provides information about the heterogeneity of any causal relationship that exists.

Finally, we test the sign of the causal relationship between culture production and local economic output, using the ratio $-(\lambda_2/\lambda_1)$, whose sign is the same as the sign of the causal relationship. Testing the sign of this ratio over the population of U.S. metropolitan areas must contend with the difficulty that $-(\lambda_2/\lambda_1)$ has an unusual (Cauchy) distribution, so we present a test based on the median value across U.S. cities, using a standard error estimated from the data by using a bootstrap technique. Further details on the methodology and the specific tests used are presented by Pedroni and Sheppard.[20]

Results

As described in detail above, the first step in applying our methodology is to verify that our levels data exhibit the unit root structure required by our approach. The two columns on the left of table 9-2 present the results from applying four tests for each of the variables y_t and c_t.

Each of the four tests suggests failure to reject the null hypothesis of a unit root, although the large magnitude of the test statistics suggests the possibility of some size distortion in our panel that may require further examination and correction for common factors across urban areas in our panel. That is true for both variables. Nevertheless, the tests do justify accepting the null hypothesis of a unit root in the data for all cities. Doing so would imply sta-

Table 9-2. *Tests for a Unit Root in and a Cointegrating Relationship between the Logs of Per Capita Income (y_t) and Per Capita Cultural Spending (c_t)*[a]

Unit root tests		Cointegration tests	
Tests for y_t		Panel tests	
LLC ρ	11.83	υ	14.94***
LLC t_ρ	17.53	ρ	-7.49***
LLC ADF	25.95	t_ρ	-9.63***
IPS ADF	37.83	ADF	-10.05***
Tests for c_t		Group tests	
LLC ρ	5.99	ρ	-1.41*
LLC t_ρ	9.91	t_ρ	-10.01***
LLC ADF	13.11	ADF	-12.65***
IPS ADF	16.98		

Source: Authors' calculations.

a. ***Significant at the 1 percent level; *significant at the 5 percent level.

tionarity for the first differences of the data, which is consistent with the visual appearance of the examples in figure 9-3. We therefore proceed to calculate seven different statistical tests for the presence of a cointegrating relationship; results for all seven are presented on the right hand side of table 9-2.

These tests also support application of our methods to these data. There is one test, the group ρ test, that suggests rejection of the null hypothesis of no cointegrating relationship, but not with a high degree of significance. The other six tests, however, are unanimous in recommending rejection of H_0 and accepting H_A with a high degree of confidence. We interpret the results of these tests as justifying confidence in the existence of a cointegrating relationship between y_t and c_t, and we proceed to the next step of estimating the cointegrating relationships and the error correction models. A separate cointegrating relationship is estimated for each of the 384 urban areas in our panel. Using the residuals from these relationships, we proceed to estimate the error-correction models described above. The models provide estimates of $\widehat{\lambda}_2$ and $\widehat{\lambda}_1$ for each MSA.

Next, as noted in the discussion of our methodology, if a long-run causal connection exists in which increases in culture c_t generate permanent changes in income y_t, then the sign of the impact is the same as the sign of the ratio $-(\lambda_2 / \lambda_1)$. This ratio is calculated for each MSA.

Table 9-3. Tests for Existence and Sign of Long-Run Causal Relation between per Capita Income and Cultural Spending[a]

	$\overline{\lambda}_2$	Test $c_t \rightarrow y_t$	$\overline{\lambda}_1$	Test $y_t \rightarrow c_t$	Median $-(\lambda_2/\lambda_1)$	σ
Group mean	0.1	0.49	-1.11	-1.8**		
Pervasively zero		1499.72***		2869.24***		
Sign test					0.0384	0.0212

Source: Authors' calculations.
a. ***Significant at the 1 percent level; *significant at the 5 percent level.

With these estimates and calculations completed for our entire panel, we are now able to complete the final step and provide summary tests for the existence of long-run causal relationships as well as the sign of the relationship in U.S. urban areas. The results are presented in table 9-3.

The first line of the table after the column headers presents the results of the group mean tests that are part of the final step in our methodology. The group means provide a test of the average relationship, over all urban areas, between increases in culture production on long-run income and also between increases in local GDP on long-run culture production. These tests suggest that we cannot with confidence reject the null hypothesis that on average there is no long-run causal relationship $c_t \rightarrow y_t$ in which increases in local culture production generate permanent changes to steady-state per capita GDP. In the context of our model, this finding is not surprising. As suggested in figure 9-3, local economies with $\overline{\tau} < \tau^*$ will experience a positive impact on steady-state GDP as a consequence of a shock to local culture production. Local economies with $\overline{\tau} > \tau^*$ will experience a negative impact. If the United States contains cities distributed on both sides of τ^*, then the average impact may well not be distinguishable from zero. On the other hand, we can reject the null hypothesis of no long-run causal relationship $y_t \rightarrow c_t$ where shocks to local GDP cause permanent changes to culture production. This result is also to be expected as long as arts and culture are valuable to the urban residents.

The second line of the table presents the results of the test to determine whether the impacts are "pervasively" zero, which is a more appropriate and direct test of whether arts and culture have a causal impact on the local economy. As discussed above, since arts and culture production is part of the local economy, it is clear that an increase in culture production will have a short-run impact because of the familiar multiplier effect. If arts and culture were simple consumption goods with no impact on productivity, the local economy would respond by assimilating this short-run impact and returning to the original steady state. The test statistic suggests rejection of the null hypothesis of no relationship in both directions with a very high degree of significance, implying that arts and culture production does have an impact on the steady-state level of local GDP. It also implies that local GDP has an impact on steady-state culture production.

We noted above that the existence of a long-run causal relationship alone does not tell us the direction of the relationship. The results so far seem to clearly recommend acceptance of the hypothesis that there exists a long-run causal connection in which increases in culture production cause permanent impacts on local GDP. What we have not determined is whether a positive shock to culture production causes a long-run increase or decrease to GDP. The final row of the table presents an analysis for that question, providing the calculation of the median across panel members of the estimated ratio $- (\lambda_2 / \lambda_1)$; in the final column of the table, the standard error of this median, obtained by re-sampling, is applied to the estimated error-correction models. The results show a positive median value, indicating that the long-run relationship $c_t \rightarrow y_t$ is such that a positive shock to culture is associated with a permanent increase in per capita GDP. The magnitude of the estimated impact is about 1.81 times the standard error, indicating that we can be reasonably confident of the result.

The individual estimates of $- (\lambda_2 / \lambda_1)$ in U.S. metropolitan areas produces a wide range in values due in part to the instability of a Cauchy-distributed random variable, but it also must be noted that the sign of the impact is likely to vary with different urban characteristics. There may be cultural norms and practices that help to determine the ways in which the arts affect labor productivity, and the scarcity or plenty with which capital is available in the urban area will be a factor. If a long-run relationship exists (as suggested by the significance of the estimated parameter $\bar{\lambda}_1$), the direction of the relationship could be negative if taking some of the resources currently spent on the arts and redirecting those resources toward some type of capital results in an increase in local GDP. That possibility cannot be discounted. To see this, we calculate the median values of the ratio $- (\lambda_2 / \lambda_1)$ for the four broad regions of the United States. The results are presented in table 9-4 below.

While these results should be interpreted with caution, they do show an unambiguous pattern. Urban areas in the Northeast region of the United States show the strongest positive relationship between culture and prosperity. Urban areas in the southern United States show a markedly different pat-

Table 9-4. *Median Sign Estimates for Long-Run Impact in U.S. Regions*[a]

Region	Median $-(\lambda_2/\lambda_1)$
Northeast	0.055
West	0.05
Midwest	0.03
South	−0.1

Source: Authors' calculations.

a. The sign of the ratio $-(\lambda_2/\lambda_1)$ equals the estimated sign of the permanent impact on per capita income arising from an increase in cultural expenditure.

tern, indicating that for those cities a locally financed increase in culture production may result in a permanent decrease in local GDP. Other decompositions of this type are possible, and it is also possible to decompose organizations into activity groups to study the distinctive impacts of performing arts, visual arts, or arts education and support organizations.

Conclusion

We regard the results presented above as important for at least two reasons. First, they address a problem that is relevant for contemporary policy in urban and regional development and that has been a source of controversy. A great deal has been written about the potential of support for arts and culture production to promote local economic development and prosperity. Much of what has been written on the subject has failed to examine, much less establish, the existence of a causal connection between culture production and local GDP. To our knowledge, this is the first study to do so. Our analysis reveals interesting results with policy implications: there appears to be a causal connection in which increases in local culture production generate permanent increases in local GDP.

Second, this analysis makes a contribution by providing further demonstration of the powerful potential of panel time-series techniques for studying issues relevant to urban and regional policymakers and economists. Time-series techniques have been regarded as a tool whose primary application is to problems for which there are data that have accumulated either over very long periods of time (like aggregate measures of output or employment) or at high frequencies (like financial market trading). Urban and regional economists have tended to focus on cross-section techniques that allow them to work with less data. Panel data, however, are frequently available for the study of urban areas, and they may provide fifteen to twenty years or more of observations from hundreds of separate local urban economies. Such data are often perfect for analysis using panel time-series techniques. We hope that this study will serve as a model for other such applications.

These results should be treated with caution. This is the first application of this methodology to analysis of not-for-profit enterprises and culture production. The techniques used have been applied to examine impacts of infrastructure and other types of public sector production in several different economies, so their application in this context is reasonable. As we move forward to explore their use in this context, it is important to check the data carefully and make adjustments for common factors that might affect all urban areas and make it difficult to isolate the separate impacts of culture production. Despite the need for caution in interpretation, we are encouraged by these results. They suggest that arts and culture production makes a difference not just because of a short-run multiplier effect but also because of its capacity to affect steady-state income levels. Properly tested, validated, and applied, the methods that we describe and demonstrate can serve as a useful guide in policymaking and allocating scarce resources.

Notes

1. Virginia Lee Owen, "The Economic Legacy of Gothic Cathedral Building: France and England Compared," *Journal of Cultural Economics,* vol. 13, no. 1 (1989), pp. 89–100.

2. Brighita Bercea, Robert B. Ekelund, and Robert D. Tollison, "Cathedral Building as an Entry-Deterring Device," *Kyklos,* vol. 58, no. 4 (2005), pp. 453–65.

3. UNCTAD, *Creative Economy Report 2008* (Geneva, Switzerland: United Nations Conference on Trade and Development, 2008).

4. Charles Lawton and Charles Colgan, *New England's Creative Economy: Nonprofit Sector Impact* (Boston: New England Foundation for the Arts, 2011).

5. Gregory H. Wassall, *Arts, Cultural, and Humanities Organizations in the New England Economy: 1996* (Boston: New England Foundation for the Arts, 1997).

6. Richard Florida, "Bohemia and Economic Geography," *Journal of Economic Geography,* vol. 2, no. 1 (2002), pp. 55–71; Richard Florida, *The Rise of the Creative Class* (New York: Basic Books, 2002); Richard Florida, Charlotta Mellander, and Kevin Stolarick, "Inside the Black Box of Regional Development: Human Capital, the Creative Class, and Tolerance," *Journal of Economic Geography,* vol. 8, no. 5 (2008), pp. 615–49.

7. Ann Markusen and others, "Defining the Creative Economy: Industry and Occupational Approaches," *Economic Development Quarterly,* vol. 22, no. 1 (2008), pp. 24–45.

8. Bruce A. Seaman, "Arts Impact Studies: A Fashionable Excess," in *Economic Impact of the Arts: A Sourcebook*, edited by Anthony Radich and Sharon Schwoch (Washington: National Conference of State Legislatures, 1987).

9. Many small communities expressed concern when, in the early days of the recession of 2008–10, the major U.S. automobile companies announced the closure of more than 3,000 dealerships. Nevertheless, few would argue that a policy of encouraging or supporting more car dealers would promote economic growth.

10. Kevin F. McCarthy and others, *Gifts of the Muse: Reframing the Debate about the Benefits of the Arts* (Santa Monica, Calif.: RAND Corporation, 2004).

11. David Canning and Peter Pedroni, "Infrastructure, Long-Run Economic Growth, and Causality Tests for Cointegrated Panels," *Manchester School,* vol. 76, no. 5 (2008), pp. 504–27.

12. Robert J. Barro, "Government Spending in a Simple Model of Endogenous Growth," *Journal of Political Economy,* vol. 98, no. 5 (1990), pp. S103–S125.

13. Robert J. Barro and Xavier Sala-i-Martin, *Economic Growth* (MIT Press, 2003).

14. Peter Pedroni and Stephen Sheppard, "Culture Shocks and Consequences: The Connection between the Arts and Urban Economic Growth," Williams College Working Paper (2012).

15. If there were no random fluctuations, then setting $\bar{\tau} = \beta/(\alpha + \beta)$ would maximize income *per capita.*

16. See Canning and Pedroni, "Infrastructure, Long-Run Economic Growth, and Causality Tests for Cointegrated Panels," Proposition 1.

17. Office of Management and Budget, *Update of Statistical Area Definitions and Guidance on Their Uses,* technical report (Washington: 2009).

18. See Canning and Pedroni, "Infrastructure, Long-Run Economic Growth, and Causality Tests for Cointegrated Panels," Proposition 2.

19. Peter Pedroni, "Critical Values for Cointegration Tests in Heterogeneous Panels with Multiple Regressors," *Oxford Bulletin of Economics and Statistics,* vol. 61, no. S1 (1999), pp. 653–70; Peter Pedroni, "Purchasing Power Parity Tests in Cointegrated Panels," *Review of Economics and Statistics,* vol. 83, no. 4 (2001), pp. 727–31; Peter Pedroni, "Fully Modified OLS for Heterogeneous Cointegrated Panels," Elgar Reference Collection, *International Library of Critical Writings in Econometrics,* vol. 9 (2002), pp. 424–61.

20. See Pedroni and Sheppard, "Culture Shocks and Consequences."

HASAN BAKHSHI, NEIL LEE, *and* JUAN MATEOS-GARCIA

10

Capital of Culture? An Econometric Analysis of the Relationship between Arts and Cultural Clusters, Wages, and the Creative Economy in English Cities

The scale of public investment in arts and cultural clusters in recent decades suggests that policymakers consider the arts and cultural sector to be an important component of the infrastructure that makes their cities better able to innovate, compete, and grow. There is empirical evidence of a strong correlation between arts and cultural clustering on the one hand and the economic performance of cities on the other.[1]

At first sight, the 2010 data for English cities presented in figure 10-1 support this view, showing a positive relationship between clustering of cultural employment (as measured by the location quotient for a city's employment in the cultural industries) and average hourly wages.[2] According to these data, workers in English cities in the 90th percentile of cultural employment clustering earned on average hourly wages of $19.29, $1.54 higher than the average wage for cities in the 10th percentile.

What happens to this relationship when we control for other characteristics of individuals and cities? What are the connections between arts and cultural clusters and the performance of their counterparts in the commercial and digital creative industries? This chapter seeks to advance our understanding of these issues in the following ways:

It draws on past research on local wage premiums to build an econometric model that tests the robustness of the relationships between arts and cultural clustering along three dimensions (occupational, industrial, and institutional) and worker wages in English cities.

We focus on England to help redress existing geographical imbalances in the empirical literature in this area, which until now has mostly

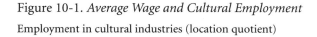

Figure 10-1. *Average Wage and Cultural Employment*

Employment in cultural industries (location quotient)

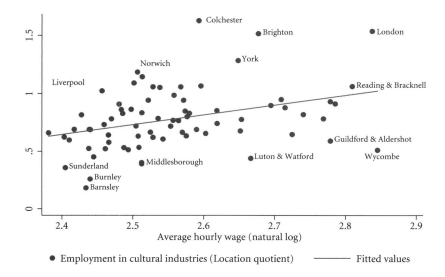

Source: Authors' calculations using 2010 Annual Population Survey (APS) and Business Register and Employment Survey (BRES) data.

been concerned with the United States. In so doing, we help to ascertain the generalizability of the U.S. results to other places where the arts and cultural industries may play a different role in urban development.[3] In this sense, it should be seen as a complement to chapters 7 and 9 in this volume, which examine similar issues with U.S. data.

We also explore the relative significance and magnitude of the relationship between different metrics of arts and cultural clustering and local economic performance as well as the interactions between arts and cultural clusters and creative industry clusters. By doing this, we aim to shed some light on the mechanisms through which arts and cultural agglomeration may contribute to local economic performance and on the relationships between different parts of the local creative economy—important issues for urban development policymakers in need of a better understanding of the interactions within their local ecosystem of creativity.[4] (These issues are also examined in chapters 7 and 3 in this volume.)

Literature Review

Arts and culture have appeared under different guises in the work of economists and economic geographers seeking to explain the spatial division of labor and geographical differences in wages, economic growth, and innovative activity. Here we overview two strands of literature that have studied the arts and culture as amenities and as sources of spillovers, respectively. We pay particular attention to what they have to tell us about the relationship between arts and cultural clustering and wages, the dependent variable in the econometric model that we specify and estimate in this chapter.

The Arts and Culture as Local Amenities

Economists studying migrations (mostly within the United States) as well as spatial differences in wages (also referred to as "urban wage premiums," such as those caused by human capital externalities in dense urban areas) have proposed that individuals balance a menu of factors when choosing among different locations in which to live and work.[5] In addition to purely economic factors (the demand for labor, going wages, and housing prices), they consider other characteristics of localities, which may act as amenities (for example, good weather) or disamenities (for example, crime). One could think of them as dimensions of the quality of life in a given place.

In this strand of literature, arts and culture are introduced as amenities—in other words, models assume that individuals are willing to sacrifice higher wages (or are willing to pay higher housing costs) for the opportunity to live in locations that have rich and varied arts and cultural offerings. That assumption means that, other variables being held equal, places with strong arts and cultural clusters should also offer lower average wages.[6] Recent studies on the rise of the "consumer city" describe museums, theaters, and other forms of commercial entertainment as important drivers of migration inside U.S. cities over the last two decades—in addition to what could be expected from improvements in productivity (and therefore higher wages) or decreases in crime (the prototypical urban disamenity).[7]

The Arts and Culture as Sources of Spillovers

Other researchers have argued that the arts and culture have a positive impact on local productivity (and therefore increase wages) and have specified various mechanisms through which that happens. We first outline the influential "creative cities" thesis advocated by Richard Florida and afterward summarize other, arguably more "active," ways in which the arts and culture may contribute to local productivity.

Creative Cities and the Creative Class

Perhaps the most influential account of—and program of research on—the role of the arts and culture in urban development is Richard Florida's "creative cities" thesis.[8] While his description of arts and culture bears a resemblance to the amenities view summarized above, Florida emphasizes migration by a "creative class" of professionals with high human capital who contribute to urban development through their entrepreneurialism and the inward investment that they attract from innovative businesses. Several studies within this framework show a positive connection between local arts and culture and local wages.[9]

This view of the role of the arts and culture in urban development has had a significant impact on local policymakers and has informed investments in "creative placemaking" through construction of distinctive "signature buildings," creation of dedicated cultural quarters and districts, and profile-raising activities such as urban branding and marketing events.[10]

The Arts and Culture as Sources of Innovation

Arts and cultural clusters have been argued to generate other positive spillovers that boost productivity—and therefore wages—in the local economy,[11] including investments in creative human capital (a labor force with skill sets and attitudes that are conducive to innovation and can improve the productivity of employees outside of the arts and cultural sector), organizational capital (ideas for innovative ways of working that can be adopted by others), and network capital (milieus that are more conducive to knowledge sharing and collaboration).[12] What is perhaps even more significant, but in a way that is harder to measure, is that the arts and cultural sector produces "expressive value"—for example, new artistic movements and aesthetic values and symbols that, it is argued, are adopted (and commercialized) by other industries.[13]

The literature suggests that spillovers such as these tend to take "short leaps," spatially as well as sectorally, because innovations and skills are more likely to be transferable between organizations that draw on similar knowledge bases.[14] One important implication of that finding is that any spillovers originating in arts and cultural clusters are likely to be most beneficial for "cognitively close" commercial creative firms and professionals.[15] That is also consistent with the "concentric circles" model of the creative economy proposed by David Throsby, which places the arts and cultural sector at the core of the creative value chain, generating "expressive value," which is then commercialized by other creative industries and eventually transferred into the wider economy through "creative innovation services" such as advertising and design.[16]

Some examples of the synergies within the "local ecosystem of creativity" (that is, between the generally nonprofit arts and cultural sector and commercial creative industries) include the crossover of ideas between artists, fashion designers, and musicians documented by Elizabeth Currid in her study of New York's "Warhol Economy," Adam Arvidsson's description of how advertisers leverage Copenhagen's artistic and cultural scene in their marketing campaigns, and the propensity for graduates of University of the Arts London to seek employment in London's creative industries.[17]

The State of the Evidence and Its Limitations

Arts and culture have received less careful attention than other amenities (and disamenities) in studies of general spatial equilibrium and urban wage premiums such as those that we touched on above. In those studies, arts and culture have been often operationalized with counts of cultural buildings (for example, museums, theaters, opera houses), which may measure only imperfectly the real strength of arts and cultural clusters and their contribution to productivity.[18]

Several studies looking specifically at the role of arts and culture as sources of spillovers, primarily within the creative cities framework, have identified significant relationships between urban economic performance and arts and cultural clusters (measured through "bohemian" indices calculated by using occupational data) in terms of income, wages, and patenting intensity, after controlling for the level of education in the local workforce and other relevant variables.[19]

These studies do, however, present two important limitations. First, they typically use cross-sectional data and therefore fail to address convincingly the possibility of endogeneity bias (the possibility that arts and cultural practitioners may be attracted to affluent and innovative places instead of generating affluence and innovation themselves).[20]

Second, they do not fully open the "black box" of creative economic development by examining the relative significance and magnitude of the different mechanisms through which arts and cultural clusters may contribute to urban growth and innovation or the extent to which different measures of arts and cultural clustering (such as occupations versus industries) are more strongly related to innovation and economic growth. Yet recent empirical studies of the geographic distribution of artistic and cultural occupations and industries have shown that artists and artistic sectors do not always cluster in the same places because large numbers of workers in those sectors are not artists themselves—and artists and cultural practitioners frequently work outside the arts and cultural sector.[21]

Establishing which—if any—mechanisms (attraction of creative professionals or innovation spillovers) and what types of cluster (occupations versus industries) play a stronger role in urban development would help policymakers prioritize scarce resources between competing arts and cultural initiatives (for example, networking versus urban branding) and guide their choice of policy goals.[22]

Methodology

According to our literature review, the direction of the relationship between arts and cultural clustering and worker wages in the cities where clusters are located tells us something about he economic role of such clusters, whether as amenities and/or as a source of spillovers. Here we present the model and data that we used to estimate this relationship.

The Model

We adapted Mincer's classic model of wages to test the impact of different measures of arts and cultural clustering on worker wages.[23] This simple model estimates individual wages as a function of personal and city characteristics (with the latter including measures of arts and cultural clustering). The model is estimated as follows, for individual i in city c:

$$(1) \quad lnWage_{ic} = \alpha + \beta_1 Individual_{ic} + \beta_2 City_c + \beta_3 Region_c + \varepsilon_{ic}$$

In this equation, *Individual* comprises a vector of individual characteristics including education, ethnicity, and migration status; *City* comprises characteristics of the city in England where the individual works, which (a very important point) include measures of arts and cultural clustering; *Region* denotes a set of Government Office Region dummies to control for wider characteristics of the region where the city is located; and ε is the residual.

The motivation for this model is straightforward: the sign of the coefficient between our measure of arts and cultural clustering and wages, after we control for other relevant individual and city characteristics, indicates whether there is a *compensating differential* for living in cities with stronger arts and cultural clustering (if the coefficient is negative) or a *cultural city wage premium* (if the coefficient is positive). The first result would be consistent with the idea that arts and cultural clustering is a local consumer good whose presence "compensates" for lower wages—that is, it acts as a local amenity. The second result would mean that, on average, workers in cities with strong cultural clusters are paid higher wages than we would expect given other individual and city characteristics. Such wage premiums are generally interpreted in the literature as indicative of higher productivity, in this case associated with the strength of arts and cultural clustering. Of course, both effects could be at play in the data; the coefficient tells only us which of the two is stronger.

By constructing our different measures of arts and cultural clustering in a consistent manner, we can also do a straightforward comparison of the sign, relative significance, and strength of their relationship with worker wages.

Before continuing, we should note two important limitations of the model. First, it does not identify shifts in the labor demand curve from the labor supply curve, which jointly determine wages. That is, while a positive coefficient on arts and cultural clustering is consistent with an increase in labor demand caused by higher productivity in cultural clusters, it could also reflect a lower labor supply (say, if arts and cultural clustering acts for some reason as an urban disamenity in the same way as congestion or crime). Reciprocally, a negative coefficient on arts and cultural clustering could be capturing a greater labor supply in cultural clusters (due to the local consumption aspects of arts and culture, which increases its attractiveness for workers) or weaker demand for labor, as if arts and cultural clustering was detrimental for worker productivity.

In stark terms, each of our two possible results can be interpreted in two alternative ways that have very different economic implications. Bearing this problem in mind, we focus, for the rest of the chapter, on the two interpretations of our coefficients (amenities rather than disamenities; positive rather than negative spillovers) that are more intuitive and better evidenced by the literature (including chapters 7 and 9 in this volume).

Even after doing that, we face a second limitation in that our model uses cross-sectional data—the significance and magnitude of the coefficients on arts and cultural clustering tell us nothing about the direction of *causality* between wages and arts and cultural clustering. For instance, while one possible interpretation of a positive coefficient is that the presence of a strong cultural cluster generates innovation spillovers, making workers in the city more productive, it may also be that highly productive, innovative, and affluent places attract—or support more effectively—arts and cultural organizations and/or practitioners.

Spatial Unit of Analysis

We conduct our analysis at the level of the U.K. "travel to work area" (TTWA). TTWAs are defined according to the 2001 U.K. census to be as close as possible to self-contained local labor markets in the United Kingdom.[24] They are defined to have a minimum "self-containment" of 75 percent, meaning that at least 75 percent of residents both live and work in the area. TTWAs are now the standard for subnational analysis in the United Kingdom.[25]

There are 168 TTWAs in our sample, representing both urban and rural TTWAs. As many of the theoretical predictions are most relevant for urban areas, we focus our testing on individuals working in the 74 urban TTWAs defined by Gibbons and others; they have an overlap with a population center of at least 100,000 inhabitants.[26] We henceforth describe these 74 TTWAs as our "cities."

Data

We drew our variables from three datasets: the Annual Population Survey (APS), the Business Register Employment Survey (BRES), and a unique dataset of cultural institutions that have registered their details on the Culture 24 (C24) platform. See table 10-1 for a summary of the variables and their sources. Our main source of data is the 2010 APS. The APS is a large-scale sample survey in the United Kingdom, covering around 300,000 people. Respondents are asked questions about their wages, labor market participation, and personal characteristics, such as their educational qualifications. As we are interested in labor market issues, we restrict our focus to observations of individuals of normal working age (16 through 64 years). We use the APS to construct both individual-level variables and city-level controls. Responses to the APS are available at the level of local authorities (LA) rather than TTWAs. Following other studies that have used these data, we allocated individuals from the LA to the TTWA level by using a probabalistic allocation method.[27]

Independent Variable (Wages)

Our measure of wages is the logarithm of the average hourly wage for individuals, calculated in the APS from the gross annual wage and the average hours worked per week. This data source may contain some extreme observations, which previous work has suggested is measurement error.[28] To deal with that, we removed observations with extremely low hourly pay (less than £1, for which there were 135 observations) and high hourly pay (greater than £100, for

Table 10-1. *Variable List*

Domain	Variable	Description	Source
Wages	Hourly pay (natural log)	Log of hourly pay	APS
Cultural and creative clustering	Cultural employment	Share of employment in cultural sectors (location quotient)	BRES
	Creative employment	Share of employment in the creative industries, excluding cultural employment (location quotient)	BRES
	Cultural institutions	Culture 24 venues per capita (location quotient)	C24
	Creative occupations	Share of the workforce in creative industries occupations (Location quotient)	APS
	Cultural occupations	Share of workers in cultural occupations (location quotient)	APS
Individual controls	Male	Whether individual is male (1) or female (0)	APS
	Experience	Years since leaving education	APS
	Experience^2	Years since leaving education, squared	APS
	Non-white	If individual is not of white ethnicity (1)	APS
	Not UK born	If individual was not born in the United Kingdom (1)	APS
	Part-time	If individual works part time (1)	APS
	Public	If self-reports as public sector worker (1)	APS
	Occupation	Nine standard occupation dummies	APS
	NVQ 0–5	One of five NVQ qualification dummies	APS
City controls (using other sources)	Population	Log of total 2010 population, calculated from local authority figures using Geoconvert	Mid-year population estimates
	NVQ4–5	Share of workforce in TTWA with NVQ4 and above	APS
	Region	One of four regional/London dummies (South, London, North, Midlands)	–

Source: Authors' compilation.

which there were 70 observations). As our data are for hourly pay, we include data for all workers regardless of total hours worked. There may still be a part-time wage penalty for part-time workers, and so in the wage regressions we used a part-time dummy variable to control for that possibility.

Individual-Level Characteristics

We controlled for relevant individual characteristics too, including experience in the labor market, measured as the number of years since an individual left full-time education (experience), and its square (experience^2); gender; and ethnicity (whether an individual was of white ethnicity). We also controlled for skills, an important determinant of labor productivity and therefore wages.[29] Since we did not have data on individual skills, we used educational qualifications as a proxy, measured by "national vocational qualification" (NVQ) levels, which are standardized measures—set out by the U.K. Department for Business, Innovation, and Skills—of the respondents' educational qualifications. In this framework, NVQ 4 and 5 are roughly equivalent to the undergraduate degree level. The base category (zero) indicates no qualifications; each subsequent qualification level, other things being equal, was expected to have a higher impact on wages.

Finally, we included variables for the nine standard occupational measures in the APS (capturing the occupation reported by an individual). There are collinearity issues in models that include both occupation and the industry in which an individual works, so we did not include both variables; we left only one. As there is evidence of a public sector wage premium in the United Kingdom, we also included a dummy variable for whether an individual worked in the public sector.[30]

City-Level Variables

We controlled for city-level characteristics that could influence wages, including population size (which we include log-transformed in order to account for potential urban wage premiums in densely populated areas), share of the population with high qualifications (that is, the proportion of APS respondents with an NVQ level of 4 or higher) to control for potential human capital externalities, and the Government Office Region for each respondent.[31]

Indicators of Cultural and Creative Clustering

We used three types of data to measure arts and cultural clustering and creative clustering in a city: occupations, employment, and institutions. Within each of these measures, we distinguished between "the arts and culture" (which constitutes the main focus of this study) and the commercial "creative industries" (which the literature suggests could be significant beneficiaries of arts and cultural spillovers).

In all cases, we used these data to construct location quotients (LQs), a standard measure of clustering used in economic geography. We calculated location quotients as the ratio between the share of a given variable (for example, employment in a sector or number of people in a given occupation) in a city and the share of the same variable in England overall. Location quotients measure the importance of a sector or occupation in the economy of a given city relative to the national average. LQs above 1 indicate above-average levels of specialization (that is, clustering), while LQs below 1 indicate below-average levels of specialization. For consistency, we constructed the LQ for cultural institutions in a city by dividing its number of cultural institutions per capita by the national average.

EMPLOYMENT CLUSTERING. We built our location quotients of employment clustering in the "arts and cultural" and "creative" sectors in a city (henceforth referred to as "cultural employment" and "creative employment," respectively) using sectoral employment data from the Business Register and Employment Survey (BRES). BRES is an annual survey of U.K. businesses carried out by the U.K. Office for National Statistics (ONS). The BRES sample (80,000 for the 2010 edition, which we used) is randomly drawn from the Interdepartmental Business Register (IDBR), which covers all U.K. businesses registered for value-added tax (VAT) and/or for pay-as-you-earn (PAYE) tax; it captures 99 percent of U.K. economic activity.[32]

In order to build our measure of cultural employment clustering, we used the 2007 standard industrial classification (SIC) codes for the performing arts used by the U.K. Department for Culture, Media, and Sports (DCMS) in its 2011 update of the Creative Industries Statistics, together with the SIC code for "libraries, archives, museums, and other cultural activities," including botanical and zoological gardens and nature reserves (SIC code 91 for the year 2007).[33] This code differs from the definition of the cultural industries used elsewhere in that it excludes from our measure of arts and culture a number of subsectors that produce creative content (as well as creative services, such as advertising or design) to be sold in the market.[34] Instead, we tried to focus on those activities lying in the core of the concentric circles model of the creative economy and those within the scope of public arts funding organizations such as Arts Council England.[35]

Our measure of creative employment clustering uses the SIC codes in the 2011 DCMS operational definition of the creative industries, excluding the

SIC codes for cultural sectors that we have included in our measure of cultural employment described above. Thus, our measure of creative industry clustering captures employment in advertising, architecture, arts markets and antiques, design, designer fashion, film, video and photography, music, publishing, software and electronic publishing, leisure software, and radio and television in English cities.[36]

OCCUPATIONAL CLUSTERING. We built our location quotients of arts and cultural and creative occupational clustering (henceforth referred to as "cultural occupations" and "creative occupations," respectively) in a given city by using data from the APS. In order to measure arts and cultural occupations, we adapted a previous definition to ensure comparability with our measure of cultural employment,[37] which consists of the following occupations: librarians; archivists and curators; artists; authors and writers; actors and entertainers; dancers and choreographers; musicians; arts officers, producers, and directors; conservation and environmental protection officers; and library assistants/clerks. For our location quotients of creative occupations, we used the standard occupational classification (SOC) codes set out in the 2011 update of the DCMS operational definition of the creative industries.[38]

Note that sample sizes are relatively small for most cities using these occupational measures; we therefore are careful to validate them by correlating them with other measures (see below).

INSTITUTIONAL CLUSTERING. We built our location quotients for cultural institution clustering in English cities by using a unique dataset provided by Culture 24, a nonprofit organization based in Brighton, England, that collects, curates, and shares cultural information online from arts and cultural venues throughout the United Kingdom. The data we used is a self-selected list of cultural institutions, including museums, public galleries, libraries, archives, heritage sites, and science centers in the United Kingdom.

We extracted the details of 4,971 English institutions from the Culture 24 database of venues as of February 2012. Each has a postcode, through which we allocated it to a city (with the exception of sixty observations for which that information was not available and which therefore were dropped). The final sample included 4,911 institutions. We used the latest government population estimates to create an indicator of "cultural institutions per capita" in each of our cities. We divided those by the number of cultural institutions per capita for England to produce location quotients of cultural institution agglomeration at the city level.

ROBUSTNESS. In order to test the reliability of the (self-selecting) Culture 24 data and the small sample of cultural and creative occupations data, we explored the correlations between the location quotients that we derived from them and those for cultural and creative employment clustering. Table 10-2 reports these pairwise correlations, along with city size and the average qualifications of the population. As the table shows, the Culture 24 data are positively and significantly correlated with three other measures of cultural and creative clustering: cultural occupations, cultural employment, and creative employment. The size of the coefficients is as expected (that is, larger for cultural measures than for creative ones), which gives us some confidence in the Culture 24 indicator as a meaningful measure of arts and cultural clustering in English cities.[39] Similarly, our cultural occupations LQs correlate closely at the city level with the other measures of creative employment.

Results and Discussion

Here we present the estimates of our models of wages using different measures of arts and cultural clustering and our individual- and city-level controls and look at the impacts of creative clustering (in terms of industries as well as employment) on urban wages. We then look at the interactions between arts and cultural clustering and creative industries wages in order to explore the possibility that spillovers that are not visible for the local economy overall may in fact be present between the arts and cultural and related commercial creative sectors, as discussed in our literature review. We conclude by discussing the robustness of our results to different specifications and controls, including housing prices at the city level.

Results from Estimating the Model

We estimated each model in table 10-3 using ordinary least squares, with wages as the dependent variable (excluding cultural practitioners and workers) and independent variables for individual characteristics, city characteristics, and measures of arts and cultural clustering.[40] Columns 1–3 display the basic results, including the variables for arts and cultural clustering, without controls, which confirm the results that we presented in figure 10-1 at the beginning of the chapter: cities with stronger cultural clusters tend to have higher average wages. Columns 4–6 include a set of individual controls. The effect of the cultural cluster measures changes dramatically. Cultural occupation clustering remains positive and significantly related to wages (though

Table 10-2. Correlation Matrix for City Characteristics[a]

Variable	Cultural occupations	Cultural employment	Cultural institutions	Creative employment	Creative occupations	City skills	Population
Cultural occupations	1.0000						
Cultural employment	0.3258***	1.0000					
	(0.0046)						
Cultural institutions (C24)	0.2724**	0.4728***	1.0000				
	(0.0189)	(0.0000)					
Creative employment	0.4693***	0.3843***	0.2324**	1.0000			
	(0.0000)	(0.0007)	(0.046)				
Creative occupations	0.4580***	0.2382	0.2461	0.6402***)	1.0000		
	(0.000)	(0.0410)	(0.0346)	(0.000			
City skills	0.5206***	0.4494***	0.4473***	0.6626***	0.6394***	1.0000	
	(0.0000)	(0.0001)	(0.0001)	(0.000)	(0.000)		
Population (natural log)	0.2073*	0.1923	-0.0349	0.4721***	0.2951	0.2763*	1.0000
	(0.0763)	(0.1007)	(0.7679)	(0.000)	(0.107)	(0.0172)	

Source: Authors' calculations.

a. Observations: seventy-four cities. Significance in parentheses. ***$p < 0.01$, **$p < 0.05$, *$p < 0.1$.

Table 10-3. Cultural Economy and Wages, Individual-Level Regressions[a]

Variable	(1)	(2)	(3)	(4)	(5)	(6)	(7)	(8)	(9)
City									
Cultural occupations	0.181***	0.255***					0.00548		
	(0.00526)	(0.00851)					(0.00923)		
Cultural employment				0.0288***	-0.0241**			-0.0498***	
				(0.00800)	(0.00975)			(0.0106)	
Cultural institutions			0.172***			-0.0263***			-0.0500***
			(0.00835)			(0.00709)			(0.00750)
City skills							0.250***	0.329***	0.392***
							(0.0577)	(0.0548)	(0.0543)
Population (natural log)							0.0215***	0.0221***	0.0197***
							(0.00397)	(0.00395)	(0.00395)
Individual skills									
Level 2				-0.000741	-0.00110	-0.00107	-0.000702	-0.00105	-0.000956
				(0.00711)	(0.00710)	(0.00710)	(0.00710)	(0.00710)	(0.00710)
Level 3				0.0877***	0.0874***	0.0875***	0.0874***	0.0872***	0.0873***
				(0.00649)	(0.00650)	(0.00650)	(0.00649)	(0.00649)	(0.00649)
Level 4				0.258***	0.258***	0.259***	0.257***	0.257***	0.257***
				(0.00677)	(0.00677)	(0.00677)	(0.00677)	(0.00677)	(0.00677)
Level 5				0.385***	0.387***	0.387***	0.384***	0.384***	0.384***
				(0.00973)	(0.00973)	(0.00973)	(0.00974)	(0.00973)	(0.00973)
Constant	2.249***	2.222***	2.304***	1.992***	2.043***	2.032***	1.639***	1.652***	1.637***
	(0.00608)	(0.00788)	(0.00744)	(0.0186)	(0.0189)	(0.0170)	(0.0517)	(0.0511)	(0.0512)
Other individual controls	No	No	No	Yes	Yes	Yes	Yes	Yes	Yes
Region dummies	Yes	Yes	Yes	Yes	Yes	Yes	Yes	Yes	Yes
Occupation dummies	No	No	No	Yes	Yes	Yes	Yes	Yes	Yes
Observations	52,250	52,250	52,250	52,250	52,250	52,250	52,250	52,250	52,250
R^2	0.037	0.026	0.010	0.469	0.469	0.469	0.470	0.470	0.471

Source: Authors' calculations.

a. The reference category, level 1, is equivalent to secondary education qualification (average attainment); level 2 is equivalent to secondary education qualification (high attainment); level 3 is equivalent to pre-tertiary qualification (Advanced Study); level 4 is equivalent to vocational qualification (Higher National Diploma); level 5 is equivalent to tertiary education. See S. McIntosh and A. Vignoles, "Measuring and Assessing the Impact of Basic Skills on Labour Market Outcomes," Centre for the Economics of Education Report (London: LSE, 2000). Dependent variable: hourly wage (natural log), excluding workers in cultural industries and occupations. Estimated with OLS. Controls are four region and nine occupation dummies. Weights applied. Robust standard errors in parentheses. ***$p < 0.01$, **$p < 0.05$, *$p < 0.1$.

considerably smaller in magnitude) after we controlled for personal characteristics such as experience, skills, and occupation. However, for both the cultural employment and cultural institution measures, the signs switch to negative and the results are statistically significant.

Columns 7–9 include other city-level variables that could influence individual wages. As expected, both the proportion of the population with high qualifications (NVQ level 4 and above) and population size have positive coefficients and are significantly associated with wages. They also have consequences for the estimated effects of the arts and cultural clustering variables: cultural occupations still has a positive sign, but it is no longer significant, whereas cultural employment and cultural institutions as measured by the Culture 24 data remain negative and significant.

This set of results supports the idea of a *compensating differential* in English "artistic and cultural" cities: that is, for a given set of individual characteristics, critically including skills, English workers appear to be willing to sacrifice higher wages in exchange for living in cities with strong art and culture offerings, which act as an amenity. Since cultural institutions and cultural employment (that is, people working in arts and cultural organizations) measures appear to be better proxies for those offerings than cultural occupation clustering (which also captures cultural practitioners working outside the arts and cultural sector), we would have expected any compensating differentials to be more visible in the case of the former two variables, and that is indeed what we found.

As discussed, our findings do not rule out the existence of positive spillovers—a labor demand phenomenon—but if there are such spillovers, it does mean that there is a labor supply effect (which we interpret as a compensating differential) that more than offsets the effect of the spillovers on wages.

Creative Industries and Wages

Table 10-4 includes measures of clustering in the commercial creative industries (both in terms of occupations and employment) to our baseline model, retaining all the individual and city controls we used in the baseline. Columns 1–3 respectively pair the results for creative and cultural occupations, creative employment and cultural employment, and creative employment and cultural institution measures.

The main results for the cultural cluster variables change little: the measure based on cultural occupations remains insignificant, while the measures based on cultural employment and the Culture 24 data stay negative and

Table 10-4. *Creative Economy and Wages*[a]

Variable	(1)	(2)	(3)
Cultural occupations	-0.0134		
	(0.00971)		
Creative occupations	0.0809***		
	(0.0106)		
Cultural employment		-0.0489***	
		(0.0108)	
Creative employment		0.0292**	0.0213*
		(0.0119)	(0.0118)
Cultural institutions			-0.0472***
			(0.00753)
Constant	1.370***	1.369***	1.350***
	(0.0603)	(0.0607)	(0.0610)
Controls	Yes	Yes	Yes
Observations	48,634	48,634	48,634
R^2	0.473	0.472	0.472

Source: Authors' calculations.

a. Dependent variable: hourly pay (natural log) excluding workers in creative/cultural occupations and industries. Estimated using OLS. Controls are four region dummies (including London), nine occupation dummies, NVQ 1–5, experience, experience2, ethnicity, migration status, part-time employment, public sector employment, city population, and city qualifications. Weights applied. Robust standard errors in parentheses. ***$p < 0.01$, **$p < 0.05$, *$p < 0.1$.

significant. However, it should be noted that the coefficients on the creative clustering measures, unlike cultural clusters, are positive and significant, which is consistent with the idea of positive spillovers from the commercial creative industries into the wider urban economy.

Cultural Economy

As highlighted in the literature review, it could be that the spillover benefits—in terms of higher productivity and wages—from strong arts and cultural clustering are primarily captured by people in cultural and creative occupations and industries. If so, we would expect to see the impacts of cultural clusters on cultural and creative wages to be higher than the city average.

We tested that possibility with a regression model that includes all the control variables used in table 10-4, a variable for whether an individual works in a creative or cultural occupation (those in creative or cultural occupations are, in this case, excluded from the standard occupational dummies that we used as controls throughout), and interaction terms between the occupation and the strength of arts and cultural clustering in the city. A positive result for these interactions would indicate that those in cultural or creative occupations earn higher relative wages in cities with strong arts and cultural clustering. The results of our estimations are presented in table 10-5. Columns 1–3 consider how wages for those in cultural occupations vary, while those in columns 4–6 wages look at workers in creative occupations.

Table 10-5 shows that after we control for education and other personal characteristics, those in cultural occupations earn significantly less than those in other occupations. Further, the results suggest a positive wage effect from urban clustering on wages in cultural occupations. Each of the three interaction terms with the city-level culture variables is positive, although only one—the interaction between "being in a cultural occupation" and "living in a city with a strong cluster of arts and cultural institutions"—is significant.

Looking at the results for people in (commercial) creative occupations, we find, after controlling for their skills and other individual characteristics, that they earn more than people in other occupations. We also find some evidence of spillovers from arts and cultural clustering into the wider creative economy—the coefficient in the interaction terms is positive for all measures of arts and cultural clustering, though again only the measure for cultural institutions is significant. Our interpretation is that those working in creative occupations in cities with high concentrations of cultural institutions tend to earn higher wages.

In short, these results are consistent with the idea of a positive effect of arts and cultural clustering on the productivity of cultural and creative workers. In this respect, although any innovation spillovers originated by arts and cultural clusters would be contained within the "creative economy" of arts and cultural and creative industries and workers, they could still conceivably flow indirectly into the wider local economy through the activities of more commercially oriented creative industries. That is because we have estimated a positive relationship between creative clustering and city wages, supporting the existence of innovation spillovers from creative workers into other sectors. Think, for example, of a web designer who uses the visual language of a painter exhibiting at a local art gallery in her redesign of the website for a local client, an ad agency that uses the "cultural capital" generated by local artists to produce a campaign for a client in the automobile industry (as related by Adam Arvidsson), or cultural districts that attract innovative media arts entrepreneurs, as shown in chapter 7 of this volume.

Testing the robustness of these findings and differentiating them from other explanations is a priority for further research. We need to be aware in

Table 10-5. *Cultural Economy and Wages for Cultural and Creative Occupations*[a]

Variable		(1)	(2)	(3)	(4)	(5)	(6)
Individual occupation	Cultural occupation	-0.312*** (0.0533)	-0.264*** (0.0397)	-0.274*** (0.0619)			
	Creative occupation				0.316*** (0.0338)	0.348*** (0.0250)	0.359*** (0.0313)
City economy measures	Cultural institutions	-0.0286*** (0.00709)			-0.0309*** (0.00710)		
	Cultural occupations		0.0209** (0.00815)			0.0178** (0.00822)	
	Cultural employment			-0.0312*** (0.00987)			-0.0320*** (0.00993)
Interaction terms	Cultural occupation * cultural institutions	0.0986* (0.0546)					
	Cultural occupation * cultural occupations		0.0304 (0.0275)				
	Cultural occupation * cultural employment			0.0530 (0.0563)			
	Cultural institutions * creative occupation				0.0710** (0.0344)		
	Creative occupation * cultural occupations					0.0252 (0.0168)	
	Creative occupation * cultural employment						0.0236 (0.0286)
	Constant	1.837*** (0.0604)	1.659*** (0.0513)	1.664*** (0.0507)	1.419*** (0.0600)	1.240*** (0.0507)	1.244*** (0.0501)
	Controls	Yes	Yes	Yes	Yes	Yes	Yes
	Observations	52,950	52,950	52,950	52,950	52,950	52,950
	R^2	0.467	0.467	0.467	0.465	0.465	0.465

Source: Authors' calculations.

a. Dependent variable: hourly pay (natural log), all workers. Estimated using OLS. Controls are four region dummies (including London), nine occupation dummies, NVQ 1–5, experience, experience[2], ethnicity, migration status, part-time employment, public sector employment, and city size. Weights applied. Robust standard errors in parentheses. ***$p < 0.01$, **$p < 0.05$, *$p < 0.1$.

particular of the possibility that arts and cultural clustering may be driven by market demand from well-paid creative professionals with high disposable incomes. However, the analysis of the relationships between commercial creative industries and nonprofit arts and culture in the Los Angeles and San Francisco regions presented in chapter 3 suggests that the causality need not go that way.

Other Robustness Checks

We subjected our model to further robustness checks, including variables such as ethnic diversity as well as the presence of cultural industries in the same locations as sectors with lower or higher wages than average (namely the manufacturing and public sectors), which could have biased our results. Overall, our main results appear to be robust to these alternative explanations.[41]

We also checked the effect of including housing prices in our model (as a proxy for housing costs); that is an important variable that is often considered together with wages in the literature.[42] If higher housing prices go hand in hand with strong arts and cultural clustering (perhaps as a consequence of gentrification), then our negative estimates of the coefficient on arts and cultural clustering would be biased. We would in fact be *underestimating* the magnitude of any arts and cultural compensating differentials, as the magnitude of the wage penalty that individuals would be willing to incur to live in cities with strong arts and cultural offerings (which also happen to have high housing prices) would be even higher than estimated. As it is, collinearity problems between city skill levels and city housing prices make it difficult for us to interpret changes in the coefficients on arts and cultural clustering once we include housing prices in our model. That makes it difficult for us to evaluate whether, once we introduce that important variable in our analysis, our interpretation of arts and culture as an urban amenity is strengthened or weakened. We do, however, note that our estimates when we do so remain in line with the results that we already reported, both in terms of sign and magnitude.[43]

Conclusions

In this chapter we explore the relationships between arts and cultural clustering and wages of workers in English cities, using three measures of arts and cultural clustering—cultural occupations, cultural sector employment, and cultural institutions—constructed respectively from official labor force and business registry survey data and a new dataset of almost 5,000 U.K. cultural institutions from the Culture 24 database.

First we sought to understand better the role of arts and culture in the economy of English cities—in particular, to evaluate their differential importance as a dimension of quality of life (that is, an urban amenity) and as a driver of productivity through innovation spillovers. When considering all workers and individual and city controls, our findings suggest that the urban amenity effects of arts and cultural clustering outweigh any innovation spillover effect. This finding is consistent with the idea of the "consumer city" where highly skilled individuals are willing to renounce higher wages in exchange for access to a rich offering of arts and culture. The fact that the sign and size of the coefficient in our measures of arts and cultural clustering mirror their intuitive validity as measures of the supply of arts and cultural goods, services, and experiences makes this interpretation appealing.

It is worth noting that this interpretation resembles Richard Florida's "creative cities" thesis, in that those highly skilled workers that he puts within the "creative class" appear to be attracted to cities with arts and cultural clusters. One could speculate that, over time, they will contribute with their skills to urban innovation and growth—in line with the findings of the human capital externalities literature and Florida's own claims—but that goes beyond the scope of our analysis here.

We also wanted to explore the interactions between nonprofit arts and cultural clusters and the commercial creative industries surrounding them. A number of qualitative studies, highlighted in our literature review, suggest that there is a strong degree of crossover and spillover between different parts of the local ecosystem of creativity, but quantitative evidence is thin. We have attempted to address this important (and policy relevant) gap in our analysis too.

Here, we find some evidence that creative workers in cities with high levels of artistic and cultural clustering do enjoy a wage premium, which is consistent with the idea that not-for-profit arts and cultural sectors may generate innovation spillovers into the commercial creative economy. Together with our estimation of a positive relationship between commercial creative clustering and wages in the urban economy overall, our results identify a potential spillover route—from the nonprofit arts and cultural sector into the commercial creative industries and from there into the wider economy—which warrants further investigation.

Our findings should be interpreted with caution, however, given the cross-sectional nature of our data and the ensuing risk of reverse causality between our relevant variables (in particular, creative worker wages and arts and cultural clustering). We also need to bear in mind those unobservable individual characteristics, such as creativity or entrepreneurialism, that may lead workers to select between different types of cities and may bias our results. Addressing these weaknesses with longitudinal data is a high priority for further research.

We also have mentioned the difficulties in identifying the consumption and production effects of arts and cultural clustering on wages, which led us to exclude some potential interpretations of our coefficients on a primarily theoretical rather than empirical basis. That is certainly undesirable. It could be addressed by using other datasets that include housing costs at the individual level, another potentially fruitful avenue for further research.

With all of these limitations in mind, we find our results to be broadly supportive of the view that there is a relationship between arts and cultural clustering and urban development. However, the relationship does appear to be subtler than is usually acknowledged. In particular, the economic impact of public investment in urban arts and cultural infrastructure may be manifest in improvements in the productivity (and wages) of creative professionals and may not be associated with higher wages in the wider economy if cultural activities serve as a compensating differential for skilled workers. This apparent complementarity between nonprofit arts and cultural clusters and the creative (and digital) industries in English cities should caution urban development policymakers against adopting a dichotomous view of their creative economy wherein nonprofit activities are seen as, at best, drivers of tourism and urban branding, while creative firms are seen as the ones that drive productivity and innovation (this may be influenced by the export base view of urban development criticized in chapter 3).

Our results support the idea that arts and cultural clusters could have impacts on the economy of English cities that go beyond tourism and urban branding—first, by attracting skilled individuals for lower wages, as the compensating differentials that we have identified suggest; second, by forming an active part of the local ecosystem of creativity in which intangible investments in skills, organizational and social capital, and new ideas make an economic contribution in the shape of innovation spillovers to for-profit creative firms. Obtaining further evidence of the robustness and magnitude of these spillovers and determining why arts and cultural clusters do not manage to capture all the external benefits that they generate—that is, why there are market failures in local ecosystems of creativity—are important topics for the research agenda going forward.

Notes

1. Brian Knudsen and others, "Density and Creativity in U.S. Regions," *Annals of the Association of American Geographers*, vol. 98, no. 2 (2008), pp. 461–78; Richard Florida, Charlotte Mellander, and Kevin Stolarick, "Inside the Black Box of Regional Development: Human Capital, the Creative Class, and Tolerance," *Journal of Economic Geography*, vol. 8, no. 5 (2008), pp. 615–49.

2. The data sources and definitions underpinning this figure are presented in detail below.

3. Robert C. Kloosterman, "This Is Not America: Embedding the Cognitive-Cultural Urban Economy," *Geografiska Annaler: Series B, Human Geography*, vol. 92, no. 2 (2010), pp. 131–43.

4. Our focus on the economic impacts of the arts and culture on local development and on the economic rationales for public investment in arts and culture should not be read as suggesting that economic impacts are the only impacts that the arts and culture have or that economic rationales are the only rationales for supporting arts and culture. In this sense, we subscribe to Ann Markusen and Greg Schrock's impassionate acknowledgment of the artistic and cultural benefits beyond the "artistic dividend." See Ann Markusen and Greg Schrock, "The Artistic Dividend: Urban Artistic Specialisation and Economic Development Implications," *Urban Studies*, vol. 43, no. 10) (2006), pp. 1661–86.

5. For a summary and critique of the general spatial equilibrium underpinning much of this research, see Thomas Kemeny and Michael Storper, "The Sources of Urban Development: Wages, Housing, and Amenity Gaps across American Cities," *Journal of Regional Science*, vol. 52, no. 1 (2012), pp.85–108. For a literature review of urban wage premiums and human capital externalities within this framework, see Benedikt Halfdanarson, Daniel F. Heuermann, and Jens Suedekum, "Human Capital Externalities and the Urban Wage Premium: Two Literatures and Their Interrelations," IZA Working Paper 3493 (Bonn, Germany: 2008).

6. Otherwise they would attract an influx of migrants, pushing wages down (or bidding housing costs up).

7. Edward L. Glaeser and Joshua D. Gottlieb, "Urban Resurgence and the Consumer City," Harvard Institute of Economic Research Discussion Paper 2109 (2006).

8. Richard Florida, *The Rise of the Creative Class* (New York: Basic Books, 2002).

9. Florida, Mellander, and Stolarick, "Inside the Black Box of Regional Development."

10. Simon Roodhouse, "Cultural Quarters: Principles and Practice" (Bristol, U.K.: Intellect, 2006).

11. Markusen and Schrock, "The Artistic Dividend"; Caroline Chapain and others, "Creative Clusters and Innovation" (London: NESTA, 2010) (www.nesta.org.uk/areas_of_work/creative_economy/assets/features/creative_clusters_and_innovation_report).

12. Kate Oakley, Brooke Sperry, and Andy Pratt, "The Art of Innovation" (London: NESTA, 2008); Jason Potts and Kate Morrison, "Nudging Innovation" (London: NESTA, 2009); Michael Storper and Anthony Venables, "Buzz: Face-to-Face Contact and the Urban Economy," *Journal of Economic Geography,* vol. 4, no. 4 (2004), pp. 351–70.

13. Adam Arvidsson, "Creative Class or Administrative Class? On Advertising and the 'Underground,'" *Ephemera,* vol. 7, no. 1 (2007), pp. 8–23.

14. Koen Frenken, Frank Van Oort, and Thijs Verburg, "Related Variety, Unrelated Variety, and Regional Economic Growth," *Regional Studies,* vol. 41, no. 5 (2007), pp. 685–97.

15. Here we follow the definition of "creative industries" given by the U.K. government: *"Those industries which have their origin in individual creativity, skill and talent and which have a potential for wealth and job creation through the generation and exploitation of intellectual property"*: Department for Culture, Media, and Sport, "Creative Industries Mapping Document" (London: 1998). The sectors included in this definition are listed later in the chapter.

16. David Throsby, "The Concentric Circles Model of the Cultural Industries," *Cultural Trends,* vol. 17, no. 3 (2008), pp. 147–64; Robert Andari and others, "Staying Ahead: The Economic Performance of the U.K. Creative Industries" (London: Work Foundation, 2007); Jonathan Haskel and others, "Innovation, Knowledge Spending, and Productivity Growth in the U.K.: Interim Report for NESTA Innovation Index Project" (London: NESTA, 2009).

17. Elizabeth Currid, *The Warhol Economy: How Fashion, Art, and Music Drive New York City* (Princeton University Press, 2007); Arvidsson, "Creative Class or Administrative Class?"; Oakley, Sperry, and Pratt, "The Art of Innovation."

18. For example, see James Rauch, "Productivity Gains from Geographic Concentration of Human Capital: Evidence from the Cities," *Journal of Urban Economics,* vol. 34 (November 1993), pp. 380–400; Kemeny and Storper, "The Sources of Urban Development"; Glaeser and Gottlieb, "Urban Resurgence and the Consumer City."

19. Knudsen and others, "Density and Creativity in U.S. Regions"; Florida, Mellander, and Stolarick, "Inside the Black Box of Regional Development."

20. Ann Markusen, "Urban Development and the Politics of a Creative Class: Evidence from a Study of Artists," *Environment and Planning A,* vol. 38, no. 10 (2006), pp. 1921–40; Michael Storper and Allen C. Scott, "Rethinking Human Capital, Creativity, and Urban Growth," *Journal of Economic Geography,* vol. 9 (2009), pp. 147–67.

21. Elizabeth Currid and Kevin Stolarick, "The Arts: Not Just Artists (and Vice Versa): New Methodological Approaches towards Understanding the Economic Composition of Arts," in *Handbook of Creative Cities,* edited by David E. Andersson, Åke E. Andersson, and Charlotta Mellander (Cheltentham, U.K.: Edward Elgar, 2011); Peter Higgs, Stuart Cunningham, and Hasan Bakhshi, "Beyond the Creative Industries" (London: NESTA, 2008).

22. Ann Markusen, "Targeting Occupations in Regional and Community Economic Development," *Journal of the American Planning Association,* vol. 70, no. 3 (2004), pp. 253–68; Markusen and Schrock, "The Artistic Dividend"; Currid and Stolarick, "The Arts: Not Just Artists."

23. See, for example, Elsie Echeverri-Carroll and Sofie G. Ayala, "Wage Differentials and the Spatial Concentration of High-Technology Industries," *Papers in Regional Science,* vol. 88, no. 3 (2009), pp. 623–41.

24. Mike Coombes and Steve Bond, "Travel to Work Areas: The 2007 Review" (London: Office of National Statistics, 2007).

25. See, for example, Stephen Gibbons, Henry Overman, and Panu Pelkonen, "Wage Disparities in Britain: People or Place?" Spatial Economics Research Centre Discussion Paper 0060 (London: SERC, 2010).

26. Ibid.

27. Max Nathan, "The Long-Term Impacts of Migration in British Cities: Diversity, Wages, Employment, and Prices," SERC Discussion Papers 0067 (London: SERC, 2011); Neil Lee, Paul Sissons, and Katy Jones, "Inequality in British Cities" (York, U.K.: Joseph Rowntree Foundation, 2013).

28. Richard Dickens, Rebecca Riley, and David Wilkinson, "The Employment and Hours of Work Effects of the Changing National Minimum Wage: Report for the Low-Pay Commission" (London: Low Pay Commission, 2009); Ian Walker and Yu Zhu, "The College Wage Premium and the Expansion of Higher Education in the U.K.," *Scandinavian Journal of Economics,* vol. 110, no. 4 (2008), pp. 695–70.

29. Allen J. Scott, "Space-Time Variations of Human Capital Assets across U.S. Metropolitan Areas: 1980 to 2000," *Economic Geography,* vol. 86, no. 3 (2009), pp. 233–50.

30. Lee, Sissons, and Jones, "Inequality in British Cities."

31. Halfdanarson, Heuermann, and Suedekum, "Human Capital Externalities and the Urban Wage Premium."

32. Caroline Chapain and others, "The Geography of Creativity" (London: NESTA, 2009).

33. That is, 2007 SIC 90010 (performing arts), 90020 (support activities to performing arts), 90030 (artistic creation), and 90040 (operation of arts facilities). See DCMS, "Creative Industries Economic Estimates: Full Statistical Release, 8 December 2011" (London: DCMS, 2011) (www.culture.gov.uk/images/research/Creative-Industries-Economic-Estimates-Report-2011-update.pdf).

34. For example, see Higgs, Cunningham, and Bakhshi, "Beyond the Creative Industries."

35. Throsby, "The Concentric Circles Model of the Cultural Industries."

36. It is worth noting that the "arts markets and antiques" category captures primarily specialized and second-hand retailers. Past research shows that it rarely co-locates with other sectors in the cultural and creative industries. Chapain and others, "The Geography of Creativity."

37. Higgs, Cunningham, and Bakhshi, "Beyond the Creative Industries."

38. SOC codes are as follows: librarians (2451), archivists and curators (2452), artists (3411), authors and writers (3412), actors and entertainers (3413), dancers and choreographers (3414), musicians (3415), arts officers, producers, and directors (3416), conservation and environmental protection officers (3551), and library assistants/clerks (4135).

39. In addition, it is significantly correlated with the proportion of the workforce qualified to NVQ level 4 and above (a standardized measure of qualifications, equivalent to degree level or above).

40. The full models passed the usual diagnostic tests for collinearity, and variables were logged to address potential heteroskedasticity. There was evidence of collinearity when models were estimated using full industry and occupation dummies, and so we limited regressions to the nine occupation dummies. However, there was little change in the results.

41. The results are available on request from the authors.

42. James Rauch uses housing expenditure at the individual level in parallel with wages as the dependent variable in two models estimated so as to identify the consumption (that is, amenity) effects of human capital externalities and compare them to its production (that is, spillover) effects. Doing that would have helped us address the identification issues described earlier in this chapter. Regretfully, the APS data do not include questions on housing costs, so we have had to include the housing price variable at the city rather than the individual level. Rauch, "Productivity Gains from Geographic Concentration of Human Capital."

43. Results available on request from the authors.

Contributors

HASAN BAKHSHI
Nesta (United Kingdom)

ELISA BARBOUR
University of California, Berkeley

SHIRI M. BREZNITZ
Georgia Institute of Technology

ROLAND J. KUSHNER
Muhlenberg College

REX LAMORE
Michigan State University

JAMES LAWTON
Michigan State University

NEIL LEE
Nesta (United Kingdom)

RICHARD G. MALONEY
Boston University

ANN MARKUSEN
University of Minnesota

JUAN MATEOS-GARCIA
Nesta (United Kingdom)

ANNE GADWA NICODEMUS
Metris Arts Consulting

DOUGLAS S. NOONAN
Indiana University–Purdue University Indianapolis

PETER PEDRONI
Williams College

AMBER PERUSKI
Michigan State University

MICHELE ROOT-BERNSTEIN
Michigan State University

ROBERT ROOT-BERNSTEIN
Michigan State University

EILEEN RORABACK
Michigan State University

MICHAEL RUSHTON
Indiana University

LAUREN SCHMITZ
The New School for Social Research

JENNY SCHUETZ
University of Southern California

JOHN SCHWEITZER
Michigan State University

STEPHEN SHEPPARD
Williams College

MEGAN VANDYKE
Michigan State University

GREGORY H. WASSALL
Northeastern University

Index

ACS. *See* American Community Survey

Adams Arts Program for the Creative Economy, 7, 60–79; and community partnerships, 66–70; establishment of, 61–64; findings, 65–76; in Fitchburg, 65, 67–73, 78–79; in Gloucester, 65, 67, 69–70, 73, 77–78; grants from, 61–62, 63–65, 66, 72, 73–74; in Hyannis, 65, 66, 68–69, 71, 73, 77; and intermediary organizations, 70–71; local government's role in, 71–73; and Massachusetts Cultural Council, 61, 62, 66–67, 69–70, 73–74, 76; methodology, 64–65; overview, 60–61

Advanced degrees, 97–98

American Community Survey (ACS), 32, 44, 63, 155

American Men of Science, 110

Americans for the Arts, 151

Andreoni, James, 85

Annual Population Survey (APS), 197, 199, 201

Art galleries, 6, 12–35. *See also* Manhattan art galleries

"The Arts, New Growth Theory, and Economic Development" (Brookings Institution), viii, 1

Arts and crafts. *See* Creative knowledge economies

Arts and Cultural Production Satellite Account, ix

Arts capacity, 36, 38–39, 43–49

Art schools, 130–33, 135–36

Arts Council England, 200

Arts districts, universities, and media arts, 8, 118–43; data on, 123–25; in economic development, 118–21; and employment, 122, 128–29, 130–35; future implications for, 136; impacts of, 125–29, 130–33; industry and occupation categories, 124–25, 137–39; and innovation, 118, 122, 128–29, 133; new media arts, 121–22; and patents, 124–25, 128–29, 133–34; research design, 123–30; robustness of results on, 129–30; unexpected results on, 133–36

Arts entrepreneurship, 8–9, 144–65; conceptual underpinnings for examining, 147–50; data on, 151–57;